Social Life

Social Life

Contemporary Social Theory

Matthias Benzer

Kate Reed

Los Angeles | London | New Delhi
Singapore | Washington DC | Melbourne

Los Angeles | London | New Delhi
Singapore | Washington DC | Melbourne

SAGE Publications Ltd
1 Oliver's Yard
55 City Road
London EC1Y 1SP

SAGE Publications Inc.
2455 Teller Road
Thousand Oaks, California 91320

SAGE Publications India Pvt Ltd
B 1/l 1 Mohan Cooperative Industrial Area
Mathura Road
New Delhi 110 044

SAGE Publications Asia-Pacific Pte Ltd
3 Church Street
#10-04 Samsung Hub
Singapore 049483

Editor: Natalie Aguilera
Assistant Editor: Eve Williams
Production editor: Katherine Haw
Copyeditor: Camille Bramall
Proofreader: Rebecca Storr
Indexer: Elizabeth Ball
Marketing manager: George Kimble
Cover design: Stephanie Guyaz
Typeset by: C&M Digitals (P) Ltd, Chennai, India
Printed in the UK

Library of Congress Control Number: 2018960846

British Library Cataloguing in Publication data

A catalogue record for this book is available from
the British Library

ISBN 978-1-4739-0783-6
ISBN 978-1-4739-0784-3 (pbk)

At SAGE we take sustainability seriously. Most of our products are printed in the UK using responsibly sourced
papers and boards. When we print overseas we ensure sustainable papers are used as measured by the PREPS
grading system. We undertake an annual audit to monitor our sustainability.

Contents

About the Authors

Matthias Benzer is Lecturer in Sociology in the Department of Sociological Studies at the University of Sheffield. He previously worked as a researcher at the Centre for Analysis of Risk and Regulation at the London School of Economics and Political Science and as a Lecturer in Sociology in the Department of Sociology at the University of Manchester. He is the author of *The Sociology of Theodor Adorno* (2011, Cambridge University Press) as well as writings on critical theory (published in the *Journal of Classical Sociology* and *Philosophy & Social Criticism*) and poststructuralist social thought. Matthias is also currently conducting research on social and political questions regarding resource allocation in the United Kingdom National Health Service.

Kate Reed is Professor of Sociology in the Department of Sociological Studies at the University of Sheffield. She is currently Principal Investigator of the Economic and Social Research Council funded project 'End of or Start of Life'? Visual Technology and the Transformation of Traditional Post-Mortem. Her research interests are focused on the areas of reproductive genetics, gender, technology and health, and social theory. Kate is the author of *New Directions in Social Theory: Race, Gender and the Canon* (2006, Sage) and *Gender and Genetics: Sociology of the Prenatal* (2012, Routledge).

Introduction

In sociology, the idea that people live in society is widely accepted. At the same time, this idea is not always made explicit in sociological research. Social theory comprises attempts to conceptualise, analyse, understand, explain, and critically scrutinise social relations and conditions. The questions that this area of sociology has addressed in the twentieth and twenty-first centuries have included whether current social conditions must be considered as radically modern, postmodern, or not at all modern, where the lines of social inequality and discrimination are drawn, how relationships of power are shaping the social world, how social relations and social interaction are to be characterised, and where the potential for the transformation of society lies, to name a few. A range of social theorists, crucially, have, in their endeavours, explicitly raised and examined the problem of living in society. In other words, they have sought to investigate human life in social relations, contexts, and conditions. *Social Life* contains expositions, explorations, and discussions of such work in contemporary social thought. The focus of the book rests on eight socio-theoretical analyses of social life: writings by Anthony Giddens, Pierre Bourdieu, Bruno Latour, Donna Haraway, Zygmunt Bauman, Jean-François Lyotard, Michel Foucault, and Jean Baudrillard. The works of these sociologists have had a tremendous impact on the sociological research of the present day. The following chapters aim to highlight, detail, and discuss the contributions and challenges of the analyses of social life put forward by these eight thinkers to sociology's ongoing quest for conceptualising and interrogating the contemporary social world.

The chapters approach the socio-theoretical ideas under discussion from two angles. Each of the social theorists in focus has developed a set of concepts, statements, and arguments for analysing and critically scrutinising contemporary social relations and conditions. The first part of every chapter concentrates on decisive elements of those conceptions of, arguments about, and inquiries into, present-day society. At no point does this amount to a summary overview either of the respective body of thought in its entirety or even of large parts of it. Instead, the first parts of the chapters identify and spotlight key components of each thinker's conception and analysis of contemporary society and explore those in detail. At issue are elements that have made particularly sustained contributions or raised particularly far-reaching challenges to sociology's project of critically examining the social world of today. For instance, an elaborate account of Foucault's thinking about power is prioritised over a summary of his major interventions from the 1960s and 1970s *tout court*. In a similar fashion, a detailed exposition of Baudrillard's distinctions between the way in which life and death are treated in symbolic exchange relationships and the way in which they are treated in capitalist society is offered instead of an overview of his entire work on the symbolic, illusion, reality, simulation, and hyperreality.

Informed by their conceptions of social relations and conditions, each of these thinkers' interpretations, examinations, and critical interrogations of the social world has, in turn, in different ways informed their investigations of particular phenomena of that world. The second part of every chapter discusses the respective theorist's analyses of the ways in which the wider social contexts in focus in the first part shape, manifest themselves in, are expressed through, and receive influence from more specific phenomena. At the centre of attention here are chiefly phenomena – or phenomena that resemble phenomena – many people are likely to have experienced immediately, may frequently hear or read about, or are simply able to imagine independently of having been exposed to sociological research. For instance, Chapter 5 explores the problem of fear in liquid modernity as it is addressed in Bauman's work, whilst Chapter 1 discusses climate change as Giddens problematises it sociologically. The aim of the second part of each chapter is to elucidate ostensibly abstract theoretical ideas about prevalent social relations, contexts, and conditions by linking them to analyses of such phenomena.

Simultaneously, the second parts of each chapter thereby pursue a further objective. What these sections are concerned with more precisely are decisive components of the eight thinkers' analyses of how wider social conditions are interrelated with particular phenomena variously, but mostly quite explicitly, associated with the ways in which people live, with living, with the question of human life. The second part of Chapter 4, for instance, engages with Haraway's thinking on immunology, that of Chapter 6 with Lyotard's considerations of the 'questions: how to live, and why' (1997: vii), and Part 2 of Chapter 8 with Baudrillard's writings on the massive extinction of life during, the suicides central to, and the ramifications of, the attacks on New York City on September 11, 2001. The growing importance of the problem of life in critical investigations of social contexts, economic relations, and political conditions, which is indicated by the ever more frequent appearance of the prefix 'bio' in designations of socio-scientific fields of study (e.g. Birch and Tyfield 2012; Lemke 2011), is widely recognised. The following chapters suggest that the ways in which social relations and contexts shape, manifest themselves in, and are affected by, specific aspects and phenomena of human life and the lives of people constitute a sustained and encompassing concern of a much wider array of sociology, especially of social theory. The objective, in other words, is to highlight and discuss how the thinkers in focus in this book intertwine analyses of social conditions with analyses of phenomena characteristic of people's lives, of living, and of life – however variously understood – in today's society. Their *œuvres* have much to offer to sociological inquiries into contemporary social life understood in this very sense.

Thematically, the aim to explore socio-theoretical analyses of the problem of living in society is not especially restrictive. In itself, it would doubtless allow, arguably call for, an engagement with a broader range of works in social theory. A further objective of the present text, however, is to explore key components of such socio-theoretical analyses in detail. An orientation by this objective precludes an inclusive, let alone an exhaustive, account of current social theory's inquiries into life in the contemporary social world. The authors readily admit that the specific problems that have occupied them in their other research, the contributions of sociology that have guided their teaching, and their respective notions of sociology's most vital concerns and conceptions today are expressed in the thematic composition of the book's chapters.

The discussions in these chapters concentrate on specific primary texts. This is consistent with the book's overall aim to engage closely and in depth with decisive elements of the conceptions, investigations, and analyses in question, which has rendered the pursuit of overviews of wide arrays of sources inappropriate. The chapters endeavour to unpack and decipher particular, often convoluted, cryptic writings – and passages in the writings – of each theorist and trace their interconnections within each *œuvre*. They contain attempts to expose, explore in detail, and discuss concepts, configurations of concepts, and arguments that constitute particular inquiries and analyses of the theorists. The first parts of the chapters draw on sources that support the reconstruction and discussion of key components of the eight thinkers' conceptions and examinations of contemporary social conditions. The second parts turn to sources that support what may be described as theoretical case studies – explorations of the theorists' inquiries into interrelations between the wider conditions at issue in the first parts and more specific phenomena linked to the problem of living in today's social world.

Of those sources, many were not originally published in English. Most of the latter first appeared in French. The approach to the sources taken – that is to say, demanded by the objectives of the book's chapters – necessitated recourse to the original language versions of some of them. It is probably prudent to declare in this context that French is not the native tongue of either author. It became nevertheless apparent that some of the published English translations of central sources of this book are more accurate than others. For instance, the English version (Lyotard 1984b) of Lyotard's *La Condition Postmoderne* (1979) is very faithful to the original text, whereas the translation (Baudrillard 1993) of Baudrillard's *L'Échange Symbolique et la Mort* (1976) is problematic in places. In the following, several directly quoted translations of passages from various sources have been modified on the basis of the French texts. The sole objectives of doing so were the correction of translation errors in some instances and greater linguistic precision in all others. For the purpose of ensuring their defensibility, some modified translations were checked against German translations (notably Baudrillard 1982b and Lyotard 1994) of the French originals where those were readily available. Translations that have been modified are marked with the designation 'trsl. modified' within the relevant in-text references.

Numerous secondary works – monographs and articles, commentaries and critiques – dedicated to many of the eight thinkers are available. It has not been possible to survey even the majority of this body of literature. All sections of this book are mainly based on engagements with primary sources rather than on explorations of secondary texts. Nonetheless, each chapter provides not only references to those secondary works that have informed aspects of the analyses presented, but also references to secondary literature that offers readers richer insights into issues that cannot be elaborated here. Moreover, recommended further readings are listed at the end of each chapter. The following eight chapters explore each theorist's ideas in turn. The ninth chapter revisits some common concerns of the socio-theoretical investigations of social life explored throughout the preceding eight.

1

Anthony Giddens: Living with Radical Modernity

PART 1: RADICAL MODERNITY

In *The Consequences of Modernity* published in the early 1990s Giddens argued that, although not yet living in a postmodern world, we were nonetheless witnessing 'the emergence of ways of life and forms of social organisation' that were different to those facilitated by 'modern institutions' (CM 52). This indicated what he refers to as a radicalised version of modernity – a future-oriented reflexive and globalised form (RW). This version of modernity is for Giddens unsettling: 'Its most conspicuous features – the *dissolution of evolutionism*, the *disappearance of historical teleology*, the recognition of *thoroughgoing, constitutive reflexivity*, together with the *evaporating of the privileged position of the West* – move us into a new and disturbing universe of experience' (CM 52–3). One of the key problems of radical modernity – climate change – according to Giddens requires radical political solutions beyond traditional politics of the left and right (BLR, TW). This chapter seeks to explore the particular dilemmas and problems that radical modernity poses for human life as outlined in Giddens's socio-theoretical framework. Focusing specifically on the potential threat posed by climate change (PCC), the chapter also examines his proposed solutions with a view to their potential to inform concrete policy.

Radicalised Modernity

Modernity tends to refer in sociology texts to 'modes of social life or organisation that emerged in Europe from about the seventeenth century onwards and that subsequently became more or less worldwide in their influence' (CM 1). According to Giddens we now stand at the dawn of 'a new era' to which the social sciences must respond and which is taking us beyond modernity itself' (CM 1). Sociologists have attempted to describe and define this era through concepts such as postmodernism, post-Fordism, postcapitalism, and so on. Post-modernism is a slippery concept and, as Giddens himself points out, can mean any number of things: that the '"foundations" of epistemology are unreliable and that "history" is devoid of teleology and consequently no version of "progress" can plausibly be defended' (CM 46). It may also refer to the emergence of 'a new social and political agenda' including an 'increasing prominence of ecological concerns and perhaps of new social movements generally' (CM 46). While Giddens acknowledges that significant social changes have occurred in society in recent decades, rather than seeing these as evidence of us living in a society beyond modernity, he argues that they actually 'provide us with a fuller understanding of the reflexivity inherent in modernity itself' (CM 49). Giddens is not alone in his attempts to suggest we are living in a modern not postmodern, society. Other theorists such as Bourdieu and Habermas also – in different ways – have sought to develop socio-theoretical positions that are at odds with postmodernity (Callinicos 1999). What is specific to Giddens's approach, however, is his focus on radical modernity. He argues that 'we have not moved beyond modernity but are living precisely through a phase of its radicalisation' (CM 51).

In order to understand the times we live in Giddens argues 'it is not sufficient merely to invent new terms, like post-modernity and the rest. Instead, we have to look again at the nature of modernity itself' (CM 3). This for Giddens includes an analytical focus on the Janus-faced nature of modernity. Modernity he argues 'is a double-edged phenomenon' (CM 7). It has created vast opportunity for 'human beings to enjoy a secure and rewarding existence' but it also has a 'sombre side' (CM 7). It was only Weber according to Giddens out of the classical theorists who acknowledged this sombre side of modernity, as Marx thought class conflict would lead to a better society: 'Yet even he did not fully anticipate how extensive the darker side of modernity would turn out to be' (CM 7). Through developing his theory of radical modernity, therefore, Giddens seeks to include a focus on its dual-edged potential, as well as suggesting sociological strategies for managing its darker side.

The dynamism of modernity

Giddens begins his theory of modernity by outlining what he calls a 'discontinuist' interpretation of modern development. In particular he wants to focus on outlining the ways in which modern institutions are different from the traditional order (CM 3, RM). The big differences between traditional and modern institutions according to Giddens are their 'dynamism' and 'global scope' (CM 16). Giddens distinguishes three dominant and interconnected sources of dynamism that underpin modernity: the first is *the separation of time and space*. This is what Giddens refers to as the condition of time–space distanciation, a means of precise temporal and spatial zoning. Giddens argues that modernity 'tears space away from place fostering relations between "absent" others', and different locales are penetrated by and shaped in terms of social influences quite distant from them (CM 19).

The second source of dynamism for Giddens is the development of dis-embedding mechanisms. Giddens refers here to the "lifting out" of 'social activity from localised contexts, reorganising social relations across large time–space distances'(CM 53). Giddens gives the example of two types of disembedding mechanisms 'symbolic tokens' (e.g. money) and 'expert sys-tems' (e.g. medicine). Expert systems refer to 'systems of technical accomplishment or professional expertise that organise large areas of the material and social environments in which we live today' (CM 27). According to Giddens 'expert systems are disembedding mechanisms because, in com-mon with symbolic tokens, they remove social relations from the immediacies of context' (CM 28). Both types of disembedding mechanisms presume, but also foster, the separation of time from space (CM 28). Essential to these disembedding systems, according to Giddens, is trust and therefore trust is involved in an essential way with the institutions of modernity.

The final source of dynamism according to Giddens is '*The reflexive appropriation of knowledge*. The production of systematic knowledge about social life becomes central to system reproduction, rolling social life away from the fixed nature of tradition' (CM 53). He argues that the reflexivity of modern social life consists in the fact that 'social practices are constantly examined and reinformed in the light of incoming information about those very practices, thus constitutively altering their character' (CM 38). Giddens argues that sociology as an academic discipline occupies a key position in the reflexivity of modernity, because sociology offers a 'generalised type of reflec-tion upon modern social life' (CM 41). 'The discourse of sociology and the concepts, theories, and findings of the other social sciences' 'reflexively restruc-ture their subject matter, which itself has learned to think sociologically'. According to Giddens therefore '*modernity is itself deeply and intrinsically sociological*' (CM 43).

The institutional dimensions of modernity

Giddens identifies four institutional dimensions of modernity – capitalism, industrialism, surveillance, and military power. These dimensions according to Giddens are irreducible to one another, each consisting of a different set of causal processes and structures. However, they work together to provide a structure for understanding some of the key features, developments, and tensions in modern societies. *Capitalism* is the first dimension that he identifies. This 'is a system of commodity production, centred upon the relation between private ownership of capital and propertyless wage labour'. It is this relationship, according to Giddens, which forms 'the main axis of a class system' (CM 55). Industrialism is viewed separately from capitalism and, for Giddens, forms the second institutional dimension of modernity: 'The chief characteristic of *industrialism* is the use of inanimate sources of material power in the production of goods, coupled to the central role of machinery in the production process' (CM 55–6).

The nation state occupies a central place in capitalist societies according to Giddens, and the administration of the capitalist system and modern society in general is coordinated control over delimited territorial arenas. In this respect capitalism depends on '*surveillance* capacities well beyond those of traditional civilisations' (CM 57). For Giddens, therefore, *surveillance* capacity constitutes a third institutional dimension associated with the rise of modernity (CM 57–8). He states that 'surveillance refers to the supervision of the activities of subject populations in the political sphere' – although not confined to that sphere (CM 58). The final institutional dimension is *military power* (control of the means of violence in the industrialisation of war): successful monopoly of the means of violence within the state. This also refers to the industrialisation of war – total war and nuclear war (CM 58). According to Giddens, 'behind these institutional clusterings lie the three sources of dynamism of modernity' referred to earlier: '*time–space distanciation*, *disembedding*, and *reflexivity*' (italics my emphasis). These facilitate the conditions for change. 'They are involved in as well as conditioned by the institutional dimensions of modernity' (CM 63).

Globalisation, trust, and risk

Modernity for Giddens is dynamic, and also inherently globalising. Globalisation therefore occupies a central role within Giddens's theory of modernity. He defines globalisation as 'the intensification of worldwide social relations which link distant localities in such a way that local happenings are shaped by events occurring many miles away and vice versa' (CM 64). Globalisation is, according to Giddens, essentially 'action at a distance' (RM 96). Giddens regards the world capitalist economy as one of four dimensions of globalisation, the nation state is the second, the world military order is the third, and industrial development: 'the most obvious aspect of this is the expansion of the global division of labour', for example difference between more and less industrialised countries) is the fourth. The media – for Giddens that is 'mechanised technologies of communication' – 'have dramatically influenced all aspects of globalisation' (CM 77). According to Giddens the point is not that 'people are contingently aware of many events, from all over the world, of which previously they would have remained ignorant'. Rather 'it is that the global extension of the institutions of modernity would be impossible were it not for the pooling of knowledge which is represented by the "news"' (CM 77–8).

A key part of Giddens's theory of radical modernity is the relationship between modern institutions and abstract systems. According to him modern institutions are bound by '*the mechanisms of trust in abstract systems*, especially trust in expert systems' (CM 83). The future-oriented nature of modernity is largely structured by trust vested in abstract systems, in particular in the trustworthiness of established expertise (CM 83–4). According to Giddens 'the reliance placed by lay actors upon expert systems is not just a matter (as was often the case in the premodern world) of generating a sense of security about an independently given universe of events. It is a matter of the calculation of benefit and risk in circumstances where expert knowledge does not just provide that calculus but actually *creates* (or reproduces) the universe of events, as a result of the continual reflexive implementation of that very knowledge' (CM 84).

What this means in a globalised modernity according to Giddens is that no one can opt out of 'the abstract systems involved in modern institutions' (CM 84). There are no others (Kaspersen 2000). In modernity 'the dangers we face no longer derive primarily from the world of nature'. Rather, threats (such as ecological decay) 'are the outcome of socially organised knowledge, mediated by the impact of industrialism upon the material environment' (CM 110). They are part of what Giddens calls the new '*risk profile*' introduced by the advent of modernity. By a risk profile he means the particular 'portmanteau of threats or dangers characteristic of modern social life' (CM 110). According to Giddens, risk and danger (like everything else) have become secularised in modernity (CM 111). He focuses on the menacing nature of the globalisation of risk, the potential, for example, of nuclear war, ecological disaster, etc. However, he argues that because we are constantly bombarded with information about global risks on an everyday basis we tend to switch off: 'Listing the dangers we face has itself has a deadening effect. It becomes a litany which is only half listened to because it seems so familiar' (Bailey cited in Giddens, CM 128). Risk discourses in this sense are, according to Giddens, background noise. Furthermore, he also states that the more we know about modern risk, the more we recognise the limits of so-called 'expert' knowledge. This according to Giddens 'forms one of the "public relations" problems that has to be faced by those who seek to sustain lay trust in expert systems' (CM 130).

Riding the juggernaut of modernity

'Radical' or 'high' modernity is according to Giddens a 'runaway world', a 'juggernaut' veering out of control. No specific individuals or groups are responsible for this juggernaut or can be compelled to 'set things right' (CM 131). While sociologists have often criticised Giddens for making sweeping generalisations in his theory of radical modernity (Kaspersen 2000), he is keen to stress that he recognises the juggernaut of modernity is not all of a piece. It is made up of diverse and contradictory forces. However, despite the bleak picture Giddens paints, it is not – according to him – all hopeless. We should not/ cannot 'give up in our attempts to steer the juggernaut' (CM 154). Giddens puts forward his notion of utopian realism, a critical theory without 'guarantees'. This theory he argues must be '*sociologically sensitive*' and '*geopolitically, tactical*', in order to '*create models of the good society*'. His focus here is on linking what he calls 'emancipatory politics' with '*life politics*, or the politics of *self-actualisation*' (CM 156). Emancipatory politics for Giddens refer to 'radical engagements concerned with the liberation from inequality or servitude'. Social movements, he argues, provide instruction to potential future transformations (e.g. labour movements, ecological movements) (CM 160–1). One of the biggest challenges we face in a radical modern world is environmental decay. 'Since the most consequential ecological issues are so obviously global, forms of intervention to minimise environmental risks' will, as Giddens argues, need to be on a global scale (CM 170). He states that an 'overall system of planetary care might be created, which would have as its aim the preservation of the ecological well-being of the world as a whole' (CM 170). Giddens ends his analysis by stressing the urgency of the need for change on a global scale with respect to environmental decay, lest we end up as a 'republic of insects and grass' (CM 173).

Radical politics

According to Giddens, the problems prevalent within radical modernity – such as ecological decay – require radical political solutions. In *Beyond Left and Right* (Giddens 1994b) and *The Third Way* (Giddens 1998) Giddens seeks to develop what he calls a radical politics of the centre, a widespread philosophy and approach for the left. He restates many points articulated in CM, that the world of the late twentieth century has not turned out as the founders of socialism anticipated. They felt that the more we collectively know 'about social and material reality', the more we will become masters of our own destiny (BLR 3). As Giddens outlines in his work on radical modernity, the world we live in today is not one subject to tight human mastery. Almost to the contrary, it is one of dislocation and uncertainty, a juggernaut veering out of control, a 'runaway world' (BLR 3, CM).

Risk again forms a central position in Giddens's work on radical politics; in this context he focuses in particular on what he calls '*manufactured uncertainty*' (BLR 4). Giddens argues that 'manufactured risk is a result *of* human intervention into the conditions of social life and into nature' (BLR 4). Manufactured uncertainty for Giddens is the outcome of 'the long-term maturation of modern institutions'. However, it has also rapidly increased as a result of 'a series of developments that have transformed society (and nature) over no more than the past four or five decades' (BLR 4). There are four main contexts in which we confront high-consequence risks coming from the extension of manufactured uncertainty. Each of these corresponds to an institutional dimension of modernity as outlined in CM. These are: the impact of modern social development on the world ecosystem, the development of poverty on a large scale, and the widespread existence of weapons of mass destruction, together with other situations in which collective violence looms as a possibility. The fourth and final source of global crisis concerns the large-scale representation of democratic rights, including the inability of vast numbers of people to develop even a small part of their human potential (BLR).

Beyond socialism and conservatism

Giddens argues that if we are to effectively address these problems posed by radical modernity we need to develop a radical political position beyond the political left or right. According to Giddens socialism and conservatism have disintegrated, and neoliberalism is paradoxical (BLR 10). Giddens poses the question: 'If the oppositional force of socialism has been blunted, must a capitalistic system reign unchallenged?' (BLR 11) He argues not. There would be several dire consequences should capitalist markets go unchecked including 'the dominance of a growth ethic, universal commodification and economic polarization' (BLR 11). A critique of these potential trends remains for Giddens essential. However, he argues that in a radical modern society it cannot be derived from a cybernetic model of socialism. Although this 'cybernetic model implicit in socialism as a whole, and developed in its most advanced way in Soviet communism was quite effective as a means of 'generating economic development in conditions of simple modernization' (BLR 66), the reflexivity inherent within a radicalised modernity, coupled with globalisation, 'introduces quite different social and economic circumstances' requiring radical political solutions (BLR 66).

According to Giddens, neoliberals have 'appropriated the future-oriented radicalism that was once the hallmark of the bolder forms of socialist thinking' (BLR 73). In contemporary society the 'conservative has become radical and the radical conservative' (BLR 73). Giddens argues that the 'main emphasis of socialist conservatism' is the turn towards the 'protection of the now embattled welfare state' (BLR 73). The critique of capitalism that Giddens develops is still focused on economic oppression and poverty but 'from a different perspective from those characteristic of socialist thought' (BLR 12). He focuses on radicalism but seeks to unhook its connection to either the political left or right: 'radicalism reverts to its original meaning as daring: it means being prepared to contemplate bold solutions to social and political problems' (BLR 49). Viewed in this way radicalism is not merely 'valued for its own sake but instead is tempered by that awareness of the importance of continuity on which philosophic conservatism exists' (BLR 50). 'Radical political programmes today', Giddens argues, 'must be based on a conjunction of life politics and generative politics' (BLR 246). He refers back to his institutional analysis of capitalism, surveillance, industrialism, and the means of violence (CM). He argues that: 'along each of these dimensions' the question that radical politics must pose is: 'what alternative sociopolitical forms could potentially exist?' (BLR 101).

Utopian realism and the third way

A framework of radical politics should, according to Giddens, be informed by utopian realism, a critical theory 'with no guarantees' (CM 154), an approach that he introduces in his earlier work on radical modernity (CM). This should relate in particular, Giddens argues, to the four overarching dimensions of modernity: combating poverty; redressing the degradation of the environment; contesting arbitrary power; and reducing the role of force and violence in social life. These, according to Giddens, 'are the orienting contexts of utopian realism' (BLR 246). Giddens attempts to outline the philosophy behind his radical politics in BLR. However, he develops more concrete proposals for how this might work in practice in *The Third Way*, focusing in particular on the role of the state. Giddens argues that while 'neoliberals want to shrink the state; the social democrats, historically, have been keen to expand it'. The third-way approach argues that it is necessary to reconstruct, the state, to go beyond those on the right 'who say government is the enemy' and those on the left 'who say government is the answer' (TW 70).

Third-way politics for Giddens advocates a new *mixed economy* (TW 99). The new mixed economy looks for a 'synergy between public and private sectors, ultilizing the dynamism of markets but with the public interest in mind' (TW 99–100). It requires a reform of the welfare state, which, although not easy to achieve, 'can be sketched out quite readily' (TW 116). A radically reformed welfare state, according to Giddens, would involve social investment in a positive welfare society' (TW 127). 'Expenditure on welfare, understood as positive welfare', would according to Giddens 'be generated and distributed not wholly through the state, but by the state working in combination with other agencies including business' (TW 127–128). Furthermore, any future welfare society according to Giddens 'is not just the nation, but stretches above and below it. Control of environmental pollution, for example, can never be a matter for a national government alone, but it is certainly directly relevant to welfare' (TW 128).

Managing the dual-edged nature of modernity

In his work on radical politics Giddens seeks again to re-emphasise the Janus-faced nature of radical modernity. He argues that unpredictability, manufactured uncertainty, and fragmentation are only one side of a globalising order. 'On the reverse side are the shared values that come from a situation of global interdependence, organized via the cosmopolitan acceptance of difference' (BLR 253). In a world where there are no others, Giddens argues that we all share common interests and face common risks (BLR 253). Giddens uses this opportunity to reinforce his arguments that we are still living in a modern world – albeit a radical one. Far from seeing the disappearance of 'universal values' (as those favouring a postmodern approach would suggest), Giddens argues: 'this is perhaps the first time in humanity's history when such values have real purchase' (BLR 253).

Giddens uses the example of ecological politics to think through ways of dealing with manufactured uncertainty. Ecological politics for Giddens is a politics of loss (of both nature and tradition). It is also for him 'a politics of recovery' (BLR 227). According to Giddens, 'we can't return to nature or to tradition' (BLR 227). However, both individually and collectively we can seek to 'remoralize our lives in the context of a positive acceptance of manufactured uncertainty' (BLR 227). 'Put in this way, it isn't difficult to see why the ecological crisis is so basic to the forms of political renewal' that Giddens discusses in his work on radical politics (BLR 227: TW). The ecological crisis 'is a material expression of the limits of modernity, repairing the damaged environment can no more be understood as an end in itself than can the redress of poverty' (BLR 227). According to Giddens, modernisation that is ecologically sensitive is not about 'more and more modernity'. Rather, it 'is conscious of the problems and limitations of modernizing processes'. It is alive to the need to re-establish continuity and develop social cohesion in a world of erratic transformation, where the intrinsically unpredictable energies of scientific and technological innovation play such an important role' (TW 67–8). Giddens attempts to offer insight into some of the problems created by modernity, as well as developing effective strategies to deal with them. The following section extends this analytical focus to his substantive sociological work on climate change. Examining his work on climate change in more depth allows for an assessment both of his core socio-theoretical concepts as outlined in CM, and his attempts to develop more concrete policy solutions (BLR, TW).

PART 2: CLIMATE CHANGE

Climate change has for some years been at the centre of a global political agenda. As numerous scholars have argued, a continued increase in the world's temperature has the potential to 'transform human and animal life as it has been known' (Urry 2009: 87). However, while climate change is at the centre of public debates about global politics (Klein 2015), according to Urry (2009) there continues to remain a limited number of good 'sociological analyses' that focus on exploring the various ways in which we can move 'societies into a different path-dependent pattern' (Urry 2009: 89). Giddens attempts to offer a sociological analysis of climate change in *The Politics of Climate Change*, which he sees as 'a prolonged inquiry into a single question'. Why do most people, most of the time, act as though a threat of such magnitude can be ignored?' (PCC 1). As will be explored in the following section, Giddens's work on climate change elaborates on certain key concepts from his earlier work on radical modernity and politics, such as the concept of risk. Giddens also seeks to offer a detailed analysis of existing climate change policies, as well as outlining his own suggestions for moving societies into new path-dependent routes.

Climate Change and Giddens's Paradox

Giddens begins his work on climate change by outlining what he calls 'Giddens's paradox', a theme that takes central place throughout the text: 'since the dangers posed by global warming aren't tangible, immediate or visible in the course of day-to-day life, many will sit on their hands and do nothing of a concrete nature about them' (PCC 2). He argues that 'Giddens's paradox affects almost every aspect of current reactions to climate change' (PCC 2). It is the reason according to him why, for most citizens, climate change is an issue that is often at the back of people's minds. Giddens's paradox effectively refers to the disjuncture between knowledge and behaviour. He uses a range of examples to illustrate what he means by this. For example, even though we know smoking is bad for us, we find it hard to face the impact that smoking may have on us in the future and modify our behaviours in the present (PCC 3). For him Giddens's paradox explains perhaps why politicians have only just woken up to the scale and urgency of the problem of climate change on a global scale, introducing a range of ambitious climate change policies.

Giddens begins his analysis by offering a summary of where debates on global climate change currently are. The first phase of global initiatives have focused on bringing climate change to the political agenda; the next focus, according to Giddens, 'must involve embedding it in our institutions and in the everyday concerns of citizens, and here, for reasons just mentioned, there is a great deal of work to do' (PCC 3). Although international organisations such as the UN, are, according to Giddens, committed to getting global reductions in greenhouse gas emissions, there is little in the way of concrete results so far (PCC 3–4). Climate change as an expression of radical modernity is 'like a "juggernaut" careering at full pace to the edge of the cliff' (Urry 2009: 89). It is difficult to see how in this context we might gain control of the juggernaut. It is not simply, according to Giddens, a question of the survival of the planet – as advocates of the green movement may argue – but rather it is about preserving a planet fit for human life and habitation. In order to gain control of this runaway juggernaut of climate change it is necessary, Giddens argues, to introduce a long-term perspective into politics, domestically and internationally, a perspective that goes beyond a politics of the left or right.

Climate change, beyond left and right

Giddens rehearses many of the arguments in his work on climate change that are articulated in both BLR and TW. Perspectives on climate change, as Giddens points out, reflect a variety of political viewpoints. Underlying these perspectives, however, remain the old left and right political divisions. 'Those who want to respond to climate change through widespread social reform mostly tend towards the political left; most of the authors who doubt that climate change is caused by human agency, on the other hand, are on the right' (PCC 49). However, it is vital in order to develop effective climate change policy according to Giddens, that we go beyond the traditional politics of the left and right (PCC 49). Giddens argues that the majority of scientists and politicians have woken up to the urgency of climate change. However, there are some who remain 'sceptics' – those who dispute the claims being made about the scale of climate change. These unfortunately, as Giddens argues, receive a good deal of attention in the media (PCC 3). Sceptics often argue that climate change is not really proven, or that there 'is nothing new about the increasing temperatures observed today', and that 'the world climate has always been in flux' (PCC 23). Other authors, writing on risk more generally, have argued that we live in an 'age of scares', climate change is just one of these (PCC 24).

Drawing on the arguments he develops in BLR and TW, Giddens argues that we need to develop a radical politics beyond traditional political divisions if we are to effectively deal with climate change. Climate change for Giddens 'is not a left–right issue'. The green movement for Giddens cannot be seen as the new socialism, 'the new red'. He argues that we need to build a long-term 'cross-party framework' (PCC 7). While appreciating that critiques of centre politics are well-worn, Giddens argues that it could be a major advantage to develop this approach in the field of environmentalism. Giddens is keen to stress that equating the political centre with an absence of radicalism only applies in the case of traditional left–right issues. He argues that 'it is entirely possible to have a "radicalism of the centre" – indeed, in terms of climate change and energy policy it is an essential concept' (PCC 114). We need to go 'beyond the rhetoric of immediate party politics' (PCC 114). For Giddens there has to be an agreement reached across different parties as the issue is too important for political point scoring. We should according to Giddens 'perhaps speak of a *concordat* rather than a consensus, because there should be a clear statement of principles that are publicly endorsed' (PCC 116).

Risk and uncertainty

The concept of risk is central to Giddens's work on both radical modernity and politics (CM, BLR, and TW). Manufactured risk and uncertainty are also central themes running throughout his work on climate change. While manufactured risk penetrates other areas of life, for example, marriage and the family (RW 27), most environmental risks such as global warming fall into the category of manufactured risk (RW 26). Giddens elaborates on his earlier conceptualisation of risk by focusing specifically on the dual nature of the concept in his work on climate change. According to Giddens 'taking risks adds edge to our lives, but, much more importantly, is intrinsic to a whole diversity of fruitful and constructive tasks' (PCC 56). It is a central part of capitalism. 'Capitalism is actually unthinkable and unworkable without it' (RW 25). According to Giddens, when it comes to tackling climate change, we need to harness the positive side of risk. We have no hope of responding effectively 'unless we are prepared to take bold decisions. It is the biggest example ever of he who hesitates is lost' (PCC 57).

Giddens seeks to pose the question: 'Where do we stand at the moment in terms of the risk posed by global warming?' (PCC 8). He begins by outlining various changes that have taken place over the past 150 years or so. For example, the levels of greenhouse gases in the atmosphere have progressively increased with the expansion of industrial production. Recent studies show the temperature of oceans rising. 'Mountain glaciers are retreating in both hemispheres and snow cover is less, on average, than it once was' (PCC 14). Giddens makes the same kinds of connections between manufactured risk and global environmental decay here that he does elsewhere (CM, BLR, TW). However, in his work on climate change he draws more directly on policy-related evidence in order to illustrate the scale of the problem. For example, he argues that the Intergovernmental Panel on Climate Change of the UN (IPCC) in 2007 stated that 'warming of the climate system is unequivocal' (PCC 15–16). They warn of the potential for the twenty-first century to be dominated by 'resource based wars', with the potential for coastal cities to become flooded. This according to the IPCC would provoke both destitution and migration on a mass scale (PCC 18).

Climate change and risk prevention

Giddens does explore some of the ways in which we might 'harness' some of the threats posed by global risk and uncertainty in his work on radical modernity and politics. For example, through the perspective of utopian realism, or via his radical politics or third-way approach (CM, BLR, TW). However, in his work on climate change he also offers a more detailed analysis of existing concrete risk prevention strategies used in this context. He examines some of the key concepts coming out of the green movement – for example, the 'precautionary principle' (PP), 'sustainability', and the principle that 'the polluter pays' (PCC 55). Giddens traces the concept of the PP back to the early 1980s, when it was used in Germany in the context of the ecological debates. 'At its simplest, it proposes that action on environmental issues (and, by inference, other forms of risk) should be taken even though there is insecure scientific evidence about them' (RW 32). 'In several European countries, programmes were initiated to counter acid rain'; however, as Giddens argues, in the UK a 'lack of conclusive evidence was used to justify inactivity about this and other pollution problems too' (RW 32).

Giddens explores the ways in which the PP has been used well beyond the green movement. It was built into the 1992 Rio Declaration[1] and into various programmes of the European Commission (PCC 55). The core meaning of PP is 'better safe than sorry' (PCC 55); however, Giddens also argues that PP 'isn't always helpful or even applicable as a means of coping with problems of risk and responsibility' (RW 32). Here he returns to his focus on the dual concept of risk. Giddens argues that the main problem with PP is that it 'concentrates only on one side of risk, the possibility of harm' (PCC 57). As Giddens argues, the notion of staying close to nature or of limiting innovation rather than embracing it isn't always appropriate. 'The reason is that the balance of benefits and dangers from scientific and technological advance and other forms of social change too' are difficult to assess (RW 32). He also states that precaution over some risks can create others, so PP can often be self-contradictory (PCC). Giddens advocates that we operate through a different type of PP, what he calls percentage principle. We have to assess risks and opportunities in relation to benefits obtained (PCC). According to Giddens, however, risks that 'shade over' into uncertainties, like those involved in global warming, mean that 'there will be an element of guesswork, perhaps large element, in whatever we do (or do not do)' (PCC 58).

Giddens provides an analysis of other climate change strategies including a focus on 'sustainable development', which he argues helped bring together two discrepant communities ('greens' and 'pro-market authors') but is none-theless 'more of a slogan than an analytical concept'. Another strategy 'polluter pays' focuses on making those who cause pollution pay through taxes. Giddens states that this is hard to pin down and has practical limits. However, polluter pays is still a 'guiding thread in bringing climate change into the sphere of orthodox politics' (PCC 67). In assessing the different ways of dealing with 'risks' posed by climate change, however, Giddens advocates that we should discard PP and the concept of sustainable development, replacing these with more sophisticated modes of risk analysis.

The role of technology and the state

Central to Giddens's analysis of climate change is technology. 'Technological innovation', Giddens argues, 'has to be a core part of any successful climate change strategy and the same is true of energy policy' (PCC 131). As argued in both BLR and TW, the state must play a key role in combating problems posed by radical modernity such as environmental decay. In his work on climate change Giddens argues that the state and government must have a significant role in making technological innovation possible 'since a regulatory framework, including incentives and other tax mechanisms, will be involved' (PCC 131). The literature on low-carbon technologies is, according to Giddens, 'a minefield of claims and counter-claims' (PCC 132). However, he returns again to his focus on the dual concept of risk, and argues that: 'Risks and problems there are plenty. Yet, as I have stressed throughout this book, it is the balance of risks we have to consider and there are no risk-free options' (PCC 132). Overall Giddens argues that there are 'no guaranteed technological solutions', hence 'radically increasing energy efficiency has to be high on the agenda' (PCC 139). Whatever happens over the next 20 years or so a diversification of energy sources will be required 'to reduce emissions and break dependence on oil, gas and coal' (PCC 140). Regardless of what technologies are backed by states, new areas of uncertainty will undoubtedly be created in the process (PCC 145).

Giddens returns to the concept of utopian realism, first outlined in *The Consequences of Modernity*. Rather than examining this concept in future-oriented philosophical terms (as he does in CM) however, he attempts to offer practical examples of what a utopian realist society could look like in his work on climate change (PCC 160). He gives examples of so-called 'utopian' societies. For example, he discusses Malmo in Sweden, a location where whole communities are built around eco-friendly policies (e.g. homes, parking, and waste). He uses the notion of utopian realism not only to explore more environmentally friendly ways of living but also travelling. He focuses in particular on cars and the need to reduce CO_2 emissions. Whilst acknowledging the potential for the growth of new modes of transport powered by renewable sources he also states that we do not know 'how quickly, new forms of propulsion for vehicles, such as electricity from renewable sources, or hydrogen, can come into use on a large scale' (PCC 161). He does also explore alternative forms of social organisation and states there may be a movement against globalisation and a return to localism driven by more effective planning strategies. This could, according to Giddens, enable us to envisage a future where we do not rely so heavily on cars (PCC 161). Whatever happens from now on Giddens states that 'climate change is going to affect our lives and we will have to adapt to its consequences' (PCC 162).

Adapting biological and social life

In order to preserve human life in the future we must, Giddens argues, adapt to climate change. Adaption, is a concept, according to Giddens, that is 'borrowed from evolutionary biology, the term 'adaptation' has come into widespread use in the climate change literature' (PCC 163). For Giddens this is not just about 'reacting to the consequences of climate change once it has occurred'. 'Adaptation as far as possible has to be anticipatory and preventative' (PCC 163). Giddens elaborates on this concept focusing on what he calls *proactive adaptation* (PA). 'PA is about diagnosing and responding to *vulnerabilities*'. Vulnerability for Giddens is all about risk: 'the risk of suffering damage to a valued activity, way of life or resource' (PCC 164). Vulnerability for Giddens stands in contrast to *resilience*. 'Resilience can be defined as *adaptive capacity*, the capacity not only to cope in the face of external changes or shocks, but, wherever possible, to respond actively and positively to them' (PCC 164). Ultimately, it is the richer countries, he argues, that must shoulder most of the responsibility for adaptation, as far 'as the developing world is concerned, just as they have to in limiting the progress of global warming' (PCC 165).

The majority of greenhouse gas emissions are produced by only a limited number of countries. According to Giddens, 'what the majority of states do pales in significance compared to the activities of the large polluters' (PC 220). Innovation at all levels has to be a key aspect of the world's attempts to contain climate change (PCC 227). Giddens argues that three things are of particular importance in dealing with climate change: states – working individually, bilaterally, or in larger groupings. According to Giddens, 'a great deal of power in world society still remains in the hands of states, and no other organizations approach them in terms of legitimacy' (PCC 227). Businesses – both big and small – must also play a role. We also need to witness the emergence of a diverse and dynamic global civil society mediated by electronic means of communication and by the ease of modern transportation. He also stresses the importance of a strong form of global governance and the need to rehabilitate the United Nations, which currently seems to have lost its way. State leaders may come to realise that it is the lack of effective global governance that is a prime reason why the dangers associated with climate change have become so acute (PCC 228). Giddens rearticulates his earlier radical political or third-way position (BLR, TW), stating that we need to go beyond a politics of either the left or right, and instead focus on developing a 'cross-party concordat' (PCC 115). This would provide 'a firm anchor for climate change as a continuing preoccupation of the "policy stream"' (PCC 115).

Giddens concludes his work on climate change by stating that, for better or worse, modern industry has unleashed a sheer volume of *power* into the world vastly beyond anything witnessed before (PCC 229). He moves from policy analysis back to social theory, reflecting again on the work of classical social theorists. He states that the enlightenment thinkers saw such capabilities as essentially benign – and as Marx argued – problems created by humans could be resolved by humans. However, others (most notably Weber) saw the powers created by industrial development as destructive or threatening the control of their creators (PCC 229). According to Giddens, this debate continues today:

> Doomsday is no longer a religious concept, a day of spiritual reckoning, but a possibility imminent in our society and economy. If unchecked, climate change alone could produce enormous human suffering. So also could the drying up of the energy resources upon which so many of our capacities are built. (PCC 230)

According to Giddens, there can be no 'going back'. 'The very expansion of human power that created such deep problems' in the first place through the process of industrial development 'is the only means of resolving them, with science and technology at the forefront' (BLR 230).

CONCLUSION

Giddens's substantive work on climate change does incorporate elements of his work on both radical modernity and politics. In *The Consequences of Modernity* he identifies climate change as one of the most pressing problems posed by radical modernity. In *Beyond Left and Right* and *The Third Way* he begins to map out a strategy to deal with environmental decay. This is something that he then elaborates on more fully in his work on climate change (PCC). A number of scholars, however, have argued that Giddens loses sight of his socio-theoretical moorings in his work on *The Third Way* (see Giddens 2000 and also Callinicos 2001) and in *The Politics of Climate Change*, both of which are aimed at a popular rather than an academic audience, and as a result his work lost credibility. For example, Giddens's theory of globalisation as outlined in *The Consequences of Modernity* afforded him the position of a respected figure in the field of globalisation. However, according to James and Steger (2014), the term Giddens's paradox (2014: 421) that he developed in PCC seemed to show a lack of integrity. The notion of Giddens's paradox to describe the core problem of climate change – the discrepancy between what people know and how they act – is not only an act of vanity on his part perhaps, but also may indicate a shift from serious sociotheoretical analysis in Giddens's work.

Throughout BLR, TW, and PCC Giddens articulated and developed his radical political position. However, it is perhaps the concept of risk that is used most consistently across all the texts explored in this chapter. Giddens continues to reinforce the message that 'our age is not more dangerous – not more risky – than those of earlier generations, but that the balance of risks and dangers has shifted' (RW 34). Giddens reinforces the message that 'we live in a world where hazards created by ourselves are as, or more threatening than those that come from outside. Some of these hazards are genuinely catastrophic', such as climate change. Others affect us as individuals much more directly, for instance, those involved in diet, medicine, or even marriage (RW 34). However, what he seeks to demonstrate is that there is 'no question of merely taking a negative attitude towards risk. Risk always needs to be disciplined, but active risk-taking is a core element of a dynamic economy and innovative society' (RW 35). Risk and opportunity, as Giddens argues, belong together; the greatest opportunities often arise from the biggest risks (PCC 230). Despite any differences identified in all the work analysed in this chapter, the message Giddens ends on in each text is not dissimilar: a mix of doomsday philosophising and of hope for the future, which he pitches through the conceptual lens of the centre ground: 'A new Dark Ages, a new age of enlightenment, or perhaps a confusing mixture of the two – which will it be? Probably the third possibility is the most likely. In that case, we all have to hope that the balance will be tilted towards the enlightenment side of the equation' (PCC 232).

Abbreviations

BLR: *Beyond Left and Right: The Future of Radical Politics* (1994b)

CM: *The Consequences of Modernity* (1990)

PCC: *The Politics of Climate Change* (2011)

RM: *Reflexive Modernization* (1994a)

RW: *Runaway World* (1999)

TW: *The Third Way: The Renewal of Social Democracy* (1998)

Selected Further Reading

The following two readings provide a good and comprehensive introduction and overview of Giddens's sociological project:

Bryant, C. G. A. and Jary, D. (eds) (2001) *The Contemporary Giddens: Social Theory in a Globalizing Age*. Basingstoke: Palgrave.

Kaspersen, L. B. (2000) *Anthony Giddens: An Introduction to a Social Theorist*. Oxford: Blackwell Publishers.

Callinicos, A. (2001) *Against the Third Way*. Cambridge: Polity Press provides a thought-provoking critique of the third-way perspective.

Note

1   United Nations, General Assembly, Rio Declaration on Environment and Development, Rio de Janeiro, 3–14 June 1992, www.un.org/documents/ga/conf151/aconf15126-1annex1.htm (accessed May 2017).

2

Pierre Bourdieu: Capital and Forms of Social Suffering

PART 1: FORMS OF CAPITAL

Bourdieu views capital as accumulated labour, 'a force inscribed in objective or subjective structures', 'the principle underlying the immanent regularities of the social world' (FC 46). According to Bourdieu, 'it is what makes the games of society – not least, the economic game – something other than simple games of chance' (FC 46). Capital for Bourdieu exists in different forms – economic, cultural, and social – which, when legitimated, are converted into symbolic capital and power. Bourdieu argues that the social position of individuals, groups, or institutions is determined by the *volume* and *composition* of capital they hold (Wacquant 2008: 268), and that the distribution of cultural and economic capital is the main source of class differentiation in society (D). Capital therefore frames his understanding of social inequality in contemporary society and, as articulated in Part 2 of this chapter, is also embedded in his work on suffering.

Habitus, Capital, and Field

The concepts of field, capital, and habitus are often perceived to be the organising concepts of Bourdieu's work (Wacquant 1989). Together these are used to formulate his socio-theoretical approach, a 'synthesis of objectivism and subjectivism, social physics and social phenomenology' (Wacquant 2008: 266). Bourdieu uses these concepts together, and it is impossible to make sense of capital without recognising its relationship to the other two. We begin our analysis, therefore, by situating his concept of capital in relation to habitus and field.

Habitus is 'the durably installed generative principle of regulated improvisations' (OTP 78). It acts as a 'system of durable and transposable *dispositions* through which individuals perceive, judge, and act in the world' (Wacquant 2008: 267). Through the habitus 'unconscious schemata' are acquired via ongoing exposure to a particular set of social conditions and through the internalisation of 'external constraints and possibilities' (Wacquant 2008: 267). It is habitus that forms a 'mediating link between individual's 'subjective worlds and the cultural world into which they are born and which they share with others' (Jenkins 1992: 75). According to Wacquant it 'is at once *structured*, by the patterned social forces that produced it, and *structuring*: it gives form and coherence to the various activities of an individual across the separate spheres of life' (Wacquant 2008: 268).

According to Wacquant (2008) 'the system of dispositions' (habitus) people acquire depends, however, on their particular endowment in *capital* (258). For Bourdieu, 'capital is accumulated labor (in its materialized form or its "incorporated", embodied form) which, when appropriated on a private, i.e., exclusive, basis by agents or groups of agents, enables them to appropriate social energy in the form of reified or living labor' (FC 46). Capital 'takes time to accumulate' and can be reproduced in 'identical or expanded form', although, according to Bourdieu, it has a tendency to persist in its existing state (FC 46). At any given point in time the structure and distribution of different types of capital represent the inherent structure of the social world, that is, a 'set of constraints inscribed in the very reality of that world, which govern its functioning in a durable way' (FC 46). In order to understand and account for the structure and functioning of the social world, Bourdieu argues for the need to acknowledge capital in all its forms and 'not solely in the one form recognized by economic theory' (FC 46). Bourdieu identifies three fundamental forms of capital:

> *economic capital*, which is immediately and directly convertible into money and may be institutionalized in the form of property rights; as *cultural capital*, which is convertible, on certain conditions, into economic capital and may be institutionalized in the form of educational qualifications; and … *social capital*, made up of social obligations ('connections'), which is convertible, in certain conditions, into economic capital and may be institutionalized in the form of a title of nobility. (FC 47)

Alongside economic, cultural, and social capital Bourdieu also uses the term symbolic capital, which is taken according to Skeggs 'to refer to the form the different types of capital take once they are perceived and recognized as legitimate. Legitimation is the key mechanism in the conversion to power. Capital has to be legitimated before it can have symbolic power' (Skeggs 1997: 8).

In contemporary societies, however, 'people do not face an undifferentiated social space' (Waquant 2008: 268). According to Wacquant (2008) 'the various spheres of life, art, science, religion, to the economy, the law, politics and so on tend to form distinct microcosms endowed with their own rules, regularities and forms of authority – what Bourdieu calls fields' (Wacquant, 2008: 208). Bourdieu defines fields as 'a network, or a configuration, of objective relations between positions objectively defined' (Bourdieu in Wacquant 1989: 39). It 'is a social arena within which struggles or manoeuvres take place over specific resources or stakes and access to them' (Jenkins 1992: 84). 'It is a structured space of positions, a *forcefield* that imposes its specific determinations upon all those who enter it' (Waquant 2008: 268). It is also an arena of struggle through which agents and institutions seek to preserve or overturn the existing distribution of capital (Wacquant 2008: 268).

Bourdieu employs this particular conceptual 'arsenal', as Wacquant refers to it, in order to explore the ways in which 'social and mental' structures are reproduced or transformed in society (Wacquant 2008: 267). Bourdieu argues that these concepts are closely linked and operate most effectively when used together.[1] As will become apparent in Part 2, it is not possible or desirable to completely isolate these concepts from one another. However, for Bourdieu it is capital – most notably economic and cultural capital – that underpins the major social divisions in contemporary social life. There is significant merit, therefore, in offering a detailed analysis of the different types of capital, which he outlines in some detail in his essay 'The forms of capital' (1986), and which is both informed by and illuminated through his substantive work on schooling and taste (Bourdieu and Passeron 1977).

Cultural Capital

Bourdieu argues that cultural capital requires familiarity 'with the dominant culture in society', and particularly 'the ability to understand and use educated language' (Sullivan 2001: 893). Cultural capital for Bourdieu can exist in three different forms:

> in the *embodied* state, i.e., in the form of long-lasting dispositions of the mind and body; in the *objectified* state, in the form of cultural goods (pictures, books, dictionaries, instruments, machines etc.), which are the trace or realization of theories or critiques of these theories, problematics etc.; and in the *institutionalized* state, a form of objectification which must be set apart because, as will be seen in the case of educational qualifications, it confers entirely original properties on the cultural capital which it is presumed to guarantee. (FC 47)

The notion of cultural capital was developed by Bourdieu originally through his own empirical research in education (Bourdieu and Passeron 1977). Cultural capital is the theoretical hypothesis that made it possible for him to explain the unequal academic achievements of children from different social classes (FC 47). In developing the concept of cultural capital Bourdieu breaks from what he argues is common-sense theory, which views academic success as related to natural aptitude. Bourdieu's approach also departs from an economic approach, which links educational success to finance (i.e. having the means to privately educate your children) and from a human capital approach, which views investments in education (e.g. in training programmes) as a means to achieve a more productive workforce.

For Bourdieu, existing approaches to educational attainment fail to account for the complex intersection of economic/cultural investment in educational attainment. They disregard 'the best hidden and socially most determinant educational investment, namely the domestic transmission of cultural capital' (FC 48). They ignore the importance of cultural capital previously invested by the family, neglecting 'the contribution which the education system makes to the reproduction of the social structure by sanctioning the hereditary transmission of cultural capital' (FC 48). In making these claims, Bourdieu has often been criticised for not being precise enough about exactly which of the resources associated with the higher class home constitute cultural capital, and how these resources are converted into educational credentials (Sullivan 2002). However, by acknowledging the interpenetration of family, cultural capital, and educational attainment in this way, Bourdieu offered a significant challenge to economic theories of capital and existing sociological work on education.

Transferring embodied cultural capital

One of the key properties of cultural capital according to Bourdieu is that 'it is linked to the body and presupposes embodiment' (FC 48). 'The accumulation of cultural capital in the embodied state' *Bildung* presumes 'a process of embodiment' (FC 48). Bourdieu argues that embodied capital is external wealth converted into an integral part of the person, into a habitus. This form of capital cannot be transmitted immediately ('unlike money' or 'property rights') 'by gift or by bequest, purchase, or exchange'. It may however be acquired unconsciously (FC 48). By focusing on the embodied nature of cultural capital, Bourdieu uniquely draws together notions of biological and cultural inheritance, the former an innate property, the latter acquired through primary socialisation. Embodied cultural capital for Bourdieu 'cannot be accumulated beyond the appropriating capacities of an individual agent' (FC 49). It decays with the biological capacity (and memory etc.) of its owner. This, for Bourdieu, is because embodied capital is linked in various ways to biological personhood 'in its singularity' and is subject to a hereditary transmission (FC 49). According to Bourdieu through the notion of embodied capital one is able to combine the prestige of innate property with the merits of acquisition, biological inheritance with socialisation. He argues that the social conditions in which such capital is transferred and acquired are therefore subtler than those of economic, capital making it function as symbolic capital (FC 49).

'The structure of the field, i.e., the unequal distribution of capital, is the source of the specific effects of capital' (FC 49). However, for Bourdieu, it is through the logic of transmission that cultural capital acquires its symbolic power (FC 49). The ability to obtain objectified cultural capital depends on the familial embodiment of cultural capital. The ability to accumulate all forms of cultural capital (embodied, objectified, and institutionalised) arises from the outset only with the children of families endowed with strong cultural capital (FC 49). Bourdieu argues that this hidden (domestic) transmission of cultural capital plays a significant role in the reproduction of different forms of capital (and subsequently an agent's position within social space). According to Bourdieu, the hereditary transmission of cultural capital 'therefore receives proportionately greater weight in the system of reproduction strategies, as the direct, visible forms of transmission tend to be more strongly censored and controlled' (FC 49). This transmission occurs through the socialisation of children within the family and therefore takes time to accumulate. For Bourdieu, 'the link between economic and cultural capital is established through the mediation of time needed for acquisition' (FC 49) of capital.

Objectified and institutional forms of capital

According to Bourdieu, 'cultural capital in the objectified state has a number of properties that are defined only in the relationship with cultural capital in its embodied form' (FC 50). 'The cultural capital objectified in material objects and media, such as writings, paintings, monuments, instruments, etc., is transmissible in its materiality' (FC 50). Bourdieu uses the example of a collection of paintings to illustrate his argument. Cultural capital can be transmitted through changes in the legal ownership of paintings along with economic capital. However, there is also the possession of the means of 'consuming a painting or using a machine', which are embodied capital, and as such is subject to the same laws of transmission (FC 50). According to Bourdieu, cultural capital in its objectified state presents itself as autonomous. It is the product of historical action and has its own laws that transcend individual desires. However, he also argues that it exists as 'symbolically and materially active, effective capital only insofar as it is appropriated by agents and implemented and invested as a weapon and a stake in the struggles which go on in the fields of cultural production' (FC 50).

This is something that Bourdieu elaborates in his work on taste (D). Here he argues that 'to appreciate' certain objective forms of capital such as 'a painting, a poem, or a symphony' presumes the 'mastery of the specialized symbolic code' (Wacquant 2008: 270). Mastery of this type of cultural capital 'can be acquired by osmosis in one's milieu of origin or by explicit teaching' (Wacquant 2008: 270). According to Wacquant (2008) when it comes through family and inheritance (as with children of cultured upper class families), this capacity is experienced as an innate inclination (Wacquant 2008: 270). He also states that the field of social classes involves the 'struggles in which the agents wield strengths and obtain profits proportionate to their mastery of this objectified capital, and therefore to the extent of their embodied capital' (FC 50).

According to Bourdieu, the objectification of cultural capital in the form of academic qualifications is one way of neutralising some of the limits of embodied capital (i.e. the fact that it decays along with its bearer) (FC 50). 'It institutes cultural capital by collective magic' (FC 51). Bourdieu argues that academic qualifications confer 'institutional recognition on the cultural capital possessed by any given agent', and in doing so 'also makes it possible to compare qualification holders and even to exchange them (by substituting one for another in succession)' (FC 51). Bourdieu also argues that this 'makes it possible to establish conversion rates between cultural capital and economic capital by guaranteeing the monetary value of a given academic capital' (FC 51). For Bourdieu, the material and symbolic profits guaranteed by academic qualifications also depend on their rarity. When qualifications become less rare they are more difficult to convert (e.g. as is the case with the expansion of higher education). In this case the investments made (in time and effort) to acquire academic qualifications may turn out to be less lucrative than was anticipated (FC 51).

Social Capital

While Bourdieu focuses in detail on cultural capital and its relationship to economic capital, he does not neglect the importance of social capital. Social capital refers to group association or membership: 'social capital is the aggregate of the actual or potential resources which are linked to possession of a durable network of more or less institutionalized relationships of mutual acquaintance and recognition – or in other words, to membership in a group' (FC 51). According to Bourdieu, this group then provides its individual members with the support of the collectively owned capital. 'These relationships may exist only in the practical state, in material and/or symbolic exchanges which help to maintain them. They may also be socially instituted and guaranteed by the application of a common name' (FC 51). According to Bourdieu, the amount of social capital possessed by an individual will therefore depend on 'the size of the network of connections he can effectively mobilize' (FC 51). It is also contingent on the volume of the capital (economic, cultural, and symbolic) that an individual possesses in their own right (FC 51). According to Bourdieu, 'the existence of a network of connections is not a natural or even a social given' (FC 52). The reproduction of social capital requires a continual effort of sociability, and 'a continuous series of exchanges in which recognition is endlessly affirmed and reaffirmed' (FC 52). Those who are richly endowed with social capital, particularly inherited social capital (e.g. as symbolised through possessing an elite family name), are more likely to be able to 'transform all circumstantial relationships into lasting connections' (FC 52).

Economic Capital and Capital Conversions

According to Sullivan (2002) sociologists have often critiqued Bourdieu for placing too much weight in his theory of capital to 'symbolic relations at the expense of material ones' (Sullivan 2002: 146; Willis 1983). This is perhaps unfair, as Bourdieu makes clear that both cultural and social capital can be derived from economic capital (FC 53). He argues that it can be assumed that 'economic capital is at the root of all the other types of capital', and that these disguised forms of capital 'conceal (not least from their possessors) the fact that economic capital is at their root' (FC 54). He argues that 'the convertibility of the different types of capital is the basis of the strategies aimed at ensuring the reproduction of capital (and the position occupied in social space) by means of the conversions least costly in terms of conversion work and of the losses inherent in the conversion itself (in a given state of the social power relations)' (FC 54). As Bourdieu argues, the conversion rate between different forms of 'capital, set by such institutional mechanisms as the school system, the labour market, and inheritance laws, turns out to be one of the central stakes of social struggles, as each class or class fraction seeks to impose the hierarchy of capital most favourable to its own endowment' (Wacquant 2008: 271).

Through his theory of capital, therefore, Bourdieu demonstrates that people are distributed in 'social space according to: the global *volume* of capital they possess; the *composition* of their capital', and the relative weight of the various forms of capital (Skeggs 1997: 8; Wacquant 2008). In his empirical work on taste and education Bourdieu emphasises the ways in which different forms of capital work together to underpin class difference in contemporary society. The following section extends this analytical focus to his broader sociological and political work on social suffering. Examining his ethnographical work on the experience of suffering in everyday life allows for an assessment of the extent to which Bourdieu's work on capital can further inform sociological analyses of how positions of disadvantage are reproduced, reinforced, and experienced in contemporary society.

PART 2: SOCIAL SUFFERING

Suffering has been described as a social experience that opposes rationality and 'exhausts the limits of practical reason' (Morgan and Wilkinson 2001: 204). Sociologists increasingly focus on conceptualising experiences of suffering in contemporary social life, particularly in the area of health and illness (Frank 2001; Kleinman et al. 1997). Bourdieu's work on social suffering belongs to a body of literature that seeks to speak to 'the experience of people living under the impact of extreme social hardships and events of political atrocity' (Wilkinson 2005: 4). *La Misère du Monde*, translated as *Weight of the World* (WOTW), is a co-authored ethnographical account of people's experiences of social suffering.[2] The book prioritises themes simultaneously central to sociology and encountered – personally or in mediated form – by large numbers of people in their daily lives, such as: poor housing and unemployment, social and symbolic forms of exclusion, intergenerational and interethnic conflict, and urban dystopia. In what follows we seek to examine Bourdieu's application of the concept of capital in this work on suffering, focusing in particular on his methodology, analysis of family and education, and social and physical space.

Researching Social Suffering in Everyday Life

In *Weight of the World* Bourdieu states: 'I am loath to engage too insistently here in reflections on theory or method' (WOTW 607). Despite this claim, however, discussions on reflexive sociology are prevalent throughout his ethnographic approach to suffering (Wacquant 1989).[3] Furthermore, it is through this discussion on the relationship between the researcher and the 'object' of research that we see elements of his theory of capital. In *Weight of the World* Bourdieu and co-authors attempt to juxtapose a sociological analysis with the individual points of view of their respondents through the direct inclusion of interview transcripts in the main text. As Bourdieu argues, it is necessary to analyse and understand respondents' points of view but without 'setting up the objectivizing distance that reduces the individual to a specimen in a display case' (WOTW 2). Bourdieu argues for the importance of juxtaposing of different points of view (the space for points of view) in research in order to 'bring out everything that results when different or antagonistic visions of the world confront each other' (WOTW 3).[4] Bourdieu argues that 'using material poverty as the sole measure of all suffering keeps us from *seeing* and understanding a whole side of the suffering characteristic of a social order' (WOTW 4). By adopting an approach that allows space for different points of view Bourdieu seeks to capture all forms of suffering including *positional suffering*, which is often taken as the point of reference for criticism ('you really don't have anything to complain about'), as for consolation ('you could be worse off you know') (WOTW 4). Through taking this approach – as will become clearer in a moment – Bourdieu is able to capture the subtle differences in the operation of various forms of capital that inform everyday experiences of suffering.

Capital and the research relationship

Bourdieu also stresses the methodological importance of acknowledging that the research relationship is first and foremost a social relationship. As such it often reflects and reproduces inequalities and hierarchies of the wider social structure. Bourdieu introduces his theory of capital directly into this discussion in this text on the research relationship. Bourdieu argues that the asymmetry in the research relationship is reinforced by 'social symmetry every time the investigator occupies a higher place in the social hierarchy of different types of capital, cultural capital in particular' (WOTW 609). He states that 'the *market for linguistic and symbolic goods* established every time an interview take place varies in structure according to the objective relationship between the investigator and the investigated or, what comes down to the same thing, the relationship between all the different kinds of capital, especially linguistic capital, with which each of them is endowed' (WOTW 609). In emphasising the operation of capital in the research situation, Bourdieu illustrates one of the ways in which the research relationship is an implicitly social one. However, he argues that sociologists have often failed to recognise this. They neglect to 'objectivize themselves' and therefore do not 'realize that what their apparently scientific discourse talks about is not the object but their relation to the object' (Bourdieu in Wacquant 1989: 33).

In order to acknowledge this relationship effectively Bourdieu argues that sociologists need to take a reflexive approach to research. However, this requires the development of an approach that goes beyond the particular type of reflexivity favoured by some American anthropologists (Clifford and Marcus 1986). According to Bourdieu, such authors spend too much time reflecting on themselves rather than their research object, opening the door potentially to a thinly veiled nihilistic relativism (Bourdieu in Wacquant 1989: 35). Bourdieu argues that the sociologist must go beyond this and objectivise her or his position in cultural production (Bourdieu in Wacquant 1989 HA). In his work on suffering, therefore, he advocates the need to adopt a particular type of reflexivity in research: 'a *reflex reflexivity* based on a craft, on a sociological "feel" or "eye", allows one to perceive and monitor *on the spot*, as the interview is actually taking place, the effects of the social structure within which it is occurring' (WOTW 608).[5] It is through the adoption of this sociological 'eye' or 'feel' that Bourdieu is able to explore the plurality of experience of social suffering in everyday life without losing sight of the effects of the wider social structure on the research relationship itself.

Social and Physical Sites of Capital

As already articulated above, Bourdieu has a multifaceted notion of social space. In contrast to Marx, he sees 'social space in modern societies not as focused around one organizing principle (relations to the means of economic production) but as a space with multiple (if interrelated) fields of competition where different forms of capital are at stake' (Couldry 2005: 356). For Bourdieu, individual action is the key site where social structure can be reproduced: social structure is not a determining force in itself. Bourdieu refers specifically to 'actions of individuals that are based on the dispositions those individuals have acquired and whose acquisition is itself structurally determined by the objective conditions in which that individual has lived his or her life (the individual's position in social space, including both inherited capital and actual resources, economic, cultural, and symbolic)' (Couldry 2005: 356). The relationship between physical (geographical) space and an agent's position in social space is present in Bourdieu's discussion of social capital in 'The forms of capital' (FC). However, the intersection of social and physical space, and more specifically the role of capital in this context, is extended in his work on suffering.[6]

According to Bourdieu, as bodies (and biological individuals) human beings are situated in a site and they occupy a place: 'The site (*le lieu*) can be defined absolutely as the point in *physical space* where an agent or a thing is situated, "takes place", exists: that is to say, either as a *localization* or, from a relational viewpoint, as a *position*, a rank in an order' (WOTW 123). 'People are constituted in, and in relationship to, a *social space* (or better yet, to needs fields)' (WOTW 124). According to Bourdieu, there is no space in a hierarchical society that is not also hierarchical and that does not articulate these unequal relationships 'in a form that is more or less distorted and, above all, disguised by the *naturalization effect* produced by the long-term inscription of social realities in the natural world' (WOTW 124). He argues that social space converts into physical space,

> but the translation is always more or less *blurred*: the power over space that comes from possessing various kinds of capital takes the form in appropriated physical space of a certain relation between the spatial structure of the distribution of agents and the spatial structure of the distribution of goods and services, private or public. (WOTW 124)

According to Bourdieu, 'the structures of social space' are inscribed 'in physical space' and cannot be changed 'except by a *work of transplantation*, a moving of things and an uprooting or deporting of people, which itself presupposes extremely difficult and costly social transformations' (WOTW 124). For Bourdieu, 'the value of different regions of reified social space' (i.e. physically realised or objectified) 'is defined in this relation between the distribution of agents and the distribution of goods in social space' (WOTW 125). The result of this is that the rarest goods and the people that own them are concentrated in particular places.

This focus on social and physical space is prevalent throughout *Weight of the World*. It is illuminated early on by Bourdieu's interview with two young boys living in a French housing project:[7] one boy – Ali – is French Algerian, the other – François – is ethnically white. Bourdieu uses interview transcripts to examine the shared position of the boys in social and geographical space. He states: 'How could readers of their interview fail to see that in fact they share every trait except ethnic origin' (WOTW 62). Whilst emphasising the similarities between the two boys, he also illustrates the differences, which relate to race, ethnicity, and access to capital:

Ali is merely a sort of François taken to the limit: the ethnic stig-
mata inscribed in a permanent way on his skin or his facial
features, as well as in his name, intensifies, or rather radicalizes the
handicap linked to the lack of certificates or qualifications, itself
linked to the lack of cultural and more specifically linguistic capital.
(WOTW 62)

In his analysis of ethnic and racial inequality (here and elsewhere) Bourdieu
emphasises the importance of socio-economic position, or at least seeks to
use the same analytical framework to study these different but intersecting
forms of inequality. However, as Lane argues, racial discrimination is the
outcome of a 'complex of tastes, aversions, prejudices and ideas', it has 'its
own autonomous logic' and requires its 'own specific tools of analysis' (Lane
2006: 153). It is the product of a complex and contradictory set of processes
that include but are not exclusive to social and economic deprivation
(McRobbie 2002). Such complexity, however, does not appear to be fully
reflected in Bourdieu's discussion of capital and ethnicity in his work on
social suffering.

Capital and physical space

In *Weight of the World* Bourdieu focuses much of his analysis of social and
physical space on Paris,[8] which he states is: 'the site of capital, that is, the site
in physical space where the positive poles of all the fields are concentrated
along with most of the agents occupying these dominant positions' (WOTW
125). This, according to Bourdieu, means 'that the capital cannot be ade-
quately analyzed except in relation to the provinces ("and provincialness"),
which is nothing other than being deprived (in entirely relative terms) of the
capital and capital' (WOTW 125). He elaborates further here on the relationship between capital and physical and social space. He argues that: 'the
ability to dominate space, notably by appropriating (materially or symbolically) the rare goods (public or private) distributed there, depends on the
capital possessed' (WOTW 127). Capital makes it possible to keep 'undesirable' people together in a far away location. It also keeps desirable people
and goods close, 'minimizing the necessary expense (notably in time)' in
appropriating them. Bourdieu argues that 'those who are deprived of capital
are either physically or symbolically held at a distance from goods' that have
the highest social value: 'they are forced to stick with the most undesirable
and the least rare persons or goods'. The lack of capital according to
Bourdieu 'chains one to a place' (WOTW 127).

Embodied capital, time, and space

Alongside capital, habitus and field are never far away from Bourdieu's analysis of social and physical space. Bourdieu argues here that: 'If the habitat

shapes the habitus, the habitus also shapes the habitat' (WOTW 128). The importance of time and acquisition were already illustrated above with reference to the hidden domestic transmission of capital and related to both biological and cultural notions of inheritance. In *Weight of the World*, embodied capital, time, and acquisition are connected again through his examination of social and physical space. Bourdieu refers here to the properties acquired through prolonged occupation of a site and sustained association with its legitimate occupants. He emphasises the importance of the relationship between location and social capital:

> This is the case, obviously, with the social capital of relations, connections or ties (and most particularly with the privileged ties of childhood or adolescent friendships) or with all the subtlest aspects of cultural and linguistic capital, such as body mannerisms and pronunciation (accents) etc. all the many attributes that make the place of birth (and to a lesser degree, place of residence) so important. (WOTW 128)

Bourdieu focuses his analysis on Paris in order to illustrate the subtle operationalisation of different forms of capital in physical space. He argues that: 'One has the Paris that goes with one's economic capital, and also with one's cultural and social capital (visiting the Pompidou Museum is not enough to appropriate the Museum of Modern Art)' (WOTW 128). Furthermore, it is not only a case of economic and cultural capital. According to Bourdieu, 'certain spaces, and in particular the most closed and most "select", require not only economic and cultural capital but social capital as well' (WOW 128–9). This is acquired through what he calls 'the *club effect*' that derives from people in 'chic' neighbourhoods coming together on a regular basis, and sharing the fact that what they have in common is the fact that they are not common (WOTW 129).

Bourdieu's focus on France is extended by other authors of *Weight of the World* to include an analysis and comparison with different geographical areas. For example, in writing about social dystopia in the American ghetto, Wacquant draws comparisons with rising urban inequality in France[9] (WOTW 130–9). Much of the analysis in the text focuses on the use of interview transcripts to illuminate the ways in which the differentiation of social space is reproduced in physical space. However, Bourdieu also includes a discussion of policy in his analysis. He argues that the differentiation of physical space can also be reinforced 'at a national level concerning housing policies, or at a local level, with regard to the construction and allocation of subsidized housing or choices for public services'. Such policies lead to for example, policies 'the *construction of homogenous groups on a spatial basis*' for example as observed in run-down housing estates (WOTW 129). By drawing on different modes of analysis Bourdieu is able to elucidate the different ways in which experiences of social inequality and suffering are reinforced through physical space.

Cultural Capital, Inheritance, and Education

As articulated above, Bourdieu often focuses in his work on cultural capital and the interaction between family background and schooling (Bourdieu and Passeron 1977). Cultural capital for Bourdieu is 'inculcated in the higher class home, and enables higher-class student to gain higher educational credentials than lower-class students' (Sullivan 2002: 145–146). In his work on suffering, Bourdieu returns to his focus on the transmission of cultural capital, education, and family. Inheritance, in particular, takes a more central role in his work on suffering. Bourdieu uses it not only to illustrate class difference, but also to demonstrate the relativity of suffering.

Capital and inheritance

Bourdieu begins his discussion with an argument on paternal inheritance. He states, first, that in order to continue and embody the paternal line it is frequently necessary to go beyond the achievements of one's father (WOTW 507).[10] Second, Bourdieu argues that 'for all social categories (though to differing degrees), the transmission of inheritance depends on the judgements' of the 'schooling system'. The schooling system for Bourdieu is brutal. It is competitive and it 'is responsible for many failures and disappointments'. In the past, it was the family that set up the parameters of inheritance, making it appear preordained (WOTW 507). In contemporary society, according to Bourdieu, 'this work also falls to schools', whose judgements and sanctions may confirm but also contradict or counter those of the family (WOTW 507). It is unsurprising, therefore, that the school is so often at the core of social suffering. Bourdieu argues that this is certainly the case with the interviewees in his study, 'who have been disappointed either in their own plans or in their plans for their children or by the ways the job market has reneged on the promises and guarantees made by the educational system' (WOTW 507).

It is worth noting at this point that Bourdieu's discussion on inheritance is focused on the father–son relationship, excluding a discussion on inheritance through the maternal line. In reflecting on issues of gender in Bourdieu's extensive œuvre, Skeggs (2004) argues that he sees the family 'as a fiction and a social artefact', in the same way that feminists do.[11] He perceives it to be a 'well-founded illusion because it is produced and re-produced with the guarantee of the state and operates as a central site of normalisation and naturalisation' (Skeggs 2004: 21). According to Skeggs, however, this does not stop him from 'normalising his own conception of the family 'by defining it as *the* universal norm, in a similar way to how he defines working-class women as closer to nature' (Skeggs 2004: 21–2). For Bourdieu 'the family functions as a field in which normalcy or the ability to constitute oneself as the universal is the capital': yet he fails to examine the ways in which 'normalcy works *differently* through gender as a form of capital' (Skeggs 2004: 22). This is certainly reflected in his discussion on inheritance in *Weight of the World*, which fails to problematise the gendered nature of inherited capital.

The family and education

For Bourdieu, the family itself is a necessary 'matrix of the contradictions and double binds that arise from the disjunction between the dispositions of the inheritor and the destiny contained within the inheritance itself' (WOTW 507–8). Inheritance is transmitted unconsciously in and by the *father's* 'whole way of being, and also overtly by educational acts aimed at perpetuating the line' (WOTW 508). However, Bourdieu is clear in his work here that successful inheritance means embodying but also going beyond the parent. The gap between parents' expectations and what the child can actually achieve is a major source of suffering (WOTW 508). Focusing more specifically on cultural capital, Bourdieu argues that if (family) connection constitutes a necessary condition for the smooth transmission of the inheritance (particularly concerning cultural capital), it is nevertheless not an adequate condition for achieving succession. 'For the holders of cultural capital above all (but also for everyone else, though to a lesser degree), succession is subject to the verdicts of school and is therefore passed on by academic success' (WOTW 509).

The transmission of cultural capital features again in Bourdieu's work in this text on schooling and secondary education more directly. Bourdieu argues that the meritocratic school system cannot deal effectively with a diversity of student intellectual strategies and as a result education often 'inflicts wounds that are likely to reactivate basic traumas' (WOTW 509). The negative judgements given by schools affect an individual's self-image, reinforced by the parents in ways 'that no doubt vary in their force and form, magnifying suffering and confronting the child or teenager with the alternatives of either conforming or quitting the game through denial, compensation, or regression' (WOTW 509). He gives the example of the manual labourer father whose 'entire existence is carried in a dual injunction' (WOTW 510). The father wants his children to succeed and be upwardly mobile on the one hand, whilst maintaining identification with himself (be like me):

> He cannot want his son to identify with his own position and its dispositions, and yet all his behavior works continuously to produce that identification, in particular the body language that contributes so powerfully to fashioning the whole manner of being, that is, the habitus. (WOTW 510)

As a result, the son/daughter is 'guilty of betrayal if he succeeds, he is guilty of disappointing if he fails' (WOTW 510). Bourdieu uses these contradictions imposed by the family to illustrate positional forms of suffering: 'The family is at the root of the most universal part of social suffering, including the paradoxical form of suffering based in privilege' (WOTW 511).

Capital, education, and schooling

Bourdieu also focuses specifically on the democratisation of the education system. According to Bourdieu, the secondary school system was until the end of the 1950s characterised by great stability based on the early and brutal elimination of students from disadvantaged families (WOTW 421). One of the biggest changes is, he argues, the democratisation of the school system – the entry into academic enterprise of social categories previously excluded (e.g. shopkeepers, artisans, farmers) (WOTW 422).[12] According to Bourdieu, it is clear that the children of the most culturally and economically disadvantaged families cannot gain access to the higher levels of the school system without significantly modifying the economic and symbolic value of educational qualifications (WOTW 423).

However, 'official diversification (into tracks or streams) and unofficial diversification (into subtly hierarchized schools or classes', ... 'also help recreate a particularly well-hidden principle of differentiation' (WOTW 424). Bourdieu argues that the 'elite students who have received a well-defined sense of place, good role models, and encouragement from their families' are in position to apply their cultural capital in top streams in good schools (WOTW 424). In contrast, students who come from 'disadvantaged families, especially children of immigrants, often left to fend for themselves, from primary school on, 'are obliged to rely either on the dictates of school or on chance to find their way in an increasingly complex universe' (WOTW 424). This, according to Bourdieu, helps to explain 'their either untimely or inappropriate use of already extremely meagre cultural capital' (WOTW 424). Bourdieu concludes his examination of education by arguing that:

> The educational system excludes as it always has, but now it does so continuously and at every level of the curriculum ... and it keeps hold of those when it excludes, just relegating them to educational tracks that have lost more or less of whatever value they once had. (WOTW 425)

The arguments Bourdieu makes about cultural capital, family, and education in *Weight of the World* are very similar to those he makes elsewhere (FC; Bourdieu and Passeron 1977). In *Weight of the World*, however, his discussion is tied explicitly to a focus on education as a source of social suffering. His position is also updated to reflect changes in education brought about by the expansion and devaluing of educational qualifications. This is easily illustrated in the UK context by the proliferation of secondary school and degree level courses such as 'music management'. Such courses appear to have little academic content and also do not provide the students taking them with specific professional qualifications. They tend, however, to be taken by those attempting to make the most of what Bourdieu calls their meagre cultural capital.

Sociological debates surrounding *Weight of the World* have often been focused on issues relating to methodology or politics. While some sociologists argue that *Weight of the World* is best read as a political tract not a socio-logical analysis (Jenkins 1992), others suggest that Bourdieu's socio-theoretical framework cannot cope with the sheer breadth and weight of topics and data presented in the text (Martuccelli 1999). However, through the analysis of capital in his work on suffering in the second part of this chapter, we have sought to show that this is not necessarily the case. Rather, through focusing on the plurality of respondents' voices Bourdieu is able to illuminate more clearly the ways in which positions of disadvantage are not only experienced, but also reinforced or reproduced in contemporary society. In *Weight of the World* Bourdieu deftly applies what he calls the sociological 'eye' or 'feel' in order to illuminate the subtle ways in which capital and suffering operate in everyday social life (WOTW 608).

CONCLUSION

There is a consistency in Bourdieu's use of capital across all of his work explored in this chapter. One of the key threads present throughout his work perhaps is the connection he makes between forms of capital, time, and acqui-sition. This is illuminated through the hidden domestic transmission of cultural capital in his work on the family and education, and through the transmission of social capital in his discussion on social and physical space. Furthermore, the embodied nature of capital appears to underpin much of his work – from his focus on the inheritance of cultural capital to the biological occupation of particular social and physical spaces. With the rapid expansion of the biomedical sciences over recent decades, the notion of embodied capital has become increasingly important in contemporary socio-theoretical discus-sions on inequality. As Webster argues, for example, the growth of genetic testing in recent decades has the potential to create new forms of (economic) inequality based on one's *genetic* capital (Webster 2007: 91). However, as his work on the family shows, embodied capital for Bourdieu is not something that is just acquired only through biological notions of inheritance, but also through primary socialisation. In developing this concept, therefore, he has offered something particularly unique to the sociological study of inequality, paving the way perhaps for the recent advancement of 'carnal sociology', which focuses specifically on the embodied and embedded nature of inequality and social action (Wacquant 2015).[13]

Whilst methodological reflexivity permeates his entire *œuvre*, capital is particularly embedded in Bourdieu's methodological approach to suffering. He seeks through his methodological strategy to illuminate a full spectrum of experiences of suffering in contemporary social life, not just those associated with profound economic hardship. However, economic capital still appears to form the bedrock of much of his analysis in his work on suffering. This per-haps mitigates some of those earlier critiques levelled at Bourdieu which suggest that he focuses too much on other forms of capital to the detriment of an analysis of material conditions (Willis 1983). However, it also means that some forms of inequality (gender, and race and ethnicity) may still appear underrepresented in his work, or that, at the very least, their analysis is often reduced to issues of economic inequality (Lane 2006; Skeggs 2004). That said, it is worth remembering here, perhaps, that capital is only one of several key concepts used by Bourdieu to illuminate social suffering. Only when it is used alongside other key concepts, such as habitus and field, can sociologists hope to expose different aspects of inequality across a range of areas of contemporary social life (Wacquant 1989).

Abbreviations

D: *Distinction* (1984)

FC: 'The forms of capital' (1997)

HA: *Homo Academicus* (1988)

OTP: *Outline of a Theory of Practice* (1977)

WOTW: *The Weight of the World* (1999)

Selected Further Reading

Wacquant, L. (2008) 'Pierre Bourdieu', in R. Stones (ed.) *Key Sociological Thinkers*. Basingstoke: Palgrave, pp. 261–77 provides a comprehensive introduction to Bourdieu's sociology. It includes a useful discussion of the concepts of habitus, capital, and field.

Jenkins, R. (1992) *Pierre Bourdieu*. London: Routledge offers a detailed and critical analysis of Bourdieu's overall sociological framework.

The edited monograph Adkins, L. and Skeggs, B. (eds) (2005) *Feminism After Bourdieu*. Hoboken, NJ: John Wiley & Sons contains varied and detailed discussions on gender and capital, and the impact of Bourdieu's work on feminism.

Notes

1 Together these concepts help Bourdieu to 'sociologize' the notion of doxa, a term originally developed by phenomenologist Husserl. These concepts emphasise the close fit between subjective worlds and objective structures. 'Each relatively autonomous universe develops its own doxa as a set of shared opinions and unquestioned beliefs' that 'bind people together' (Wacquant 2008: 270).

2 Bourdieu is the lead author for WOTW. The text is nearly 700 pages long and includes chapters by 20 different authors. It is impossible to explore all of these chapters in detail. We have drawn on a range of chapters by Bourdieu to illuminate his use of capital. However, where appropriate we also refer to chapters by other authors.

3 Sociological reflexivity is not the central focus of this chapter. For further discussion, see Bourdieu and Wacquant (1992).
4 See 'Space of points of view' (WOTW 1–5).
5 See 'Understanding' (WOTW 607–26).
6 See also Bourdieu (1995).
7 See Bourdieu's chapter 'The order of things' (WOTW 60–77).
8 See Bourdieu's chapter 'Site effects' (WOTW 123–9).
9 See also the chapter by Lois Wacquant 'Inside the zone' (WOTW 140–67) and the chapter by Phillippe Bourgois 'Homeless in El Barrio' (WOTW 168–79).
10 See chapter on 'The contradictions of inheritance' (WOTW 507–13).
11 There is a significant body of feminist literature on Bourdieu. See Skeggs (2004).
12 See chapters 'Outcasts on the inside' (WOTW 421–6) and 'They were the days' (WOTW 427–40).
13 For a discussion on the development of carnal sociology, please see Waquant (2015).

3

Bruno Latour: Rethinking Modern Social Life

PART 1: BEYOND MODERN SOCIAL CONDITIONS

In *We Have Never Been Modern* Latour offers an alternative approach to the theorisation of modernity. Latour is not suggesting – as radical modernists or postmodernists do – that we are simply living in a radical or postmodern society. Rather he seeks to problematise the very idea that we have ever been modern (WHNBM). Latour also seeks to offer an alternative socio-theoretical view to the concept of the social in *Reassembling the Social*. Rather than seeking to use the word to develop social explanations, he focuses instead on networks and associations, including those involving both humans and non-humans (RAS). This chapter seeks to explore his analytical approach to these two key concepts, also examining their manifestation in *An Inquiry into the Modes of Existence* – his comparative anthropology. With the threat of ecological decay looming on a global scale, Latour seeks in AIME to revisit many of the questions he poses in his earlier works, such as: if we were never modern then what were we and what are we to become (AIME 11)?

Were We Ever Modern?

Socio-theoretical explanations of the development of society tend to rest on the premise that we have been through or are currently still living in a period of modernity. For Latour these dominant accounts of modernity fall short. He is not aiming here to offer an alternative socio-theoretical vision of modernity itself as theorists such as Giddens have done in their work on radical or high modernity. Nor is he attempting to suggest – as postmodernists such as Lyotard do – that there has been a radical rupture with modernity. Both Giddens and Lyotard in different ways assume that modernity has existed in some form and at some point in time. For these theorists and many others the society we currently occupy is either a radicalised version of modernity or a new type of society beyond modernity. Latour is arguing for something quite distinct. He seeks to problematise the existence of modernity. He begins by highlighting the plurality and contradictions often inherent in definitions of modernity:

> Modernity comes in many versions ... yet all its definitions point, in one way or another, to the passage of time. The adjective 'modern' designates a new regime, an acceleration, a rupture, a revolution in time. When the word 'modern', 'modernization', or 'modernity' appears, we are defining, by contrast, an archaic and stable past. (WHNBM 10)

Latour also argues that the word 'modernity' refers to two distinct sets of practices that have nonetheless become blurred:

> The first set of practices, by 'translation', creates mixtures between entirely new types of beings, hybrids of nature and culture. The second, by 'purification' creates two entirely distinct ontological zones: that of human beings on the one hand; that of nonhumans on the other. Without the first set, the practices of purification would be fruitless or pointless. Without the second, the work of translation would be slowed down, limited, or even ruled out. (WHNBM 10–11)

According to Latour the first set of practices corresponds to what he calls 'networks' and the second to what he names as the modern critical stance (WHNBM 11). Latour argues that, providing we treat the two practices of translation and purification as distinct, then we can consider ourselves as 'truly modern' (WHNBM 11). However for Latour: 'as soon as we direct our attention simultaneously to the work of purification and the work of hybridization, we immediately stop being wholly modern, and our future begins to change' (WHNBM 11). It is at this point that Latour questions whether we have, in fact, ever been modern. This is because we become aware, on reflection that the two sets of practices have already been at work historically, and therefore our past also begins to change (WHNBM 11). Finally, Latour argues 'if we have never been modern – at least in the way criticism tells the story – the tourtuous relations that we have maintained with the other nature-cultures would also be transformed' (WHNBM 11).

The problem for Latour, which he returns back to again and again, is the relationship between humans and non-humans, and the ways in which modernity or being modern denies the simultaneous emergence of non-humans. According to Latour 'modernity is often defined in terms of humanism' (WHNBM 13). However, he also argues that this definition 'overlooks the simultaneous birth of "nonhumanity" – things, or objects, or beasts – and the equally strange beginning of a crossed-out God, relegated to the sidelines' (WHNBM 13). Modernity develops from the combined creation of these three entities (the birth of man, non-humanity, and God relegated to the sidelines). This combined creation is simultaneously masked and the three entities are treated separately (WHNBM 13). At the same time that these are being separated however 'underneath, hybrids continue to multiply as an effect of this separate treatment' (WHNBM 13). According to Latour, 'the common text that defines this understanding and this separation is called a constitution' (WHNBM 14).

The modern Constitution

Latour refers to what he calls the *modern Constitution*, which he spells with a capital 'C' to distinguish it from the notion of a political constitution. He uses it to define humans and non-humans, their attributes, relationships, abilities, and groupings (WHNBM 15). Latour begins by drawing on a seventeenth-century debate in philosophy between Hobbes (political philosophy) and Boyle (natural philosophy, physics, and chemistry) that arose over Boyle's air-pump experiments.[1] In his *Leviathan*[2] Hobbes simultaneously redraws the boundaries between different fields of physics, theology, psychology, law, biblical exegesis, and political science. Boyle on the other hand concurrently redesigns scientific rhetoric, theology, scientific politics, and the hermeneutics of facts. According to Latour:

> Together, they describe how God must rule, how the new King of England must legislate, how the spirits or the angels should act, what the properties of matter are, how nature is to be interrogated, what the boundaries of scientific or political discussion must be. . . (WHNBM 29–30)

Latour presents the arrangement that came out of the debate as 'being laid down in a "modern Constitution" that separates the powers of politics and science' (de Vries 2016: 124). He argues that this composition stayed in place 'for centuries because the internal, intellectual structure of this Constitution shields it from criticism and change' (de Vries 2016: 124). What Latour refers to here, however, is not a political constitution (such as we might think about in relation to the American political system, for example) and the separate powers of government. Rather the Constitution that Latour has in mind focuses on separating the powers of 'nature' (the domain of the natural sciences) on the one hand, and 'society' (values, human interaction, politics, and culture) on the other (de Vries 2016: 125).

At the heart of the modern Constitution, according to Latour, lies a paradox: when 'we consider hybrids we are dealing only with mixtures of nature and culture' (WHNBM 30). However, when we reflect on the work of purification, then nature and culture are separated (WHNBM 30). This is precisely what Latour is aiming to understand. The key point of the modern Constitution, according to Latour, is that 'it renders the work of mediation that assembles hybrids invisible, unthinkable, unrepresentable' (WHNBM: 34). The point that Latour is trying to make – and one that distinguishes his work from dominant socio-theoretical accounts of modernity – is that the modern Constitution allows for the creation of hybrids whilst simultaneously pretending that these hybrids don't exist. Latour argues that moderns are not actually unaware of what they do. Rather, he is saying that 'what they do – innovate on a large scale in the production of hybrids – is possible only because they steadfastly hold to the absolute dichotomy between the order of Nature and that of Society, a dichotomy which is itself possible only because they never consider the work of purification and that of mediation together' (WHNBM 40).

Modernity as illusion

In making the case that we were never modern however, Latour does not suggest that modernity is an illusion. Modernity according to Latour 'is a force added to others that for a long time it had the power to represent, to accelerate, or to summarize – a power that it no longer entirely holds' (WHNBM 40). For Latour, 'the modern Constitution exists and indeed acts in history', 'but it no longer defines what has happened to us' (WHNBM 40). Modernity is about the development of humanism, it is also about the development of progress and mastery of humans over nature. However, according to Latour, what the moderns have actually succeeded in doing is creating more and more hybrids. According to Latour, moderns think that they have been successful because 'they have carefully separated Nature and Society (and bracketed God), whereas they have succeeded only because they have mixed together much greater masses of humans and nonhumans, without bracketing anything and without ruling out any combination!' (WHNBM 41). By making this case Latour seeks to offer a unique and original socio-theoretical alternative to existing theories of modernity.

Latour moves away from a focus on social relations in his work. He argues that the modern Constitution facilitates the creation of collectives rather than societies made up of only social relations (WHNBM 43). Despite making this case Latour is clear, however, that the position he seeks to advance is not one that could be described as postmodern: Postmodernism does not offer solution. 'It lives under the modern Constitution, but it no longer believes in the guarantees the Constitution offers. It senses that something has gone awry in the modern critique, but it is not able to do anything but prolong that critique, though without believing in its foundations' (WHNBM: 46).

According to Latour, if we focus closely on the production of hybrids and the simultaneous 'work of elimination of these same hybrids', we then realise that 'we have never been modern in the sense of the Constitution'. According to Latour, postmodernism is unfeasible therefore as postmodernists claim to come after a time that hasn't even begun (WHNBM 46–7).

Entering a non-modern world

If we have never been modern or postmodern, then what kind of world are we living in or entering into? Latour concludes this work by tackling possibly the most difficult question: 'the question of the nonmodern world that we are entering', he argues, 'without ever having really left it' (WHNBM 130). As we enter this non-modern world that we have never actually left, Latour wants to know what attributes of the 'moderns' we might want to hold on to. 'The moderns' greatness' for him stems from a range of things including: their 'proliferation of hybrids, their lengthening of a certain type of network', their 'daring', 'research', and 'their innovativeness', as well as their 'youthful excesses', 'the creation of stabilized objects independent of society' and 'the freedom of a society liberated from objects'. All of these features, according to Latour, 'we want to keep' (WHNBM 133).

In seeking to develop a way forward Latour outlines what he thinks is worthy of retention: *'to retain the production of a nature and of a society that allow changes in size through the creation of an external truth and a subject of law, but without neglecting the co-production of sciences and societies'* (WHNBM 134). According to Latour this would involve using premodern categories to conceptualise the hybrids, whilst holding on to the moderns' final outcome of purification 'that is, an external Nature distinct from subjects' (WHNBM 134). In moving forward, Latour also wants to retain some aspects of postmodernism because, according to Latour, postmodernists have 'sensed the crisis of the moderns and attempted to overcome it'. He stresses that: 'take away from the postmoderns their illusions about the moderns, and their vices become virtues – nonmodern virtues!' (WHNBM 134). What Latour seeks to do in this work is simply reestablish symmetry between science and technology and human beings. According to Latour, nature and society are not two opposites, 'but one and the same production of successive states of societies–natures, of collectives' (WHNBM 139).

In WHNBM Latour aims to highlight the ways in which science studies have sought to reevaluate the division of labour between science and politics (WHNBM 144). Latour argues that we often ascribe ourselves disciplinary labels as sociologists, historians, scientists, philosophers, or anthropologists. But to such disciplinary labels 'we always add a qualifier: of science and technology', 'science studies', or 'science technology and society' (WHNBM: 3).

Rather than science studies appearing as an adjunct to social theory, however, Latour shows the value of placing it at the centre of socio-theoretical frameworks. Latour seeks to demonstrate throughout the text that there is something missing from existing social explanations and that is non-human entities or 'quasi-objects' as Latour calls them. Quasi-objects link the two poles between nature and society (WHNBM 55). They are agents (not operators) that bring people together in particular relations as well as drawing people into relations with other non-human entities (WHNBM: 51–55). This inclusion of non-human entities in his analysis and the movement beyond focusing solely on human social relations is primarily what distinguishes Latour's socio-theoretical framework from many others. Overall Latour suggests that 'modernism was not an illusion, but an active performing. If we could draft a new Constitution, we would, similarly, profoundly alter the course of quasi-objects' (WHNBM 144–5).

Reconfiguring the Social

In WHNBM Latour offers a way of conceptualising the development of society that is quite distinct from most other socio-theoretical approaches. He also offers an alternative approach to conceptualising the social. The 'social' is one of the defining concepts of social theory and sociology more generally. In *Reassembling the Social* (RAS) he seeks to rethink the meaning of the concept. According to Latour, 'when social scientists add the adjective "social" to some phenomenon, they designate a stabilized state of affairs, a bundle of ties that, later, may be mobilized to account for some other phenomenon' (RAS 1). For Latour, there is nothing problematic about using the concept in this way 'as long as it designates what is *already* assembled together, without making any superfluous assumption about the *nature* of what is assembled' (RAS 1, italics in original). Latour states that problems arise when 'social' begins to refer to a type of material, as if the adjective were roughly comparable to other terms like 'wooden' or 'steely' (RAS 1). For Latour it is at this point that the word's meaning breaks down as it now refers to two very different things: 'first, a movement during a process of assembling; and second, a specific type of ingredient that is supposed to differ from other materials' (RAS 1).

In RAS, Latour aims to 'show why the social cannot be construed as a kind of material or domain'. He also wants to dispute the project of providing a 'social explanation' of some other 'state of affairs' (RAS 1). He seeks, rather, to use the term to trace connections, which he believes was the original purpose of the term. Once this has been achieved, then the social sciences, according to Latour, can resume their traditional goal but with tools better suited to the task (RAS 1–2). Latour wants to: 'scrutinise more thoroughly the exact content of what is "assembled" under the umbrella of a society' (RAS 2). For Latour this appears to be the only way to remain faithful to the original aims of sociology, this 'science of the living together' (RAS 2). In *Reassembling the Social* he argues that we need to define the discipline of sociology. Latour takes us back to the original Latin or Greek definition 'socio-logy', which means the 'science of the social'. According to Latour there are problems with this definition, as scientific and technical enterprises 'bear little relation with what the founders of the social sciences had in mind when they invented their disciplines' (RAS 2). Science, according to Latour, was all about progress during the modernising period. However, as science has expanded it has been brought into much more of a co-extensiveness with society. This has resulted in changes to the actual meaning of science and society. For Latour 'neither science nor society has remained stable enough to deliver the promises of a strong "socio-logy"' (RS 2). He argues that it is time to 'modify what is meant by "social"' (RAS 2). He wants to 'devise an alternative definition for "sociology" while still retaining this useful label' and in doing so remaining true to its 'traditional calling' (RAS 2–3). This offers quite a significant departure from most existing socio-theoretical approaches.

What is society?

Sociology has sought to establish the existence of a specific sort of phenomenon ('society', 'social order', 'social practice', 'social dimension', or 'social structure'). According to Latour, in order to establish this sphere it has been important to distinguish it from others (such as law, science, politics etc.). Once the domain of 'society' had been defined the aim of sociology has been to 'shed some light on specifically social phenomena – the social could then explain the social' (RAS 3). This version of social theory has, according to Latour,

> become the default position of our mental software that takes into consideration of the following: there exists a social 'context' in which non-social activities take place; it is a specific domain of reality; it can be used as a specific type of causality to account for the residual aspects that other domains (psychology, law, economics etc.) cannot completely deal with. (RAS 3–4)

In this sense, according to Latour, 'the social sciences have disseminated their definition of society as effectively as utility companies deliver electricity and telephone services' (RAS 4). There is, according to Latour, an alternative approach to understanding the social. This second approach however does not claim there is anything specific about the social order, social context, or social dimension of any sort (RAS 4). For Latour 'the second position takes as the major puzzle to be solved what the first takes as its solution, namely the existence of specific social ties revealing the hidden presence of some specific social forces' (RAS 5). Latour argues that 'it is possible to remain close to the original intuitions of the social sciences by redefining sociology not as the 'science of the social', but as the *tracing of associations*' (RAS 5). According to Latour, here the 'social does not designate a thing among other things, like a black sheep among other white sheep, but *a type of connection* between things that are not themselves social' (RAS 5). This is important and is what really distances his approach from many other socio-theoretical frameworks. Latour argues that this may seem to 'dilute' sociology to a means for representing all aggregates 'from chemical bonds to legal ties'. However, he argues that this is precisely the point that this alternative division of social theory would like to make. This is because 'all those heterogeneous elements *might be* assembled anew in some given state of affairs' (RAS 5).

By widening his approach of the social to include non-humans (objects and animals etc.) Latour also seeks to problematise our understanding of 'collectivity' (of the notion of 'we'). According to Latour we no longer know what 'we' means as we are 'bound by ties that don't look like regular social ties' (RAS 6). Latour states that the overall project of what we are supposed to do as a collective is thrown into doubt and the notion of belonging enters a crisis. Another notion of social therefore has to be developed (RAS 7). A new version of 'the social' must be '*much wider* than what is usually called by that name, yet *strictly limited* to the tracing of new associations and to the designing of their assemblages' (RAS 7). Latour therefore seeks to 'define the social not as a special domain, a specific realm, or a particular sort of thing, but only as a very peculiar movement of re-association and reassembling' (RAS 7).

The social cannot be a safe and unproblematic category. According to Latour 'having rendered many useful services in an earlier period, what is called "social explanation" has become a counter-productive way to *interrupt* the movement of associations instead of resuming it' (RAS 8). In the traditional explanation the social is perceived 'to be made essentially of social ties' (RAS 8). However, the alternative explanation recognises that 'associations are made of ties which are themselves non-social' (RAS 8). Sociologists have traditionally 'imagined that sociology is limited to a specific domain', whereas, according to Latour (and the alternative explanation), 'sociologists should travel wherever new heterogeneous associations are made' (RAS 8).

Actor network theory (ANT)

The first approach he calls 'sociology of the social', the second approach, and the one he seeks to advance, he calls 'sociology of associations' (RAS 9). The name for the latter approach is 'actor-network-theory'. According to Latour, this is 'a name that is so awkward, so confusing, so meaningless that it deserves to be kept' (RAS 9). Latour has written extensively on ANT, in his work on Pasteur (Latour 1988) for example and elsewhere.[3] According to Latour the task of a social scientist is no longer to 'impose some order', nor is it to 'limit the range of acceptable entities' or 'teach actors what they are', or to 'add some reflexivity to their blind practice'. Rather '"you have to follow the actors themselves" (RAS 11–12). 'ANT. . . is a technique for detecting how connections between heterogeneous, human and non-human, entities make up a state of affairs that we used to call "social"' (de Vries 2016: 88).

It is the inclusion of non-human actants and agents in his analysis that really differentiates this approach to theorising the social from many other socio-theoretical approaches. 'Actants can be concrete or abstract'. According to Latour 'a good ANT account is a narrative or a description or a proposition where (de Vries 90) all the actors *do something* and don't just sit there' (RAS 128). Latour uses the term actant in order to permit 'agency for *anything* non-human' (de Vries 88). This does not just relate to science; for example, some people insist that they are being moved by divinities, spirits, and voices (RAS 236). Latour draws on a range of concepts to advance his ANT. In particular he uses terms such as intermediary and mediator. 'An *intermediary* is what transports meaning or force without transformation; *mediators* on the other hand, 'transform, translate, distort, and modify the meaning or the elements they are supposed to carry' (RAS 39; see also de Vries 90). An actor network refers to an assembly of actants who are 'networked' and defined by another actant through the translations they are involved in (de Vries 2016: 92). According to de Vries ANT 'introduces new terminology – such as "oligopticon"[4] – 'to account for the common experience of the annoying fact of society. That is, that individual actions and relations take place within a society (or economy and culture) 'that is perceived as a realm that guides and constrains individual actions' (de Vries 2016: 98).

Latour makes it clear that ANT 'is not an alternative theory *in* sociology' (i.e. it is not a theory competing with for example, Giddens's theory of structuration, de Vries 88). ANT rather 'is an alternative *to* the "sociology of the social", an alternative social science, a technique for redescribing the social world by tracing the associations of humans and nonhumans that make up a "collective"' (de Vries 2016: 88). The incorporation of non-human objects and entities into his analysis is a theme running throughout Latour's work – as we have already seen in WHNBM. Latour has often been criticised for the ways in which the same properties appear to be ascribed to both humans and non-humans in his work. According to Winner (1993) this fails to account for the intentionality that distinguishes humans from many other animals or objects. As will be explored in Part 2 however, Latour continues to extend his focus on non-human and human actants and agents, networks and associations in his comparative anthropology.

PART 2: DIFFERENT MODES OF LIVING

The current global ecological crisis is a reoccurring theme in Latour's more recent work. In *An Inquiry into the Modes of Existence* (AIME) for example, published 20 years after WHNBM he argues that we must choose between 'modernising' and 'ecologising'. Ecological problems force us, according to Latour, to reanalyse the values of the so-called moderns, to pose a series of questions: 'If we have never been modern, then what has happened to us? What are we to inherit? Who have we been? Who are we going to become? With whom must we be connected? Where do we find ourselves situated from now on?' (AIME 11). Latour refers to AIME as a comparative anthropology of the moderns.[5] As we explore in this section, Latour seeks to show us that there is not one outside world, but rather a plurality of worlds that relate directly to the key institutions that frame our lives (Muecke 2012). According to Latour the Earth is a plural collective. With the current threat of global ecological crisis, the key question we must face now is: how can this plural world we currently live in work as a collective to achieve common goals (de Vries 2016)?

Ecological Politics and Gaia

The questions that Latour poses to the moderns in AIME are set within the context of the ecological crisis. He states that: 'the scope of the ecological crises obliges us to reconsider a whole set of reactions, or rather conditioned reflexes, that rob us of all our flexibility to react to what is coming' (AIME 7). Since he wrote WHNBM ecological problems have been a serious concern for Latour. In *Politics of Nature* he reconfigured 'political ecology' and the role of science in democracy (de Vries 2016: 194). In AIME he seeks to develop his work on this further:

> For more than twenty years, scientific and technological controversies have proliferated in number and scope, eventually reaching the climate itself. Since geologists are beginning to use the term "ANTHROPOCENE" to designate the era of Earth's history that follows the Holocene, this will be a convenient term to use from here on to sum up the meaning of an era that extends from the scientific and industrial revolutions to the present day. (AIME 9)

Latour argues for a shift in the nature of the relationship between humans and the Earth throughout his work. This focus, however, becomes more pressing given the current ecological crisis. According to Latour, in light of the 'planetary negotiation that is already under way' we need to reflect on all the 'values that the notion of modernization had at once revealed and compromised' (AIME 17, de Vries 148). Latour argues that we are now called to appear before Gaia, 'the odd, doubly composite figure made up of science and mythology used by certain specialists to designate the Earth that surrounds us' (AIME 9). Gaia is a truly global entity that 'threatens us even as we threaten it' (AIME 9).

The name Gaia comes from Greek mythology – the primordial Greek goddess, the personification of the Earth. According to de Vries (2016) the novelist William Golding suggested Gaia to British Scientist James Lovelock as a potential 'name for his hypothesis that living organisms regulate the terrestrial atmosphere' – 'the balance between the levels of oxygen and carbon dioxide that makes life on Earth possible' (de Vries 2016: 195). Latour argues that if we (humans) through the expansion of transport, the development of industry, and large-scale livestock breeding 'continue to emit too much carbon dioxide, the subtle balance between oxygen and carbon dioxide will be disturbed. Gaia, "the living Earth", will be endangered', with devastating effects (de Vries 2016: 195). However, according to Latour 'there is only one Earth, but Gaia is not One' (Latour, cited in de Vries 2016: 195).

In order to effectively tackle climate change, we need to work collectively. Latour argues that we must choose between modernising and ecologising. This is a point he has been articulating since the publication of *Politics of Nature* (PON) in 2004. In PON Latour outlines the values of the politics that he thinks will be required. In contrast AIME 'suggests a platform for the diplomatic exchanges that will be necessary, if war, violence, and ecological catastrophe are to be avoided'. The purpose of AIME is to 'offer the moderns a clearer view of themselves' and other peoples (de Vries 2016: 199). In this text, however, Latour seeks to present 'a positive, rather than merely a negative, version of those who "have never been modern" (AIME xxvi; see also de Vries 199).

Latour focuses here on what he sees as 'the work of redescription', which he feels 'may allow us to give more space to *other values* that are very commonly encountered but that did not necessarily find a comfortable slot for themselves within the framework offered by modernity' (AIME 11). He gives the examples here of politics or religion, or law. According to Latour these are values that:

> the defences of Science in all its majesty had trampled along its way but which can now be deployed more readily. If it is a question of ecologizing and no longer of modernizing, it may become possible to bring a larger number of values into cohabitation within a somewhat richer ecosystem. (AIME 11)

According to Latour the intensity of the world's ecological problems is undeniable, and like others Latour argues that new ways of thinking about the world are needed. We need a deeper common sense than the modern Constitution offers. 'Once we have a clearer idea of our values', we may move forwards 'to explore our plural world' (de Vries 2016: 200–201). It is overall a positive message that Latour seeks to reinforce in his comparative anthropology: 'what risk do we run ...? The world is young, the sciences are recent, history has barely begun, and as for ecology, it is barely in its infancy: Why should we have finished exploring the institutions of public life?' (PON 227–8; de Vries 2016: 201).

A Plurality of Types of 'Beings'

Latour extends many of the themes from WHNBM and RAS in AIME, in particular the move beyond a focus on social relations to include other types of 'being' and other forms of life. At the end of part one of the text, according to Latour, 'we shall know how to speak appropriately about a plurality of types of beings by relying on the guiding thread of experience, on empiricism as William James defined it: nothing but experience, yes, but *nothing less than experience*' (AIME xxv). Rather than drawing on ethnographic detail to articulate his argument as Latour does in other work however,[6] in AIME the argument is set up by introducing a fictitious female anthropologist. The anthropologist proceeds by questioning the puzzles left by the moderns as they have tried 'to account for values in a wide variety of domains – science, technology, religion, politics, law, fiction, their emotions, morality, and the economy' (de Vries 2016: 152).

Latour encourages the fictitious anthropologist that he creates to distinguish between *being-as-being* and *being-as-other* (de Vries 158). Being-as-being 'seeks its support in a **SUBSTANCE** that will ensure its continuity'. In contrast, beings-as-other 'depend not on a substance on which they can rely but on a SUBSISTENCE that they have to seek out at their own risk' (AIME 162; see also de Vries 159). Introducing the notion of being-as-other allows us to explore 'how many *other forms of alterities* a being is capable of traversing in order to continue to exist' (AIME 163). By distinguishing being-as-being and being-as-other, according to de Vries Latour appears to give '(individual) *existence* pride of place over *substance* (essence)' (de Vries 163). Latour continues to focus on ontology as he seeks to move '*pluralism* from the level of language, culture, and society to the level of ontology' (reality) (de Vries 2016: 163).

From actor networks to modes of existence

According to Latour, ANT focused on redescribing 'each of the central institutions of contemporary societies by following the heterogeneous network of associations that make them up'. Through this process 'it has been shown that the grand narrative of modernization does not do justice to the very institutions developed by the Moderns'. A comparative anthropology, according to Latour, needs to have common ground (which actor networks provide) 'but also requires an instrument to make the differences among collectives emerge anew'.[7] He argues that in conjunction with research on networks another line of inquiry into modes of existence must be pursued in order to capture the 'various ways in which those associations were binding entities together'. According to Latour, 'such an inquiry into modes of existence (AIME) feeds on the research on networks, but tries to qualify the mode in which those networks expand' (all quotes taken from http://www.bruno-latour.fr.node/328).[8]

According to Norton, to speak of modes of existence 'is to inquire both into the existence of things (and, thus, to do ontology) and into all the relations into which things enter, as well as the behaviors and values they exhibit, in order to exist' (Norton 2013: 2). Modes of existence frame Latour's conceptualisation and understanding of contemporary life. There are crossovers between the different modes of existence and a tendency for each to want to be dominant (Muecke 2012). However, the 'principle of irreduction' that is at the heart of Latour's philosophy and the starting point of ANT – 'nothing is, by itself, either reducible or irreducible to anything else' (POF 158) – prevents this from occurring (Muecke 2012).

Latour returns again to ANT – the world 'is made up by actor networks, by actants relating, translating, and defining each other' (de Vries 156). Latour identifies a number of concepts – stages through which modes of existence pass. For Latour, each mode of existence has its own hiatus, trajectory, felicity/infelicity conditions, beings to institute, and alteration. According to Latour, however, each translation is an abstract, whereby a small discontinuity, a *hiatus*, needs to be practically overcome. The right *conditions of felicity* must be present in order for an actor network to function well. Furthermore, something is allowed to pass along the *trajectory* of associations that are established (de Vries 2016: 163).

A mode of existence is identified therefore by specifying the characteristics (see also de Vries 48–9) listed below:

- *Hiatus*, a disruptive condition that needs to be overcome. According to Latour 'every instance of continuity is achieved through a discontinuity, a HIATUS' (AIME 100).

- *Trajectory*, the continuity it allows through the results of these transformations.

- 'every leap across a discontinuity represents a risk taken that may succeed or fail; there are thus FELICITY and INFELICITY CONDITIONS proper to each mode' (AIME 100).

- The *beings* that are instituted and passed through and the alteration of beings-as-other it allows (i.e. the way these are transformed).

As Latour argues, 'the result of this passage, of this more or less successful leap, is a flow, a network, a movement, a wake left behind that will make it possible to define a particular form of existence, and consequently particular

BEINGS' (AIME 100). In the book 15 modes of existence are identified by Latour, which is the number that he claims is necessary to get an image of modern life 'as a whole with a satisfactory *resolution*' (AIME 479–80; see also de Vries 181).

The modes of existence

The 15 modes of existence are as follows: reproduction [REP], metamorphosis [MET], habit [HAB], technology [TECH], fiction [FIC], reference [REF], politics [POL], law [LAW], religion [REL], attachment [ATT], organisation [ORG], morality [MOR], network [NET], preposition [PRE], and [DC] for double click. The characteristics for each mode are summarized in what Latour calls a 'pivot table' (AIME 488–9). According to de Vries for 'each mode, the table specifies by what *hiatus* and *trajectory* it is distinguished; what its *conditions of felicity* and infelicity are; what beings are instituted; and, finally, to what alteration being-as-other is subjected' (de Vries 2016: 181).

In part one of the text, Latour examines the first few modes of existence to be encountered in the inquiry: network [NET], preposition [PRE], reference [REF], and reproduction [REP]. In addition he introduces double click [DC], 'which is an allusion to the digital mouse' (AIME 93). [DC] is not 'a proper mode of existence', but rather an adversary who pushes the notion that information can be shifted from one context to another without any need for translation' (Norton 2013: 2). [NET] and [PRE] are modes that appear to lead the way to other modes. While the [NET] mode identifies a collection of associations, [PRE] modes identify the differences between networks. Joined with [DC] these modes make up the final of five groups of modes, each group containing three modes. [TEC], [FIC], and [REF] 'provide alternative descriptions of science, technology, and fiction. [POL], [LAW] and [REL] offer descriptions of politics, law, and religion as modes of existence' (de Vries 2016: 184). There is no time or space to cover each of these modes in detail; here we will just look at a few.

The three modes of existence of the first group, [REP], [MET], and [HAB], 'are the ones that have been at most elaborated by other collectives and most ignored by our own' (AIME 288). According to de Vries by introducing them Latour has widened the area for discussions between the moderns and other peoples. For example, [MET] focuses on how to take into account experience that 'under the modern Constitution may be viewed as psychogenetic'. Its hiatuses might be described as emotional shocks and crises (de Vries 2016: 185). In common sense terms, when a person experiences an emotional shock (bereavement, relationship breakdown), their life continues but often in a radically different form. However, when Latour discusses [MET] he is not just referring to human beings but also to non-humans, spirits, and divinities. Through introducing [MET] Latour helps to break down distinctions between us (moderns) and them (others). According to Latour: 'the modernist believes that the others believe in beings external to themselves, whereas he "knows perfectly well" that these are only internal representations projected onto a world that is in itself devoid of meaning' (AIME 187; see also de Vries 185).

Given that Latour identifies [POL], [LAW], and [REL] as distinct modes of existence, why does he not do this for economics? Latour does not present this as a separate mode of existence. Latour explicitly distinguishes his work from existing critiques of capitalism. What is required in its place, according to Latour, is 'an alternative account that neither endorses nor deplores capitalism', but rather deconstructs the modern concept of the economy (Norton 2013: 4–5; AIME 385). One of the reasons for not identifying the economy as a separate mode of existence runs parallel to the reasons he set out in *Reassembling the Social* 'to abandon the concept of "Society". Like "Society", "the economy" mixes up process – a specific way of assembling collectives – and the outcome of these processes' (de Vries 2016: 188). This is where ANT is useful: it provides us with 'the language to account for the economy as process, rather than as something already given as hard economic facts determined by the laws of the market (de Vries 2016 189; Norton 2013).

CONCLUSION

According to Norton (2013) AIME draws together much of Latour's previous work to present 'a comprehensive relational metaphysics, an "ont-ecology" with the power to constructively and creatively confront the many challenges to which modern thought has led us' (Norton 2013: 5). AIME is not an easy text to navigate. It is philosophically complex and confusing at times. Furthermore, although ecological concerns – and the implications that these have for contemporary forms of life – provide the background for the book's aims and argument, the substantive concerns posed by climate change are often buried by the book's philosophical focus. There is, however, consistency across all the works examined here. We certainly see many of the themes that are present in both WHNBM and RAS in AIME. AIME was published 20 years after WHNBM, and, as articulated in Part 2 of this chapter, can be seen as a direct attempt to address many of the questions he raised in his earlier text. There is however one important distinction: while WHNBM has a somewhat negative message overall, Latour seeks in AIME to offer a positive version of those who 'have never been modern'. He seeks in AIME to ask whether we can defend the values that we keep close to us – the values 'that the notion of modernization had at once revealed and compromised' in the 'planetary negotiation that is already underway over the future of [these] values' (AIME 17; see also de Vries 201)? In order to do this Latour argues that we need a new philosophical vocabulary. He presents AIME as a 'provisional report' on these issues (AIME xix, 476; see also de Vries 157). But he leaves us with more questions than answers. What have we learnt from our explorations into modes of existence? Can the inquiry lead to diplomatic arrangements with other peoples (AIME 477–80)?

According to de Vries (2016) Latour in his earlier work emphasises the 'heterogeneity of what makes up our world', 'suggesting that in order' to get a realistic picture 'of the world we must rid ourselves of the 'established distinctions' emerging from 'the primarily epistemological concerns of Western philosophy' (e.g. distinctions between 'nature' and 'society', humans and non-humans) (de Vries 2016: 153). Ontology rather than epistemology is still central to the argument Latour makes in AIME and he continues to show that practices are made out of heterogeneous components. Latour also suggests that ANT is still the most appropriate tool to describe them. As de Vries (2016) notes, however, while most of Latour's earlier work focuses on describing how actor networks are created, his focus in AIME is on what has passed in the actor networks that make up science, politics, law, religion: 'so under the word "network" we must be careful not to confuse what circulates *once everything is in place* with the *setups* involving the heterogeneous set of elements that allow circulation to occur' (AIME 32). Throughout his work Latour does provide us with the tools to problematise our existing understandings of 'modern' and 'social' life, moving beyond a socio-theoretical focus on human social relations. This is perhaps where his strongest contribution to social theory lies.

Abbreviations

AIME: *An Inquiry into the Modes of Existence* (2013)

POF: *The Pasteurization of France* (1988)

PON: *Politics of Nature* (2004)

RAS: *Reassembling the Social: An Introduction to Actor-Network-Theory* (2005)

WHNBM: *We Have Never Been Modern* (1993)

Selected Further Readings

The following text provides a detailed and critical overview of Latour's œuvre: de Vries, G. (2016) *Bruno Latour*. Cambridge: Polity.

Michaels, M. (2016) *Actor Network Theory: Trials, Trails and Translations*. London: Sage offers a comprehensive account of ANT.

Lynch, P. and Rivers, N. (eds) (2015) *Thinking with Bruno Latour in Rhetoric and Composition*. Carbondale, IL: Southern Illinois University Press, an edited collection, explores the use and relevance of Latour's work across disciplines, focusing in particular on writing and rhetoric.

Notes

1 Boyle played a significant role in the development of scientific methodology. His air-pump experiment relates to the association he made between the pressure and volume of gas within a closed system.
2 Hobbes's *Leviathan* was first published in 1651. It relates to the structure of society and legitimate government, it is regarded as one of the first and also most influential examples of social contract theory.
3 ANT is frequently associated with Michael Callon, Bruno Latour, and John Law. See Michaels (2016) for an overview of ANT and its relationship to sociology.
4 'Oligopticon' for Latour refers to a site for the manufacture of social structures (e.g. legal system) (RAS).
5 AIME is a large text accompanied by a bilingual website and readers are encouraged to contribute to the website, to 'extend the work ... with new documents, new sources, new testimonies, and most, important, to modify the questions by correcting or modulating the project in relation to the results obtained' (AIME xx).
6 See, for example, Latour and Woolgar (1986).
7 See www.bruno-latour.fr/node/328 the companion website to AIME.
8 See www.bruno-latour.fr/node/328

4

Donna Haraway: New Modes of Sociality

PART 1: CYBORGS AND PARTIAL PERSPECTIVES

One of the distinguishing features of Donna Haraway's social theory is the emphasis she places on the role of non-human actants and agents, namely animals and technology. When social theorists talk about the social, what they often really mean, Haraway argues, is the study of social relations and history. Haraway develops the concept of the cyborg in order to displace the social from its 'exclusive location in human doings' (Gane and Haraway 2006: 142). She states that she is 'serious about the temporalities, scales, materialities, relationalities between people and our constitutive partners, which always include other people and other critters, animal and not, in doing worlds' (Gane and Haraway 2006: 143). What she makes clear in the development of her concept of the cyborg is that one cannot attempt to theorise contemporary social conditions without understanding the relationship between humans and other, non-human forms. She uses the deconstruction of the boundaries between humans and non-humans to develop her analysis of contemporary social life as well as to sketch out her specific blueprint for social change. The following outline of Haraway's concept of the cyborg frames her socio-theoretical vision and, as we will explore, underpins the development of her epistemological focus on what she calls 'partial perspectives'.

Cyborg Theorising

The cyborg is the metaphor through which Haraway carefully illustrates the contemporary human condition. Her clearest and most enduring statement of the concept comes in 'A cyborg manifesto' originally published in 1985. Haraway states that many of the entities appearing in her work have been birthed through the reproductive apparatuses of war, and that this is particularly true of 'A cyborg manifesto' (Haraway 2004a: 3). She writes that: 'For me, the "Cyborg Manifesto" was a nearly sober socialist-feminist statement written for the *Socialist Review* to try to think through how to do critique, remember war and its offspring, keep ecofeminism and technoscience joined in the flesh, and generally honor possibilities that escape unkind origins' (Haraway 2004a: 3). In an interview with Nicholas Gane, Haraway (Gane and Haraway 2006) argues that the manifesto is a feminist theoretical statement, a coming to terms with the social conditions of our times and a treatise that outlines how to move forward. The central question of the manifesto, which is a direct play on Lenin's 1902 tract, is: 'What is to be done' (Gane and Haraway 2006: 136)?

The 'cyborg is a cybernetic organism, a hybrid of machine and organism, a creature of social reality as well as of fiction (CM 149)'. In developing the concept, Haraway continually blurs the boundaries between reality and fiction: 'Social reality is lived social relations, our most important political construction, a world-changing fiction' (CM 149). The cyborg is also Janus-faced: it is both a source of inequality and a potential facilitator of social change. According to Haraway the cyborg era is a fairly recent one. It is, however, impossible to pinpoint when exactly it came into being. It could date from the late nineteenth century, or from the 1930s, or from the Second World War, or even after that. She is keen to point out that how it is dated depends on how one chooses to foreground the concept (Gane and Haraway 2006: 146). Implicit within this focus is Haraway's position on the development of society and her approach to modernity and post-modernity. She argues that there can be no logical development of society that can be charted from the period of the Enlightenment through to modernity and post-modernity. For Haraway, there are no beginnings and endings: we have only ever been in the middle of things (PM 77). At the start of the manifesto Haraway states that in the late twentieth century 'we are all chimeras, theorized and fabricated hybrids of machine and organism; in short we are cyborgs. The cyborg is our ontology; it gives us our politics' (CM 150). Haraway argues that her Cyborg Manifesto should be read as 'an argument for *pleasure* in the confusion of boundaries and for *responsibility* in their construction' (CM 150). This focus on boundary transgressions and the possibility and potential inherent in their deconstruction form the central tenet of Haraway's social theory.

Deconstructing Western universalism

In her development of the concept of cyborg Haraway moves away from theoretical claims about universality and objectivity. For Haraway, the cyborg is completely committed to partiality. She uses the cyborg to deconstruct the existing binaries of Western thought. She focuses her analysis on the dualisms that have been used to denigrate women and keep them confined to the domestic sphere (e.g. public/private, nature/culture).[1] The cyborg for Haraway collapses and transforms these dichotomies. She argues that the 'cyborg is a creature in a post-gender world' (CM 150). It is oppositional and utopian. However, it 'is not innocent' but deeply rooted within the 'monster' of global capitalism. Haraway locates the development of the cyborg in Cold War rhetoric, in financial investment in military technology,[2] and in cybernetics.[3] During this era, technological development and research became directly inter-linked with business interests and financial investment (Gane and Haraway 2006: 139). The cyborg for Haraway therefore is 'a military project, a late capitalist project in deep collaboration with new forms of imperial war' (Gane and Haraway 2006: 139). Haraway, however, wants to utilise the subversive potential of the cyborg. She argues that, while the cyborg is deeply embedded in global capitalism, it also opens up radical possibility (Gane and Haraway 2006: 139). As she states:

> The main trouble with cyborgs, of course, is that they are the illegiti-mate offspring of militarism and patriarchal capitalism, not to mention state socialism. But illegitimate offspring are often exceedingly unfaith-ful to their origins.[4] Their fathers, after all, are inessential. (CM 151)

Haraway signals three crucial boundary breakdowns central to her conceptu-alisation of the cyborg (although she tends to concentrate on the first two). These are: the boundary between human and animal, the boundary between animal–human (organism) and machine, and the boundary between the physi-cal and non-physical world (CM 151–2). The cyborg is about transgressed boundaries, and Haraway continually focuses on the dual potential of these transgressions. She argues that from one perspective a cyborg world with its rapid technological advancement could signal the further militarised control of populations across the globe. However, viewed from another perspective, a cyborg world might indicate new and more egalitarian social arrangements that celebrate new kinships between animals, humans, and machines, and that accept a partial rather than an objective view of the world (CM 154). This almost dialectical tension lies at the heart of her socio-theoretical vision. The boundary transgression that is so central to the conceptualisation of the cyborg could lead to the development of progressive politics but could also lead to the creation of further oppression for minority groups. She articulates this argu-ment through socialist feminism. She argues 'that most American socialists and feminists see deepened dualisms of mind and body, animal and machine, ideal-ism and materialism in the social practices, symbolic formulations, and physical artefacts associated with "high technology"' (CM 154). However, rather than seeing technology simply as a form of domination, Haraway argues that it offers potential ways to resist oppression. She seeks to use the cyborg myth to imagine other alternative more egalitarian versions of society. She argues for 'a politics rooted in claims about fundamental changes in the nature of class, race and gender in an emerging system of world order analogous in its novelty and scope to that created by industrial capitalism' (CM 161).

Communication, technology, biology

Central to Haraway's conceptualisation of the cyborg is the relationship between language, technology, and biology. While communication and language have formed a central focus of much existing social theory, her inclusion of biology and technology distinguishes Haraway's socio-theoretical approach from many others. She argues that information and communication technology along with biotechnologies are the crucial tools for recrafting bodies in the current era (CM 164). These technologies are transforming social relationships and the social conditions in which people live. In particular, for Haraway these are the tools that have the potential to fundamentally transform the position of women in society. She argues that 'these tools embody and enforce new social relations for women worldwide' (CM 164).

Haraway contends that:

> communications sciences and modern biologies are constructed by a common move – *the translation of the world into a problem of coding*, a search for a common language in which all resistance to instrumental control disappears and all heterogeneity can be submitted to disassembly, reassembly, investment, and exchange. (CM 164)

She continually states that humans are living in what can be termed as 'disassembling times' where their entire way of being is constantly deconstructed and reassembled in new ways through advances in science and technology. 'In communications sciences, the translation of the world into a problem in coding can be illustrated by looking at cybernetic (feedback-controlled) systems theories applied to telephone technology, computer design, weapons deployment, or data base construction and maintenance' (CM 164). In this context solutions to problems are based on 'determining the rates, directions, and probabilities of flow of a quantity called information' (CM 164). In modern biology, she uses examples from molecular genetics, ecology and sociobiology, evolutionary theory, and immunobiology to illustrate the problem of coding. She states that organisms have been translated into problems of genetic coding and read-out (e.g. DNA printing). Haraway argues that organisms no longer exist as objects of knowledge, but have become information-processing devices (CM 164). Haraway uses these examples to argue that it is science and technology that are fundamentally responsible for transforming contemporary social conditions. In making this case, Haraway is also quick to point out that it is largely economics that forms a central domain of these transformations (CM 165).

Production and reproduction

While Haraway's conceptualisation of the cyborg is focused on the relationship between humans, animals, and machines, processes of economic production still form the centre of her theorisation of contemporary social conditions. For Haraway, production is caught up with technology, biology, and processes of reproduction. While feminists have long criticised malestream social theory for its inability to acknowledge the relationship between production and reproduction, Haraway adds a further dimension to this through her exploration of technology. She argues that 'microelectronics mediates the translations of labor into robotics and word processing, sex into genetic engineering and reproductive technologies, and mind into artificial intelligence and decision procedures' (CM 165). According to Haraway 'Communications sciences and biology are constructions of natural–technical 'objects of knowledge in which the difference between machine and organism is thoroughly blurred; mind, body, and tool are on very intimate terms' (CM 165). She argues that the new biotechnologies go beyond human reproduction, redefining and revolutionising industry such as agriculture. For Haraway, science and technology provide fresh sources of power, requiring new sources of analysis and political action.

Haraway consistently argues against technological determinism – her position on this is perhaps best articulated in relation to her focus on production and reproduction. For example, she states that it is often argued that new technologies have caused the development of the homework economy. However, Haraway is quick to point out that the homework economy[5] is made possible (not caused) by new technologies. She relates the development of robotics, for example, to putting men out of work in developed countries and exacerbating failure to generate male jobs in developing contexts (CM 168). At the same time, there has been a feminisation of work. In the context of sex and reproduction, Haraway argues that 'new technologies affect the social relations of both sexuality and of reproduction, and not always in the same ways' (CM 168–9). The intimate ties of sexuality and instrumentality, of private satisfaction on one hand and utility on the other reinforce male and female gender roles. Haraway refers to these as sociobiological stories that 'depend on a high-tech view of the body as a biotic component or cybernetic communications system' (CM 169). A central part of this, Haraway argues, is the medicalisation of pregnancy and childbirth – whereby women's bodies become permeable, subject to both 'visualisation' and 'intervention'. Haraway argues that: 'sex, sexuality, and reproduction are central actors in high-tech myth systems structuring our imaginations of personal and social possibility' (CM 169).

The cyborg and social change

In detailing the development of technology one thing that is crucial to Haraway and perhaps demarcates her position from other feminist perspectives of the time is that she acknowledges the potential for change inherent in human

couplings with other actants and agents. She wants to move away from a somewhat nostalgic position articulated by socialist feminists that less technologically
driven times were less oppressive for women. Some virulent forms of oppression
have been lost through advances in technological development. She argues that:

> ambivalence towards the disrupted unities mediated by high-tech cul-
> ture requires not sorting consciousness into categories of 'clear sighted
> critique grounding a solid political epistemology' versus 'manipulated
> false consciousness', but subtle understanding of emerging pleasures,
> experiences, and powers with serious potential for changing the rules
> of the game. (CM 172–3)

This is centrally important to Haraway's approach to social change.

Haraway uses the concept of the cyborg to describe contemporary social
conditions. She also uses it, however, to outline her blueprint for social change
through the metaphor of science fiction. She argues that 'certain dualisms have
been persistent in Western traditions', such as self/other, mind/body, culture/
nature, male/female, and so on (CM 177). She states that these dualisms have
been central to the oppression of 'women, people of colour, nature, workers,
animals, in short, domination of all constituted as others, whose task is to mirror
the self' (CM 177). With reference to the relationship between self and other
Haraway argues that in existing Western thought the 'self' is perceived as the
autonomous powerful 'God' like figure, while the 'other' is multiple with no clear
boundaries or power (CM 177). For Haraway, high-tech culture challenges these
dualisms in novel and interesting ways. The relationship between human and
machine is unclear, as is the relationship between self and other, mind and body.
Whether people refer to themselves in formal discourse (e.g. in terms of humans'
biology) or in daily practice (e.g. home/work), Haraway argues that people find
themselves to be 'cyborgs, hybrids, mosaics, chimeras' (CM 177). For Haraway,
there is no 'ontological separation in our formal knowledge of machine and
organism, of technical and organic' (CM 177–8). Overall, Haraway tries to make
two key points through the development of her cyborg perspective: first, that 'the
production of universal, totalizing social theory is a major mistake that misses
most of reality'. Second, she articulates the need for humans to take 'responsibility for the social relations of science and technology'. This is not about
demonising technology. Rather, it means 'embracing the skilful task of reconstructing the boundaries of daily life, in partial connection with others'. The
cyborg, she concludes, can help humans find 'a way out of the maze of dualisms'
in which they have 'explained' their 'bodies and ... tools' to themselves (CM 181).

Partial Perspectives

If the concept of the cyborg represents Haraway's ontological framework, then
the partial perspectives must be viewed as her epistemology. Cyborgs themselves are based on partiality, and cyborg visuality offers only a partial

perspective. In order to study and understand the cyborg world, sociologists need to develop an approach that reflects this partiality, somewhere between scientific objectivity on the one hand and postmodern relativism on the other. Haraway argues that in these disassembling times 'some of us have tried to stay sane' by 'holding out' for 'a feminist version of objectivity' (SK 578). The problem according to Haraway is the dilemma of attempting to maintain 'an account of radical historical contingency for all knowledge claims and knowing subjects', whilst at the same time cultivating 'a no-nonsense commitment to faithful accounts of a "real" world' (SK 579). According to Clough and Schneider what she is trying to articulate here is that as well as revealing the 'historical and ideological specificity of scientific practices' and 'deconstructing their absolute authority', feminists should also seek to offer a 'better account of the world' (SK 579; see also Clough and Schneider 2001: 342). She states that such an account comes with the acknowledgement of the 'irreducible difference and radical multiplicity of local knowledges' (SK 579; see also Clough and Schneider: 342).

Haraway accepts a version of scientific realism; however, this version of realism is expressed 'in partial visions or partial perspectives'. She wants to move away from postmodern relativist accounts. In particular, she wants to move away from what she calls the 'god trick – that is, seeing everything, everywhere, from nowhere' (Clough and Schneider 342). According to Haraway, partial views are not a universalising vision, a view from above. She argues that feminists do not need 'a doctrine of objectivity that promises transcendence'. However, for Haraway there needs to be a global network of connections that include the possibility 'partially to translate knowledges among very different–and power–differentiated–communities' (SK 580). She states that: 'We need the power of modern critical theories of how meanings and bodies get made, not in order to deny meanings and bodies, but in order to build meanings and bodies that have a chance for life' (SK 580).

Feminist objectivity

In developing what she calls the partial perspective, Haraway attempts to develop an approach between radical constructivism and feminist empiricism. She does acknowledge that 'it is, of course, hard to climb when you are holding on to both ends of a pole, simultaneously or alternatively' (SK 580). In this essay, she uses vision as a metaphor. Among many feminists 'vision' has been viewed as a source of oppression for women. She seeks to reclaim vision, however, arguing that it 'can be good for avoiding binary oppositions' (SK 581). Haraway argues for the 'embodied nature of all vision' (SK 581). She argues that feminist objectivity 'means quite simply *situated knowledges*' (SK 581). For Haraway, it is only the partial perspective that can promise objective vision. In short, the argument that she is seeking to articulate in this essay is 'an argument for situated and embodied knowledges'. She argues against 'unlocatable, and so irresponsible, knowledge claims' (SK 583). As with the development of the concept of the cyborg, Haraway attempts to create a path between universal generalisation on the one hand and postmodern relativism on the other. Clough and Schneider (2001: 342) argue that this is an epistemo-logically demanding perspective, as one must attempt to see from the perspective of those on the margins without romanticising or appropriating the vision of those who are less powerful (SK 583–4). Along with many other feminists, Haraway wants to argue for 'a doctrine and practice of objectivity that privileges contestation, deconstruction, passionate construction, webbed connections, and hope for transformation of systems of knowledge and ways of seeing' (SK 584–5). She clearly wants to take a stance against relativism at the same time, though. In sum, Haraway argues for a politics and epistemol-ogy of location. Through this perspective, 'partiality and not universality is the condition of being heard to make rational knowledge claims' (SK 589). Haraway situated knowledges require that the object of knowledge be pic-tured as an actor and agent, not as a screen or a ground or a resource, never finally as slave to the master that closes off the dialectic in his unique agency and his authorship of "objective" knowledge' (SK 592). Indeed this notion of agency underpins her broader socio-theoretical vision. Haraway argues that agency has the potential to transform the entire project of social theory; by acknowledging the agency of objects of knowledge we can avoid making false claims to objectivity and universality (SK 592–3).

The production of bodies

One of the key facets of Haraway's conceptualisation of the cyborg is her focus on the boundary transgressions between humans and animals and humans and machines. In her manifesto, she also makes reference to the boundaries between the physical and non-physical. However, a thorough articulation and analysis of this particular binary remain elusive in the context of the manifesto. It is discussed in the context of her epistemological work on partial perspectives (SK 595–6). In her discussion and development of the partial perspectives, Haraway returns to her focus on biology and, more specifically, the production of bodies. She draws on the work of Katie King (1987), a feminist literary theorist, who examines the ways in which poems are produced as objects of knowledge. Haraway applies this approach to understanding the 'production and reproduc-tion-of bodies and other objects of value in scientific knowledge projects' (SK 595). First, Haraway asks whether bodies can be generated and produced in the same way that Romantic late eighteenth-century poems were. It is here that Haraway develops another key concept, the notion of *material-semiotic* actor. The concept of material-semiotic is Haraway's attempt to translate the third dualism outlined in 'A cyborg manifesto', the relationship between the physical and non-physical (Gane and Haraway 2006: 147). The concept of material-semiotic actor is used by Haraway to 'portray the object of knowledge as an active, meaning – generating part of apparatus of bodily production, without *ever* implying the immediate presence of such objects' (SK 595). Haraway argues that 'like "poems", which are sites of literary production where language too is an actor independent of intentions and authors, bodies as objects of knowledge are material-semiotic generative nodes' (SK 595). Bodily boundaries materialise in social interaction (SK 595). Haraway argues that 'boundaries are drawn by mapping practices; "objects" do not pre-exist as such (SK 595). In short, Haraway seeks to examine the ways in which bodies are produced through different types of discourse and practice. Haraway argues that 'various contending biological bodies emerge at the intersection of biological research and writing, medical and other business practices, and technology such as visualization technologies' (SK 596). She states that feminist embodiment, partiality, objectivity, and situated knowledges 'turn on conversations and codes at this potent node in fields of possible bodies and meanings' (SK 596). Bodies emerge as creations of both fact and fiction in Haraway's work on the cyborg and partial perspectives. As will be explored in Part 2 of this chapter, Haraway's work on immunology provides fertile ground for a more detailed examination of her discursive analysis of the body, as well as enabling in-depth reflections on her wider socio-theoretical vision.

PART 2: IMMUNE SYSTEM DISCOURSE

Whether we are talking about war, migration, or the proliferation of diseases such as AIDS, the immune system or immunity from contagion forms 'the symbolic and material linchpin around which our social systems rotate' (Esposito 2011: 2). This has led a number of scholars across the humanities and social sciences to study the immune system in scientific and public discourse, as well as its role in clinical practice. For example, feminist epistemologies have increasingly been applied to scientific discourse in order to 'assess competing claims of immune function within a feminist context' (Weasel 2001: 27). The immune system has figured frequently throughout Haraway's work. As she states: the immune system is a 'potent and polymorphous object of belief, knowledge, and practice' (BPB 200). It is the perfect example of the 'networked consciousness of the cyborg age', and a good example of what Haraway means when she denies there is such a thing 'as the abstract' (Kunzru 1996: 4). A critical reflection on her use of cyborg and partial perspective in her work on the immune system can shed light on Haraway's approach to biopolitics along with her conceptualisation of the relationship between self and other.

Cyborg Theory and Immune System Discourse

In 'The biopolitics of postmodern bodies' (BPB) Haraway explores the often competing popular and technical languages that construct biomedical, biotechnical bodies and selves in scientific culture in the 1980s. She takes the immune system as the focus of the essay and observes that 'immune system discourse is about constraint and possibility for engaging in a world full of

"difference", replete with non-self' (BPB 211). According to Murray (2007)
Haraway does not deny the clinical importance or significance of the immune
system. She views it as an 'iconic mythic object' in which there is a close inter-
connection of 'myth, laboratory and clinic' (BPB 201; see also Murray 2007:
159). The immune system

> is an elaborate icon for principal systems of symbolic and material
> "difference" in late capitalism. Pre-eminently a twentieth century
> object, the immune system is a map drawn to guide recognition and
> misrecognition of self and other in the dialectics of Western biopoli-
> tics. That is, the immune system is a plan for meaningful action to
> construct and maintain the boundaries for what may count as self and
> other. (BPB 200)

According to Haraway 'the immune system is imaged as a battlefield' and 'the
self' as a 'stronghold' (Murray 2007: 159). It provides a picture of relationships and 'a guide for action in the face of questions about the boundaries of
the self and about mortality' (BPB 210–11).

Haraway returns to several of the key themes present in the development
of the cyborg and partial perspectives. In particular, she argues that bodies are
not born but made. She argues that discourses of immunology are particularly
powerful mediators of the experiences of illness and death in contemporary
society. In the essay Haraway reintroduces readers to the notion of the material-
semiotic actor, which she begins to develop in her work on partial perspectives.
She argues that bodies 'are not ideological constructions' and are 'always radically historically specific' (BPB 204). For Haraway, 'bodies have a different kind
of specificity and effectivity', and 'invite a different kind of engagement and
intervention' (BPB 204–5). She repeats the argument that she outlined earlier:

> 'Material-semiotic actor' is intended to highlight the object of knowl-
> edge as an active part of the apparatus of bodily production, without
> *ever* implying the immediate presence of such objects or, what is the
> same thing, their final or unique determination of what can count as
> objective knowledge of a biomedical body at a particular historical
> juncture. (BPB 205)

Haraway argues again that 'bodies as objects of knowledge are material-
semiotic generative nodes. Their boundaries materialise in social interaction'
(BPB 205). However, in her work on immunology she focuses more specifically
on the ways in which biological bodies surface 'at the intersection of biological
research, writing, and publishing' (BPB 205). She extends her analysis to
examine the ways in which bodies are also made through 'medical and other
business practices', and through 'cultural productions of all kinds, including
available metaphors and narratives' (BPB 205). Furthermore, Haraway explicitly examines the ways in which they are made through technology; for

example, visualisation techniques that bring to life 'killer T cells and intimate photographs of the developing fetus' (BPB 205).

The cyborg, communication, and immunology

The cyborg is central to the focus of her argument in this essay. She extends her conceptualisation of the cyborg in a section in this essay entitled 'Cyborgs for earthly survival' (BPB 209). In the 'bio politics of postmodern bodies', Haraway elaborates on the notion of the cyborg as text, machine, body, and metaphor. This is again theorised through her focus on communications. She begins to unpack in more detail here the ways in which the cyborg 'not only blurs the boundaries between human beings, animals, and machines, but also that between between body and language' (Munnik 1997: 112). According to Haraway, modern technology textualises reality. In making this argument, she returns again to the issue of coding that appears in 'A cyborg manifesto' (CM 164). She argues that it is possible to see how technology textualises the body in biological discourses of the body. These discourses increasingly 'tends to conceive of the body primarily as expressing or bearing the genetically coded information of DNA molecules' (Munnik 1997: 112). Immunology is used by Haraway to illustrate this textualisation of the body (BPB 199–233). The entire discourse of immunology is permeated by notions of coding and decoding. For example, a virus in this discourse is a 'clever invader that sets out to produce an entirely new text that eventually is recognised as "foreign"' (Munnik 1997: 113; BPB 221). Immunology is about the immune system 'defending the body against invaders from the outside, which must therefore be able to establish the difference between friend and foe, health and sickness' (Munnik 1997: 113). Immunologists recognise this 'as a process involving original texts, textual corruptions, and the ability to recognize alien texts as such' (Munnik 1997: 113). Haraway sees the immune system above all as an object in contemporary scientific narratives that is used to create and maintain the boundaries between self and other – a war narrative (BPB 200). However, this is problematic for cyborgs who are themselves hybrids and who therefore do not need to defend their original selves from the other: 'their sickness stories have no need to be war narratives' (Munnik 1997: 113).

The central focus on communication in this essay is illustrated by an example from a study by Winograd and Flores on understanding *computers and cognition*, which is about the operation of computer systems in artificial intelligence. A key idea in this study is 'communication *breakdown*, which Haraway then adopts, in her essay in immunology as a metaphor for illness' (Munnik 1997: 113). Winograd and Flores show that breakdowns play a vital role in human understanding. They should not be viewed as a negative situation that should be avoided. Rather, they should be viewed as 'a situation of non-obviousness, in which some aspect of the network of tools that we are engaged in using is brought forth to visibility' (Winograd and Flores 1986 cited in BPB 211). A breakdown exposes the node of relations essential for us 'to accomplish our task'. . . 'to anticipate the form of breakdowns and provide a space of possibilities for action when they occur' (Winograd and Flores 1986 in BPB 211). Haraway draws 'a connection here between the political (war) narrative and the prevailing immunological narrative' (Munnik 1997: 114). She demonstrates how Winograd and Flores's interpretation highlights a radically different type of narrative than the existing one:

> This is not a Stars Wars[6] or Strategic Computing Initiative relation to vulnerability, but neither does it deny therapeutic action. It insists on locating therapeutic, reconstructive action (and also theoretic understanding) in terms of situated purposes, not fantasies of the utterly defended self in a body as automated, militarised factory, a kind of ultimate self as Robotic Battle Manager meeting the enemy (not self) as it invades in the form of bits of foreign information threatening to take over the master control codes. (BPB 211)

She returns again to the arguments made in her work on the cyborg and partial perspectives that in these completely denaturalised systems another opportunity for political action is uncovered. She argues that it is up to cyborgs to develop truthful narratives such as that of Winograd and Flores. 'The construction or "writing" of such a denaturalized narratives is one form of political action needed to disarm the state' (Munnik 1997: 114; BPB 209–11).

The cyborg and biopolitics

The argument Haraway articulates in this essay on the immune system should be read as her specific take on biopolitics. This is something that is implicit in the development of the concept of the cyborg in the manifesto, and in her introduction to the term material-semiotic in her work on partial perspectives. However, Haraway uses her work on the immune system to illustrate this position more fully. In particular, in this essay Haraway emphasises 'the dual potential that biopolitics holds for destruction or affirmation' (Esposito 2011: 145–7). Like Foucault, Haraway 'takes the centrality of the body as a specific object of biopower', however she does so from a 'material-semiotic' perspective through which she deconstructs the unitary character of the body (Esposito 2011: 146). In contrast to Foucault, Haraway approaches the body from the perspective of its deconstruction and multiplication, prompted by the rapid increase in the 'new bionic, electronic, and information technologies' (Esposito 2011: 146). This, according to Esposito (2011: 146), should be viewed as a 'real paradigm shift in interpretation': 'If in the 1930s the discursive regime on the body attained its ultimate ideological solidity in the concept of "race", and around the 1970s it was reconceived by Foucault in terms of "population" today it must be looked at from the standpoint of its technical transformation' (Esposito 2011: 146). Haraway does not lose sight of 'the actual relations of power into which the management of the living being is inscribed and which tends to change continuously' (Esposito 2011: 146). However, Haraway goes beyond this by arguing that the 'connection between politics and life is radically redefined by the unstoppable proliferation of technology' (Esposito 2011: 146). In conversation with Gane, Haraway herself expands on this, stating that 'Foucault's formulation of biopower remains necessary but it needs to be enterprised up' in light of this cyborg world in which we live. She argues that Foucault's 'sense of the biopolitics of populations has not gone away, but it has been reworked' and 'mutated', and in short 'technologized' (Gane and Haraway 2006: 148). As with the argument first articulated in the manifesto, therefore, the dual-edged potential of the cyborg is reinforced in her biopolitics essay. The cyborg articulated here thus continues to be poised as a potential source for radical change as well as a source for the continued and enhanced unequal structuring of social relations.

Producing Nature, Producing Knowledge

The immune system also plays a key role in Haraway's essay 'Promises of monsters' (PM 63–124). The immune system is used in this context to further revisit and illustrate various elements of her work on cyborg theory and partial perspectives. It also extends her focus on the relationship between self and other and illuminates her position on modernity and postmodernity. Haraway argues that one of the key aims of this essay is to reclaim vision from the ways it has been used in the past to oppress minority groups – she wants to remake vision for activists and advocates engaged in political action (PM). This is very similar to her original development of the partial perspective in 'Situated knowledges' (SK) where she states that she wants to reclaim vision for feminist theory. In promises of monsters, Haraway wants to use vision to see the world from the perspectives of socialist feminists and anti-racist environmentalism, and science for the people (PM).

The main focus of the essay is what she terms artifactualism. She refers again to the central tenet of her work on the production of bodies in both 'Situated knowledges' (SK 595) and 'The biopolitics of postmodern bodies' (BPB 205), arguing that organisms are not born but made (PM 67). She focuses her analysis this time on the production of nature. She argues that many think that the postmodern world is *denatured*. However, Haraway holds that the world has not been denatured as such; rather the contemporary world is merely a particular production of nature. In global capitalism, 'the whole world is remade in the image of commodity production' (PM 66). She returns again to her initial argument in 'A cyborg manifesto' on the importance of relationships between humans and other actants and agents. She argues that nature is made through a co-construction between humans and non-humans (PM 66). In promises of monsters, Haraway develops a path somewhere between materialism, constructivism, and postmodernism. She is keen to distinguish her approach from postmodernism. She argues that postmodernists tend to view the entire world as 'denatured and reproduced in images or replicated in copies' (PM 66). Haraway departs from this and argues that 'organisms emerge from a discursive process' (PM 67). In the essay she advances the same themes outlined elsewhere in this chapter, that 'biology is a

discourse, not the living world itself' (PM 67). She again stresses the importance of other actants and agents in this context. Humans, she argues, 'are not
the only actors in the construction of the entities of any scientific discourse'
'machines' and 'other partners' are 'active constructors of natural scientific
objects' (PM 67).

The production of bodies

The term 'material-semiotic actor' again plays a central role in promises of
monsters. She uses it to 'highlight the object of knowledge as an active part of
the apparatus of bodily production' (PM 67). As argued earlier, for Haraway
'"objects" like bodies do not pre-exist as such' (PM 67); the same argument is
applied in this context to nature. It cannot 'pre-exist as such, but neither is its
existence ideological' (PM 68). Haraway argues that 'nature is a common
place and a powerful discursive construction' (PM 68). She again rehearses the
same arguments about politics and the potential for change. She argues in this
essay that 'perhaps our hopes for accountability for techno-biopolitics in the
belly of the monster turn on revisioning the world as coding trickster with
whom we must learn to converse' (PM 68).

In 'Promises of monsters', Haraway develops what she calls the four-
square cyborg in order to 'play havoc with some of the finest technology of
structuralist and poststructuralist analysis' (Haraway 2004a: 4). This square
consists of four categories: real space (Earth), outer space (the extra-terrestrial),
virtual space (science fiction), and inner space (the biomedical body (PM 78)).
This last category, 'the biomedical body', will form the central focus of this
analysis and in particular her work on the immune system. Haraway argues
that the immune system is a construct of an elaborate 'apparatus of bodily production' (PM 68). But, she argues that 'neither the immune system nor any other
of biology's world-changing bodies – like a virus or an ecosystem – is ghostly
fantasy' (PM 68). She focuses here on the artefactual production of nature.

By doing so she makes another important theoretical statement that again
further develops her work on the partial perspective. She emphasises the cor-
poreality of theory, asserting that overwhelmingly theory is embodied (PM
68). She seeks to place the lived body at the centre of social theory not apart
from it. She also states that lives are built just as technologies are. Because of
this she argues that 'we had best become good craftspeople with the other
worldly actants in the story' (PM 68). She restates her argument that this is
not about the rationalist progress of science in potential league with progressive politics (PM 77). However, she is also quick to point out that this is not
about the social construction of science and nature that situates agency on the
side of humanity. She makes reference to Bruno Latour in this essay to elaborate her position on the development of society and argues that the modern
will not be superseded by or infiltrated by the postmodern (PM 77). She agrees
with Latour in maintaining that 'belief in something called the modern' has
always been 'a mistake'. Haraway makes a very important point here: there is

an 'absence of beginnings, enlightenments, and endings' (PM 77). She states that: 'the world has always been in the middle of things, in unruly and practical conversation, full of action and structured by a startling array of actants and of networking and unequal collectives' (PM 77).

Haraway returns to the connections she makes between language and biology in immune systems discourse. In this essay, however, she grounds her argument in a range of examples, from print media to medical texts through to examples from the entertainment industry. Thus, Haraway illustrates and extends her earlier argument that the immune system is used as a battle ground metaphor, referring to science sections of newspapers and magazines. She gives the example of the *National Geographic*, which openly punned on the notion of Star Wars in its use of the phrase 'Cell Wars' (Jaret in PM 101). Medical texts on the immune system also abound with militarised metaphors. However, what is interesting about immune system discourse is that it works both ways. As Haraway says, it is not just the 'imagers of the immune system' discourse that learn from military cultures, 'military cultures draw symbolically on immune system discourse'. She draws on a range of examples to support and illustrate her arguments here; for instance, the Disney World thrill ride called 'Body Wars'. She argues that 'immune system discourse is about the unequally distributed chances of life and death' (PM 102). She states, however, that this is not just about death' but also life; for example, '*living* with AIDS' (PM 103).

Theorising the self and other

In 'Promises of monsters' Haraway also emphasises the ubiquitous nature of the immune system. She states that with about 10^{12} cells, the immune system 'has two orders of magnitude more cells than the nervous system' (PM 103). The immune system is regenerated throughout life from the pluripotent stem cells. The immune system starts with embryonic life and is there right through the lifecourse. It is dispersed across the body in various tissues and organs, and 'a large fraction of its cells are in the blood and lymph circulatory systems and in body fluids and spaces' (PM 103). Haraway stresses that the immune system is a very dispersed system with a flexible communication system, she argues that: 'The immune system is everywhere and nowhere. Its specificities are indefinite if not infinite, and they arise randomly; yet these extraordinary variations are the critical means of maintaining bodily coherence' (PM 104). Haraway uses the immune system here to further elaborate on her conceptualisation of the relationship between the self and other. Haraway argues that the immune system is a highly dispersed system yet despite such dispersal it is responsible for holding the body together. She uses the immune system here as a metaphor for self and other, alluding perhaps to a more fluid or liquid sense of self (Murray 2007: 162). However, Haraway uses this conceptualisation to position her approach against traditionally postmodern approaches. According to Murray, in postmodern theories the self is portrayed as 'more fragmented in terms of symbolic consistency and narrative texture, and is characterized by ambiguities, ambivalence, discontinuity, dread, flux, multiplicity – and turmoil. The 'self' may be recognised as a composite of contending discourses, practices, representations, images and fantasies' (Murray 2007: 162 referring to Elliot 2001). However, despite these ambiguities and contradictions, for Haraway there is something that holds the self together. In illustrating this point through the immune system, Haraway again avoids the relativism of postmodern conceptualisations of the self, thus again delineating her specific socio-theoretical contribution.

CONCLUSION

In the conclusion to her essay 'Promises of monsters' Haraway states that:

> The whole argument of 'The Promises of Monsters' has been that to 'press enter' is not a fatal error, but an inescapable possibility for changing maps of the world, for building new collectives out of what is not quite a plethora of human and unhuman actors. (PM 110)

This is perhaps the principal argument underlying all of the essays examined in this chapter. For Haraway a theory of society does not rest on an examination of the relationship between individual and society. Rather it includes meaningful relationships between humans and other organisms and technology. Furthermore, to engage with other non-human actants and agents does not necessarily lead to greater inequality but can open up new possibilities for social change.

There are of course those who have questioned whether the cyborg, which is made up of both fact and fiction, really does have the political potency that she ascribes to it (Munnik 1997: 115). However, this critique is perhaps a little unfair. What Haraway tries to show through the development of the concept of the cyborg is that one can imagine a better and fairer world. Such a world for Haraway has the potential to be realised one day through the expansion of new biological, technical, and social relationships. This is the central premise upon which the concept of the cyborg is based and through which the epistemology of the partial perspectives is built. It is also the position that is illuminated by Haraway's work on the immune system: first, through an elaboration of her position on biopolitics; and second, by illustrating her theory of the relationship between the self and other. While the manifestation of the concept of the cyborg and partial perspectives in her work on the immune system is reasonably clear, there is perhaps a lack of analytical clarity between the actual concepts themselves. This, coupled with Haraway's rather abstruse essay style, often makes it difficult to analyse the manifestation of each individual concept in Haraway's work effectively. However, to make this criticism is perhaps to miss the point, as for Haraway boundaries both real and imagined must be transgressed in order for meaningful and egalitarian ones to be reconstructed. This after all is perhaps the most powerful contribution that Haraway makes to contemporary social theory.

Abbreviations

BPB: 'The biopolitics of postmodern bodies' (1993)

CM: 'A cyborg manifesto' (1991)

PM: 'Promises of monsters' (2004b)

SK: 'Situated knowledges' (1988)

Selected Further Readings

The following two readings offer short but comprehensive introductions to Haraway's works:

Reed, K. (2006) *New Directions in Social Theory: Race, Gender and the Canon.* London: Sage, pp. 132-6.

Clough, P. T. and Schneider, J. (2001) 'Donna J. Haraway', in A. Elliot and B. S. Turner (eds) *Profiles in Contemporary Social Theory.* London: Sage, pp. 338-48.

For a more detailed and critical account of her cyborg theory, see:

Munnik, R. (1997) 'Donna Haraway: Cyborgs for earthly survival', in H. Achterhuis (ed.) *American Philosophy of Technology.* Bloomington and Indianapolis, IN: University of Indiana Press, pp. 95-118.

Notes

1 For a feminist discussion on binary thought and women's oppression, see Oakley (1979).
2 The Cold War era is commonly defined as the period commencing at the end of World War Two and ending with the collapse of communism (1946–1991). For a discussion on the relationship between Cold War politics, technological investment, and the military, see Mackenzie (1993).
3 Cybernetics is a transdisciplinary field that focuses on the study of regulatory systems and their structures. The systems that come under study are diverse including: biological, cognitive, mechanical, and social.
4 Some authors have suggested that Haraway is often too quick to dispense with the notion of origin and history. Kirby (1997), for example, argues that origin cannot be separated from the question of identity itself.
5 The discussion of homework presumes a particular set of relations of production. According to Leach (1998) a homeworker is someone 'who receives work for which she is paid by the piece from the supplier, the latter being responsible for the disposal of the finished product. In industrialized societies there is also a tendency to use a category of "home-based work"'. This refers to work such as childminding, small business ventures, etc. (Leach 1998: 97). Haraway (in CM) uses the term to explore the exploitation of female labour in developing nations as well as the feminised nature of work in industrial contexts.
6 Stars Wars refers to the Strategic Defence Initiative (SDI) developed during Ronald Reagan's US presidency. This was a proposed missile defence system intended to protect the US from nuclear attack.

5

Zygmunt Bauman: Liquid Social Life

PART 1: LIQUID SOCIETY

Zygmunt Bauman's conception of contemporary social reality turns on his distinction between 'solids' and 'fluids' such as 'liquids' (LM 1–2). A solid, he clarifies, generally maintains its 'shape': its 'spatial dimensions' are definite; 'time' has limited relevance for it. A liquid is always about 'to change' 'shape': it takes up a 'space' only momentarily; for a liquid, 'the flow of time' is essential. 'Fluids' are also more mobile, and thus commonly considered 'lighter', than 'solids'. Bauman argues that the current stage of 'modernity' can be captured by the 'metaphors' of '"fluidity" or "liquidity"' and that this 'phase' is, in many respects, new (LM 2).

> The kind of modernity which was the target, but also the cognitive frame, of classical critical theory strikes the analyst in retrospect as quite different from the one which frames the lives of present-day generations. It appears 'heavy' (as against the contemporary 'light' modernity); better still, 'solid' (as distinct from 'fluid', 'liquid', or 'liquefied'); condensed (as against diffuse or 'capillary'); finally, systemic (as distinct from network-like). (LM 25)

Bauman draws this distinction in numerous ways, in respect of multiple domains of modern society. Whilst an exhaustive survey is beyond this chapter's scope, reconstructing his distinction in view of individualisation and modernisation as well as in view of the changing relationships between time and space and between capital and labour is indispensable for an exposition of his conception of contemporary social conditions.

Individualisation

One of the domains in relation to which Bauman develops his distinction of liquid from solid modern society is 'individualization' (LM 31). Prior to the onset of modernity *tout court*, he argues, people were '"born into" their identities' (LM 32). Among the principal 'frames' that defined the scope of what humans could choose to do in their lives were 'hereditary estates' (LM 6). Estates were ascribed to people (LM 6, 32), 'inherited' (LM 33) rather than '"joined"' (LM 32). The 'frames of estates' were rigid (LM 32, see also 6). People could hardly 'contest' their position (LM 33, see also 6). Modernity, by contrast, is inseparable from individualisation. In fact, Bauman insists that the two are 'the same social condition' (LM 32). Individualisation, he explains, involves making 'human "identity" ... a "task" and charging the actors with the responsibility for performing that task ...' (LM 31). Throughout the modern era, people have had to attend to 'the self-constitution of individual life' and to the establishment and maintenance of relationships 'with other self-constituting individuals' (LM 49; see also Davis 2016: 78, 94).

Bauman distinguishes specifically early modern conditions, though. Whilst 'the estate-order' was declining (LM 33, see also 6, 32), new 'frames', especially the modern '*classes*', were forming (LM 7). They came to define the 'life projects and life strategies' people could conceivably engage in. The class frames were the 'ready-made niches' of the young modern era (LM 7; see also Blackshaw 2008: 120–1). Yet now the individual herself or himself had 'to find the appropriate niche' (LM 7) and work on 'conforming to the emerging class-bound social types and models of conduct' by 'imitating' (LM 32), obeying 'rules' (LM 7), and keeping to 'the norm' (LM 32). Moreover, individuals had constantly to reaffirm their class 'membership' (LM 32). Crucially, though, class frames, too, were rigid (LM 7). 'Class', but also, for example, 'gender hung heavily over the individual range of choices', like '"facts of nature"'. People's ability 'to escape' the confines of their class was severely limited (LM 33). This illustrates Bauman's more encompassing view that whilst 'modernity' has been a project of liquefying 'deficient', often already unstable 'solids', its objective initially was to forge better, more durable ones (LM 2–3). Installed in place of its 'defunct ... predecessor', the 'industrial order' as a whole was built for the eons (LM 143–4). 'New solids were to be ... constructed'; and who- and whatever had been 'set afloat' when the previous context was undone was 'to be ... "re-embedded"', notably workers (LM 142–3; see also Poder 2008: 100–1).

In today's 'fluid and light' phase of the modern era, people must continue to partake 'in the individualizing game' (LM 34; see also Blackshaw 2008: 120–1). They also still draw 'on society for the building materials and design blueprints' of life (LM 7). But the present is characterised by a whole range of 'patterns and configurations' with conflicting 'commandments' and pliable constitutions. The 'patterns' are not '"self-evident"' anymore, leaving the end point of each individual's efforts of self-constitution 'underdetermined' (LM 7). In fact, individuals themselves are increasingly responsible for configuring 'patterns of dependency and interaction', which, in turn, are as difficult to hold 'in shape' as any fluid (LM 8; see also Poder 2008: 101). The frames 'postulated and pursued' today resemble '"musical chairs"' with their propensity to switch 'positions' or disappear abruptly. Individuals must repeatedly reorient themselves and are always in transit, with no hope of arriving at a 'final destination' (LM 33–4).

In solid modernity, Bauman continues to draw his distinction along very similar lines, some people made laws, planned routines, and determined 'ends', whilst others – 'other-directed men and women',[1] namely – carried out those activities in pursuit of these goals. The former included 'authorities' such as 'leaders' and 'teachers' (LM 63). Everyone else could concentrate on 'learning and following the rules set down for them' (LM 59). By contrast, liquid modernity, which knows, instead of a 'Supreme Office', only competitions 'for supremacy' among multiple 'offices', has no – and certainly not only one – answer to 'the question of objectives' (LM 60). Rather than gauging 'means' in view of a 'given end', people are likely to spend the majority of their time 'agonizing about the choice of goals' (LM 61). And it is the task of each 'individual' alone to discover 'what she or he is capable of', to enhance these skills as much as possible, and to choose the goals most consistent with these abilities (LM 62). The present conditions allow for multiple 'law-proffering authorities', which undermine one another (LM 63–4). The era of 'great leaders' giving people directions, instructions, and orders is over. Nowadays, a great number of 'individuals' offer various 'advice' on and 'examples' for living one's life. Every person must examine this range of suggestions and choose themselves which 'example to imitate', and the 'responsibility for the consequences of investing ... trust in this example rather than another' is theirs alone (LM 30; see also Campain 2008: 201; Davis 2016: 54–5, 78, 100–2; Poder 2008: 101, 104). Bauman differentiates sharply 'between leaders', who must 'be followed', and the 'counsellors' so frequently encountered today, who 'need to be hired and can be fired' (LM 64).

Modernisation

Bauman develops his distinction between the two modernities further in view of what he terms 'modernization'. Perpetual modernisation, a desire for '"clearing the site"' for 'a "new and improved" design', constitutes a distinctive characteristic of the whole of modernity (LM 28). From the outset, Bauman writes with reference to Peter Gay, a mode of procedure according to a medical model was envisaged: 'diagnose the ailment, ... design the therapy course, apply it, and make the ill healthy again – or even healthier ... than ... before' (LL 130–1). The people of modernity have never been able to terminate these endeavours, because for modern society '[f]ulfilment is always in the future' (LM 28).

However, crucially, 'early' modernity still harboured 'the belief' that the transformations of history might – be it in a day, be it in a thousand years – reach a conclusion in the form of a 'good society' in which 'needs' are met, 'order' is immaculate, and 'all contingency' and 'ambivalence' of humans' activities have been eliminated (LM 29, see also 143; Poder 2008: 101). In the eyes of the key 'characters' of that phase's 'story' – a privileged few, Bauman points out, rather than the whole population (LL 133–4) – overcoming 'the world as found' and installing another meant striving for the '*perfect* world' which would warrant no additional changes (LL 132–3). Moreover, they imagined that a better management of 'the world' could help realise 'greater happiness' for 'all humans' and understood the quest for it as 'a *collective task*', a joint project of conceptualising and constructing 'a better world' (LL 132).

Twenty-first century society, Bauman holds, is unquestionably 'modern' in that it still pursues constant '*modernization*' with an 'unquenchable thirst for creative destruction' (LM 28; see also Poder 2008: 100). The 'motif' resounding in the chants of 'ministers' everywhere is 'modernize, modernize, change or perish'. The 'characters' central to the narratives of the modernities of the year 2000 and of the year 1800, respectively, share an inability to 'stand still' and a dissatisfaction 'with what is' (LL 131). Yet although the desire for change of both types of characters has been fuelled by the vital sustenance that the assurance of the transformability of 'what is' lends to 'the hope of satisfaction' (LL 131–2), contemporary 'modernity' can be told apart from 'early' modernity by the 'swift decline' of any 'illusion' that consummate conditions might ever be achieved (LM 29; see also Poder 2008: 101). When the 'heroes' of today's 'story' – and these are now 'all' the 'players' – do not downright 'resent the thought of ever stopping', they keep their minds off any ultimate goals, conscious of their being in the dark about the moves that their modernisation endeavours would require beyond the immediate next 'step' now engaging them completely (LL 133–4). In their eyes, 'change is an end in itself' (LL 133). No longer looking to a link between 'happiness' and a 'state of the world', they are convinced that the escape from misery hinges on each person's work on her- or himself, thus conceiving it as an entirely '*private task*' (LL 132). Nowadays, the chores of modernisation tend to be 'left to individuals' management and individually administered resources' (LM 29).

Time and Space

Bauman's aforementioned introduction to solids and liquids with reference to time and space already indicates that these dimensions are important for his investigations. Indeed, the key quality of modernity, 'from which all other characteristics follow', he surmises, '... is the changing relationship between space and time' (LM 8). This transformation leads Bauman to affirm and further specify his distinction between the two modernities.

Technological component

In 'pre-modern' epochs, Bauman argues, time and space were 'locked in a ... one-to-one correspondence' (LM 8–9). Questions about the distance between two locations could be answered with reference to the length of time it took 'human or animal muscles' to travel it: '"Far" and "long", just like "near" and "soon", used to mean nearly the same: just how much or how little effort it would take for a human being to span a certain distance – be it by walking, by ploughing, or harvesting' (LM 110). In the specific sense that no king could traverse a distance in any less time than anyone else, inequality was minimal (LM 112).

The onset of modernity coincided with the dissociation of time and space (LM 8, 112). Of central importance were inventions of transport technologies that enabled people to travel given 'distances' in ever 'less time' (LM 111, see also 9). 'Time was different from space because, unlike space, it could be ... manipulated' by human-made means (LM 111). Those disposing of better means of transport could travel the same distance more quickly, and thus seize a larger 'territory', than everyone else (LM 112).

The technological contraction of the time of movement for the purpose of seizing ever wider spaces, the fortification of these spaces, and populating them with things became characteristic modern endeavours (LM 112–14, see also 9). Bauman mentions the growing size of factories, numbers of employees, and volume of machines, as well as imperial expansion (LM 113–14). 'Wealth and might' were augmented by enlarging 'the place they occup[ied]', 'protected by protecting that place' (LM 115), and, crucially, 'tied to their place', that is, 'immovable' (LM 114). Controlling such spaces, in turn, hinged on 'neutralizing' time's 'inner dynamism': on carving time up into segments of equal length and establishing 'monotonous and unalterable sequences' – in factory work, for instance – so that nothing would happen sooner than planned (LM 115). These time–space configurations were decisive for solid or '*heavy* modernity' (LM 113).

Modernity's current phase is distinct from its heavy stage not because it has steered the development of the time–space relationship in a new direction, but because it has radicalised its already ongoing development. Tendentially (LM 119), Bauman emphasises, in this 'software' or 'light modernity' (LM 118), 'space may be traversed, literally, in "no time"' (LM 117). At the speed of 'electronic signals', far away localities can now be 'acted upon'. Crucially, if, to argue with Georg Simmel, the value of anything hinges on what must be sacrificed to obtain it, then, continues Bauman, where 'no time needs to be ... "sacrificed" ... to reach ... places, places are stripped of value in the Simmelian sense' (LM 117). Plus, insofar as not an instant is required for getting anywhere, no location 'has "special value"'. In these conditions, it is difficult to justify investment in gaining 'access to', and in the 'management' and 'cultivation' of, any place (LM 118).

Power component

Whilst Bauman thus clearly understands the modern condition as decisively shaped by technological developments and the changing time–space configuration, he closely associates these with transformations in social power relationships characteristic of modernity's unfolding.[2] Foucault's analysis of panoptic spaces conceived in the 1700s and 1800s, such as factories, schools, and prisons (1991: 195–228), serves Bauman as a cardinal reference point. In the panopticon, every inmate was immobilised, trapped in a cellular space (LM 9–10). First, inmates were aware that they could be watched all the time but unsure whether their supervisors were occupying their posts at any particular time (LM 9–11, see also 26). Second, 'the flow of [their] time' was strictly 'routiniz[ed]'. The supervisors were mobile to an extent that supported 'their domination' in the former respect, but 'routinization', among other duties, required them to remain present in the spaces of confinement. Hence, crucially, panoptic space was one of 'mutual engagement and confrontation between the two sides of the power relationship' (LM 10; see also Davis 2016: 100–1, 105n7; Poder 2008: 101).

The recent successes in humans' endeavours to increase 'the speed of movement', argues Bauman, are having a deep impact on contemporary power relations. Now that devices such as mobile phones allow a 'command' to travel from anywhere to anywhere in no time, no part of the exercise of power requires those exercising it to stay put in any specific location. The 'power-holders' are able to remove themselves from proximity to those on whom power is exercised, which brings the panoptical arrangement to an end: 'The end of Panopticon augurs *the end of the era of mutual engagement:* between the supervisors and the supervised, capital and labour, leaders and their followers, armies at war' (LM 10–11; see also Campain 2008: 202–3).

Capital and Labour

The social relationship arguably most important to Bauman's analyses of modernity's solid and liquid phases is that between capital and labour. He describes the former phase as simultaneously that of 'heavy capitalism' and that of the '*dependency*' of 'capital and labour' on one another, which 'tied them' permanently to each other (LM 145; see also Poder 2008: 101).

'Heavy capitalism was obsessed with bulk and size' (LM 58): with gigantic factories populated with masses of workers and huge machines (LM 144) behind insurmountable walls (LM 58). Henry Ford, Bauman remarks citing Daniel Cohen, gave his workers a 100% raise specifically in order to bind them to his factory (LM 58, 144). 'Routinized time', too, as already mentioned, 'tied labour to the ground' (LM 116; see also Davis 2016: 100–1). And 'labour' bound to the workplaces, together with the gargantuan and heavy sites and tools of production, kept 'capital' immobile (LM 116). Emphasising labour's '*embodied*' quality, Bauman points out that to 'mov[e] around' and 'hire ... labour' employers needed to move and hire 'labourers', and 'to control the work process' they needed 'to control the workers'. This 'brought capital and labour face to face' (LM 120–1; see also Davis 2016: 101n6). The relationship between the two was characterised by daily struggles and occasional intense clashes that took the form of direct confrontations (LM 116, CL 14, 19). Yet since neither could do without the other and both were aware that they required 'solutions' agreeable to both, clashes and 'bargaining' could reinforce their 'unity' (LM 146–7). Moreover, both needing the exchange of labour for wages, both had to be maintained in a condition 'fit for that transaction', and both 'had "vested interests" in keeping the other side in the right shape' (LM 145). A key element of their 'settlement' (LF 164), 'the state' contributed to keeping 'capitalists' able 'to buy labour' (LM 145) and to stimulating the 'expansion of the capitalist economy' as well as to 'rehabilitating labour' (LF 163) and to ensuring that the jobless were prepared for being 'called back into active service' (LM 145, see also CL 7–8). Generally, workers of that era had a degree of certainty: an 'apprentice' starting to work for Ford, for example, could look forward to a lifetime of 'employment' in an enterprise whose life expectancy was even longer (LM 146).

Liquid modernity, by contrast, is witnessing the emergence 'of light ... capitalism' (LM 149). Whereas the ability to work still cannot be fulfilled without 'the presence of capital' (LM 121), capital's 'reproduction and growth' are now 'largely independent from the duration of any particular local engagement with labour'. Their bonds are 'loosening' (LM 149; see also Campain 2008: 202–3; Davis 2016: 66–7; Poder 2008: 106).

In the current 'software era', which is contemporaneous with the '"disembodiment"' of the 'labour' fuelling 'capital', capital need no longer manage cumbersome control and training apparatuses. Hence, it is not 'tied' down and 'into direct engagement' with the workers anymore. Today's 'capitalists' are keen to jettison unnecessary weight, especially the 'onerous' duty of managing countless employees (LM 121–2; see also Campain 2008: 202–3; Poder 2008: 101). Unburdened from 'bulky machinery and massive factory crews, capital travels light' – 'briefcase', notebook, mobile (LM 150, see also 58). It is able to reach virtually any place, need not remain anywhere longer than is satisfactory, and can always swiftly move on (LM 58, 121–2; see also Campain 2008: 202–3; Davis 2016: 101n6, 105). A firm 'engagement' would only hamper 'movement' and 'competitiveness', leaving opportunities potentially to improve 'productivity' unused (LM 150–1).[3] Capital's ability to move rapidly from one locality to another allows it to issue the 'threat of' – for any locality devastating – 'capital disinvestment'. Politics on the ground responds by 'deregulation', and the people's capacity and will 'to put up an organized resistance' is corroding (LM 150, see also LF 159; Campain 2008: 202–3). Bauman adds that 'profits' no longer flow from things but from '*ideas*', which 'are produced only once'. Rendering them 'profitable' does not hinge on a large workforce 'replicating the prototype', but on a large crowd of 'consumers'. When capital arranges its journeys, it is therefore ever less concerned about whether a locality provides a workforce, whose '"holding power" ... on capital' is, as a result, atrophying (LM 151). Today's employee, finally, experiences 'uncertainty', a world of 'work on short-term contracts, rolling contracts or no contracts' under the sign of '"Flexibility"' in which people will change employment increasingly frequently (LM 147; see also Campain 2008: 202–3; Poder 2008: 106).

Politics and Individualisation

Bauman's analysis of the relationship between capital and labour constitutes one component of his multifaceted investigation of the political dimension of contemporary social conditions. Bauman also highlights the present obstacles to the transformation of liquid society for the better. Whilst a complete account of this part of his work cannot be given here, an argument in connection with 'individualization' (LM 34) may illustrate the kinds of dilemmas he attempts to tackle.

It is doubtful, emphasises Bauman, that people can spare themselves 'frustration' by their own individual means (LM 34). Nonetheless, individuals today concentrate 'on their own performances' rather than on the social conditions in which the 'contradictions' of their lives are generated (LM 38). Indeed, the frustrated are advised to blame themselves and their personal shortcomings (LM 34). As a consequence, Bauman argues citing Ulrich Beck (1992: 137), people come to live '"... *biographical solution[s] to systemic contradictions*"': the latter are 'socially produced', but the obligation to deal with them is 'individualized' (LM 34; see also Davis 2016: 133–6). Yet '"biographic solutions to systemic contradictions"' do not exist (LM 38).

The liquid age, Bauman insists, is sustaining a chasm 'between the right of self-assertion' and the power over the social conditions that determine whether 'self-assertion' is 'feasible' (LM 38, see also 39). The 'individual' does not presently control 'the resources' that proper 'self-determination' would require (LM 40). No individual is free to determine 'the range of choices and the agenda of choice-making' (LM 51; see also Davis 2016: 51, 75–8, 136–7; Poder 2008: 103). Bauman concedes that individual capacities amalgamated 'into a collective stand and action' might provide 'a remedy' (LM 35; see also Campain 2008: 203). However, the message disseminated everywhere is that the individual 'is the master of his or her own fate' (LM 39, see also 64; Davis 2016: 133–6). The primary lesson of observing others today is that everybody is exposed to 'risks ... to be ... fought alone'. People have become 'sceptical' of appeals to the '"common good"' or the '"good society"', asking only that everybody be allowed to pursue their own path. 'Sharing intimacies', 'worries', 'anxieties', Bauman argues drawing on Richard Sennett, is now virtually the only mode of forming 'communities', which are correspondingly transient (LM 36–7; see also Campain 2008: 203–4; Davis 2016: 135–7). Today, he adds, 'communities' also often form with reference to 'celebrities', those 'liquid modern characters' whose celebrity Daniel Boorstin ascribed to their '"… well-knownness"' (LL 49–50). Yet a celebrity's 'notoriety' rarely lasts; celebrity-centred 'imaginary communities' require 'no commitment' and are fragile, always prone to disband (LL 50). The 'colonization of the public sphere by the private', continues Bauman, has in fact become the foremost barrier to liberation (LM 51, see also 37, 39). Personal problems 'will not congeal' and form 'a "common cause"', so 'individual grievances' do not easily coalesce 'into shared interests', let alone 'joint action' (LM 35; see also Davis 2016: 67, 135–6). In this situation, replenishing 'public space' with substance becomes a key emancipatory 'task' (LM 39, see also 41). What needs addressing is the problem of turning 'private problems into public issues' and of 'recollectivizing the privatized utopias' in order to transform them into 'visions of the "good society"' (LM 51; see also Campain 2008: 203; Davis 2016: 132–5, 138).

PART 2: LIQUID LIVING

Whilst the problem of life in contemporary social conditions can be heard to reverberate throughout Bauman's examinations of liquid modernity, he also raises this problem explicitly. What goes by 'the name of "modernity"', he says, is 'our bizarre way of life' (LL 130). '"Liquid life"', he specifies, 'is a kind of life that tends to be lived in a liquid modern society… Liquid life, just like liquid modern society, cannot keep its shape … for long' (LL 1). Like his depiction of liquid society, Bauman's portrayal of the liquid life seeks to capture a wide range of its properties. His problematisation of individuality and of life's modernisation, the concept of the consuming life, and his analysis of contemporary fears contain some of his decisive considerations.

Individual Life

Bauman's emphasis on individualisation renders it unsurprising that he identifies the problem of individuality as a key characteristic of the liquid life. Bauman understands individuality as a typically modern problem. When the 'capacity' of 'the community' to 'regulat[e] the lives of its members … matter-of-factly' according to standards or norms was waning, the 'shaping' of people's conduct was coming to light as something to be chosen (LL 20). The 'normative powers' of modern society did not take control over the sphere of 'interpersonal relations'; such ties could henceforth be established and severed 'freely'. A person's 'individuality is asserted and daily renegotiated' in that 'face-to-face' sphere. More specifically, the very idea of being 'an "individual"' is inextricable from that of taking 'responsibility' for one's 'interaction'. This 'responsibility' can only be thought if it is assumed that people 'have the right to choose' how to 'proceed'. In fact, in contemporary society, such 'free choice' is also a 'duty' (LL 21). This right and duty notwithstanding, for many people 'practising … free choice' is, of course, often out of 'reach' (LL 22).

For Bauman, 'individuality' is truly a problem. It contains 'an *insoluble* contradiction': both the 'cradle' and the 'destination' required by individuality is 'society' (LL 18). That one 'be an individual', namely distinct, is, he emphasises, a central 'demand' of contemporary 'society' on all people indiscriminately: 'individuality is a "universal must"'. In turn, so as to demonstrate their 'individuality' persuasively, people cannot but utilise 'tokens' that are 'shared' and 'commonly recognizable' (LL 16; see also Davis 2016: 142–3). As might be expected, in trying to construct their individuality, people 'listen' out for signals emitted by their innermost 'feelings', the supposed quintessence of '"uniqueness"' (LL 17). However, purchasing assistance for decoding these signals, they all too often end up with 'recipes for individuality ... peddled wholesale' (LL 18).

According to Bauman, '[c]onsumerism' has certainly become a vital strategy for responding to the social demand on everyone to build, maintain, and renew 'their individuality'. Pointing to the advertising slogan '"Be yourself – choose Pepsi"', he argues that people's effort to stand out constitutes 'the main engine' of the 'production' of commodities *en masse* and of their 'consumption' by the masses (LL 23–4). Everybody seeks to form 'the friable stuff of life' into an 'identity' – a word one cannot dissociate from a vague notion of 'consistency' (LM 82). Yet insofar as nobody's identity is now fixed, 'it is the ability to "shop around" in the supermarket of identities' that supports the realisation of notions of identity (LM 83). The inhabitants of this 'liquid modern world' tour its shopping centres for 'publicly legible identity badges' (LL 34; see also Davis 2016: 56–7, 63–4, 73). Here people appear 'free' to assemble and disassemble 'identities' as they wish. In actual fact – as another brazenly frank advert, this time for a 'brand of hair conditioner': '"All unique; all individual; all choose X"', reveals – they must buy 'mass-produced' goods bought by thousands of others for building their particular identities, whilst the 'life' they want for themselves is more often than not a life they have seen on one of the many 'screens' surrounding them (LM 83–4, see also LL 86–7; Davis 2016: 73, 76–80, 86; Poder 2008: 102). This is evidently a tricky situation.

Modernising Life

Indeed, people's longing to be different can support the 'mass consumer market' only in 'a consumer economy' in which articles quickly become outdated. A contemporary strategy for rendering oneself distinct consists of divesting oneself of goods 'relegated from premiership league' and acquiring the latest faster than others (LL 24). However, the situation thus remains tricky with regard to consistency. Today, the objects out of which identity is constructed are made not to last, 'standards' are highly 'flexible', and 'identities' are inevitably 'unstable', so that the individual ends up perpetually having to readapt rapidly to 'the changing patterns of the world "out there"' (LM 85–6).

In this respect, individual identity is a site of the modernisation of life. From Bauman's aforementioned contention that modernisation is increasingly focused on the individual rather than on social conditions it may be inferred that identity constitutes a key site of modernisation. 'Life in a liquid modern society', he argues, '... must modernize' (LL 3). In the fluid present, one's 'assets' and 'abilities' quickly become 'liabilities' and 'disabilities' (LL 1). People live in dread of becoming laden with what has become outmoded and of not keeping step 'with fast-moving events'. Accordingly, 'getting rid of things' is now a vital activity (LL 2). '"Creative destruction" is the fashion in which liquid life proceeds'. For a life, to modernise means precisely to continue to rid oneself 'daily of attributes ... past their sell-by dates' and to undo one's present 'identities' (LL 3). People are enabled and obliged to deactivate their 'past', to strive for fresh starts, to go through an entire 'series of families, careers, identities' (CL 100–1). Bauman reads the growing prominence of 'cosmetic surgery' as an expression of the current appeal of '"serial births"'. Scores of people have come to use such interventions regularly as tools for periodically reconstructing their 'visible self'. Each of the consecutive surgical procedures allows the individual to respond to today's 'fast-changing standards' and successively replace 'an image that has outlived its utility or charm' with 'a new public image' and, if possible, 'a new identity' (CL 101). Personal 'identity' is 'living through' a number of chapters steered by the need to obliterate one's 'history' instead of the will to design a 'future'. It means endeavouring 'to embrace' whatever is deemed necessary 'today' accompanied by the knowledge that all of this may well be considered problematic 'tomorrow'. Individual identity is always tied to its own respective 'present'. As its only stable – yet possibly even solidifying – kernel remains *homo eligens*, a human being continuously choosing without ever having definitively chosen (LL 33).

It is indispensable to add, however, that for Bauman this activity of constructing and repeatedly refreshing an individual identity manifests economic inequality: hinging on consumption in the above sense, this activity is clearly very expensive, open exclusively to those with substantial means (LL 25). A sizeable 'remainder' of the population is shut off from the 'costly extras' required for preparing trendy 'identity cocktails'; given 'no choice', they must accept 'identity concoctions' – however bland – 'as they come' (LL 35; see also Davis 2016: 87–9, 92–6; Poder 2008: 102, 110).

Life in the Market

As the foregoing considerations already strongly indicate, Bauman understands liquid modernity as the phase of 'the society of consumers' (CL 68, see also LL 80, LM 73). The 'consumer society' values people mainly according to 'capacities and conduct' relevant to 'consumption' (LL 82, see also LM 76). It compels them to choose 'a consumerist lifestyle and life strategy' (CL 53). Formerly, in the 'society of producers and soldiers', people were 'trained' to adapt to their assigned station, bear 'drudgery' and 'routine', and agree 'to working for the work's sake'. That society sought to render people 'fit' to operate on 'the factory floor and the battlefield' (CL 54). In the consumer society, by contrast, everybody is supposed to approach 'consumption as a vocation'

(CL 55). From an early age, people are meant to develop a fitness for operating in shopping centres (CL 54).

Shopping and non-satisfaction

'The code in which our "life policy" is scripted', Bauman asserts, 'is derived from the pragmatics of shopping' (LM 73–4, see also LL 83). 'Shopping' – that is, 'scanning' what is on offer, inspecting the items, considering prices in relation to one's funds or 'credit limit', and selecting – takes place everywhere today, not just in 'shops'. It is what people do for 'food, shoes, cars', of course, but also 'for new and improved examples and recipes for life'. They '"shop" for the skills' required for winning a livelihood, for instance, or 'for ways to earn the love of the beloved' and for cheap ways of splitting up with them, as much as for the best sound systems (LM 73–4, see also LL 87–8; Blackshaw 2008: 119–20; Davis 2016: 73, 76–8; Poder 2008: 104). This extension of 'consumer patterns', Bauman surmises, is probably due to the pervasive '"marketization" of life processes' characteristic of contemporary society (LL 88).[4]

Contemporary 'consumerism', however, is not primarily a matter of meeting 'needs', which were once considered scarcely malleable (LM 74–5). Even 'desire', which lends itself more easily to being inflated but is expensive for sellers of commodities to cultivate in people, is making way for the still more flexible '"wish"' as the 'stimulant' of consumption (LM 75–6). 'Life' in a producer society, argues Bauman, was 'regulated' by norms (LM 76). People needed a certain minimum to be able to work and could not easily want what lay beyond a socially permitted maximum. The key issue was 'conformity'. 'Life organized around consumption' is not 'normatively' modulated but 'guided by seduction', continually expanding 'desires', and fickle 'wishes' (LM 76). What matters chiefly now is 'adequacy': being able 'to develop new desires' that match ever novel 'allurements' (LM 77).

The 'case' of the society of consumers is underpinned by 'the promise to satisfy human desires' like no formation before it (LL 80). Indeed, whereas in the producer society people still considered it decent to postpone gratification, the period between 'wanting' and 'getting' has contracted (LL 83, see also CL 85–6, 98, LM 155–60). In the former formation, emphasis rested on the principle of forgoing instant 'rewards' for the sake of 'future benefits' and 'individual rewards for the benefit of the "whole"', for example, the 'nation' (CL 69). Liquid modernity's consumer society, by contrast, posits the 'obligation … to choose' – though presenting it 'as *freedom* of choice' – and 'to seek pleasure and happiness' (CL 74–5; see also Davis 2016: 74). However, if people were ever convinced that their 'desires' have been wholly met, the prospect of 'satisfaction' would cease to lure them to the shops (LL 80), 'consumer demand' might deteriorate, and 'the consumer-targeted economy' might stop turning (LL 81; see also Poder 2008: 105). The latter is driven by a '"buy it, enjoy it, chuck it out" cycle' (CL 98). It thrives on the enduring 'non-satisfaction of desires' (LL 80, see also 92). To a 'society' which states that its principal

'purpose' is 'customer *satisfaction*', Bauman argues from an only slightly different angle, any permanently '*satisfied* consumer' poses a threat. So 'the
ethical guideline of the consuming life' must instruct 'to avoid *staying
satisfied*' (CL 98).

Bauman mentions several ways in which 'non-satisfaction' is sustained (LL
80). What is acquired might certainly simply fail to create the 'fulfilment' it
promised (LM 72). But even if gratification ensues, it will, owing to the inex-
haustible amount of further 'seductive ... offer[s]', be short-lived (LM 72, see
also 73). In particular, holds Bauman, goods that are essential and up-to-date
one day are rivalled by novel products the next and become inessential, out-
of-date, or worse, and ready to be discarded (LL 85–9, see also CL 102–3).
Articles heavily promoted today can even be maligned in the harshest terms
tomorrow (CL 96–7, 99–100, LL 80). Finally, gratification itself will produce
'new needs/desires/wants' (LL 80). Reports that some skincare products have
caused skin problems and thus boosted 'consumer demand' for the next versions of such articles provide an illustration (LL 81, see also LM 74). Of
course, if people are to consume to help stimulate the economy, they must
have money or credit (CL 78–9). In fact, in the society of consumers, '"living
on credit"' is meant to become 'second nature' (CL 79; see also Blackshaw
2008: 125).

Ultimately, Bauman holds, the inhabitants of the consumer society
approach their entire 'social setting' and all the 'actions' it arouses under the
direction of the '"consumerist syndrome"'. The term 'syndrome' designates
here a bundle of *inter alia* 'attitudes', 'cognitive dispositions', and 'value
judgements' (LL 83; see also Blackshaw 2008: 117–18; Poder 2008: 106).
'The consumerist cultural syndrome' involves the valuation of 'transience'
and 'novelty' over 'duration' (CL 85, see also LL 83). Belongings are desired
and deemed useful only for a short while; they are sought to be got rid of
soon after they are acquired (CL 85–6, LL 83–4). People try to avoid keeping
things for too long, happily 'consigning' them 'to waste' (CL 86, LL 84).
'Fully fledged consumers' are relaxed, even positive, about the objects' 'short
lifespan', perceiving their flaws at the same time as heralds of 'new joys' (CL
86, LL 84).

Consumers as commodities

A proper understanding of life in the consumer society, Bauman accentuates
though, hinges on recognising not only that individuals are consumers, but also
that many 'inhabit' markets as '*commodities*' (CL 6, see also 57, 62), notably, of
course, labour markets (CL 10). As mentioned, Bauman, drawing on Jürgen
Habermas, argues that until recently 'the capitalist state' – responding to the
requirement that 'capital' be able and keen to purchase 'the commodity' 'labour',
and that the latter remain capable of catching the attention and securing the
'approval' of 'potential buyers' – was vital in 'encouraging capitalists to spend
their money on labour' as well as in 'making labour attractive to capitalist

buyers' (CL 7). Yet whereas states still support 'capital' in many ways, 'the recommoditization of *labour*' is undergoing 'deregulation and privatization' (CL 8–9, see also 62). Education and healthcare, for example, are increasingly provided by private suppliers, and individuals themselves are responsibilised for rendering 'labour sellable', for instance by obtaining skills (CL 9, see also 57–9). Simultaneously, people are ever busier '*marketing*', '*promot[ing]*' themselves as '*commodities*' (CL 6). To 'become a subject', Bauman asserts, one must become 'a commodity', and to maintain one's 'subjectness', one must constantly revive 'the capacities expected and required of a sellable commodity' (CL 12).

Now, Bauman describes this '*transformation of consumers into commodities*' as the consumer society's primary characteristic (CL 12). This is not to say, however, that it outweighs the constitution of humans as consumers in characterising that society. Rather, the two are inseparable. For it is, in turn, precisely by consuming that people render themselves distinct 'from the mass of indistinguishable objects' and able to draw the attention of buyers (CL 12, see also 79). From Bauman's perspective, 'consumption' constitutes 'an investment' in articles that can influence one's '"social value" and self-esteem', an investment in one's '"saleability"' (CL 56–7). In fact,

> [t]he crucial, perhaps the decisive purpose of consumption in the society of consumers ... is not the satisfaction of needs, desires and wants, but ... *raising the status of consumers to that of sellable commodities...*
>
> It is by their potency to increase the consumer's market price that the attractiveness of consumer goods – the current or potential objects of consumers' desire triggering consumer action – tends to be evaluated. (CL 57)

Bauman specifies humanity's 'passage' into the consumer society as the 'colonization of life by the commodity market'; market 'laws' have become the 'precepts' of 'life' (CL 61–2). Humans turn to the market for the means they have to deploy 'in making themselves "fit for being consumed" – and so market-worthy'. Consumers consume consumer articles to accomplish a mission '"outsourced"' to private, 'individual' 'consumers', namely the consumers' own '"commoditization"' (CL 62). Competing with everyone else, they are supposed to strive for their 'optimal selling price', better 'ratings', or a superior ranking in some 'league table' (CL 62–3).

Living with Fear

Bauman considers the liquid life problematic not only due to individualisation and modernisation or due to the consumerist syndrome and commodification, but also, perhaps above all, because life in contemporary conditions involves suffering. He has already been shown to accentuate the non-satisfaction that characterises people's lives today. Yet Bauman is particularly concerned with the fears that pester people, describing the contemporary epoch as one 'of fears' (LF 2; see also Davis 2016: 51). Some beset specific groups, others everyone in the world (LF 20), and combating 'fears' has become 'a lifelong task' (LF 8). The 'dangers' fuelling them are now thought to accompany 'human life' constantly (LF 8). Fears can emanate from a range of objects and daily surroundings, from nature as well as fellow humans – both 'threatening' to wreck 'our bodies' and 'homes' (LF 4). Moreover, Bauman points to a fear-inducing sphere of simultaneously 'natural and human' calamities, of market debacles, of firms dissolving 'together with dozens of services ... and thousands of jobs', of plane crashes etc. (LF 5). Contemporary 'fears', diagnoses Bauman, stir a 'feeling of impotence': people have virtually no notion of where their fears come from, do not know how to protect themselves against them, let alone 'preven[t]' or 'figh[t]' the 'dangers', and are unable even to envisage the necessary 'tools' and 'skills' (LF 20). '"Fear"' stands here for 'our *uncertainty*', not knowing what exactly 'the threat' is and what one should do about it (LF 2).

Existential tremors

Bauman's discussion of what he calls existential tremors contains key components of his multifaceted analysis of 'liquid modern fears' (LF 21). The variety of today's dangers notwithstanding, people's 'insecurity', Bauman holds, centres on the 'fear' of 'humans' doing harm (LF 131). Most people harbour the notion that other people are 'a source of existential insecurity'. This is unsurprising in contemporary society, especially, as people are compelled 'to pursue their own interests' and hence unlikely to count on much 'disinterested compassion and solidarity' from others (LF 132). Among the 'horrifying ... fears' of today are those 'of being left behind', 'of *exclusion*' (LF 18). The British television shows *Big Brother* and *The Weakest Link* (LF 22–8), Bauman claims, are 'moral tales' for the inhabitants of the 'liquid modern world' (LF 28). They convey the 'truths' that individuals are threatened with social expulsion, but 'that blows hit at random', that causal connections between people's actions and what happens to them are extremely faint at best, and that hardly anything, if anything at all, can be done to 'stave off' the 'fate' of 'eviction' (LF 28, see also 18–19, 47; Blackshaw 2008: 129).[5] Such 'tales', Bauman states, instil 'fears' that come to 'penetrate and saturate the whole of life', to suffuse 'body and mind' (LF 28–9).

Individuals, elaborates Bauman, are indeed living in the 'presence of ... [e]xistential tremors' (LF 133). He describes as 'shaky' the supposed underpinnings of 'life prospects', people's employment and employers, 'partners' and friendship 'networks', and social status and 'self-confidence'. '"Progress"' has come to mean 'the threat of relentless ... change', whereby a moment's 'inattention' can lead to definitive 'exclusion' (LL 68, see also LF 3–4, 19–20, 139, 148; Blackshaw 2008: 128–9; Poder 2008: 105). However, crucially, the focus of contemporary 'fears' is shifting to 'areas of life' which, whilst reassuringly 'within sight and reach', are 'largely *irrelevant* to the genuine source of anxiety' (LF 133, see also 4).

Bauman places this shift of focus within a wider historical context:

> The long crusade against socially begotten and gestated terrors culmi-
> nated in collective, state-endorsed insurance against individually
> suffered misfortune (like unemployment, invalidity, disease or old
> age), and in collectively guaranteed provision, similarly countersigned
> by the state, of the amenities essential to individual self-formation and
> self-assertion, which was the substance, or at least the guiding objec-
> tive, of the social (misnamed as 'welfare') state. (LF 157)

Yet this 'social state' is pulling back. Few in contemporary politics reiterate
the 'promise', made in 1933 by US president Roosevelt, of an age in which
nothing but fear would need to be feared. People are once more pestered by
'fear of social degradation', ultimately 'of poverty and social exclusion' (LF
157, see also 1; Davis 2016: 92–3). Owing to the cutbacks in the social
state's collective efforts to insure individuals against 'misfortune', 'security'
is increasingly at the mercy of 'market' caprices and 'global forces' (LF 134).
People are having to try to solve 'socially produced' problems individually
through 'solitary actions', deploying their own private means, which cannot
but fall short. The 'messages' released by 'political power' create perspectives
of still further 'privatization of troubles' and thus still greater 'uncertainty',
rather than of 'collectively assured existential security'. They motivate people
to funnel their attention on their *safety* (LF 136, emphasis added; see also
Davis 2016: 67–9, 92–4). For Bauman, the latter term chiefly points to
'material, bodily ... aspects of security' (LF 138); by 'safety', he means 'shel-
ter from ... threats to one's own person and its extensions' (LF 134), for
example, 'homes and their contents' (LF 138, see also 3, 158; Poder 2008:
105–6). Indeed, since individuals can neither decelerate the aforementioned
inexorable 'change' nor tell and determine where it is going, they concentrate
instead on what they 'can, or believe [they] can, ... influence'. They endeavour to spot '"the five symptoms of depression"', avoid 'cigarette smoke' and
direct sunlight, build a protective arsenal of CCTV, 'SUVs', and 'martial arts'
skills etc. (LL 68–9, see also LF 143; Davis 2016: 68, 161–5).[6] People aspire
to obtaining the means necessary to gain 'control' in this *safety* sphere, leaving other fear-emitting spheres – which could not be controlled through
individual efforts anyway – 'unattended' (LF 138–9). The actions upon those
life 'areas' onto which the focus of 'fears' is shifting are insufficient for deac-
tivating the 'genuine sources' of fears and allaying 'the original anxiety' (LF
133–4, see also 139).

Bauman specifies the curtailment of the function of the state in this context. Assessing globalisation, Richard Rorty notes: '"... the economic situation
of the citizens of nation states has passed beyond the control of the laws of
that state ..."'; '"... a global overclass ..."' now takes the key '"economic decisions ..."' independently '"of the legislatures ... of any given country ..."'
(cited in LF 146). Bauman includes 'extraterritorial capital', whose relationship

with labour was discussed above, together with 'its neoliberal acolytes' in that class (LF 147). He affirms:

> ... society is no longer adequately protected by the state; it is now exposed to the rapacity of forces the state does not control and no longer hopes or intends to recapture and subdue – not singly, not even in combination with several other similarly hapless states. (LF 147; see also Davis 2016: 51, 65–7)[7]

Much of the state's power is dissolving 'into global space', whilst much of the state's 'political acumen and dexterity' is being transferred to each person's '"life politics"'. The thus ever slimmer state is largely confined to operating as 'a *personal safety state*'. The latter's 'political formula' revolves increasingly around pledges 'to defend' individuals against 'the threat of a paedophile let loose, a serial killer, an obtrusive beggar, mugger, stalker, prowler, poisoner of water and food, terrorist ...'; it revolves ever less around the promise, made by the '*social state*' of the relatively recent past, to protect people from 'social degradation' (LF 148, see also 4, 158; Davis 2016: 51, 67–8).

Fear of death

Like in several *œuvres* engaging this book, in Bauman's writings the problem of life in contemporary society raises that of death. Bauman's sociological considerations of death predating *Liquid Modernity* are quite well known (see e.g. Tierney 1997: 56–62). The analysis of the fear of death in his later work retraces in an intriguing way the contours of the liquid social condition and the liquid life led within it.

The 'fear of death', asserts Bauman, is both humans' and animals' '"original fear"'. However, only the human being experiences also a '"secondary fear"' fuelled by the constant consciousness of the certainty of death, the 'knowledge' that eventually, inevitably, he or she will die (LF 30, see also 50). Death, an '*irreversible*' termination that issues into an unending 'absence', concretises the graspable 'meanings' of the notions of 'finality' and 'eternity' (LF 42, see also 29–30). The 'cultures' of humankind, in turn, constitute contrivances for rendering '*life with the awareness of mortality liveable*' (LF 31; see also Tierney 1997: 56–7).

Among several 'strategies' (LF 49, see also 31–9), Bauman lists the '*banalization*' of death (LF 39). The passing of somebody 'near and dear', with whom one had an '"I-Thou"' connection, who cannot be wholly 'replaced', creates a sense of the '*finality* and *irrevocability*' that all deaths revolve around (LF 43). In fact, argues Bauman, any severance of 'an interhuman bond', which involves losing 'a partner', the 'disappearance' of something special, bears 'a stamp of "finality"', allowing for an indirect 'death experience' (LF 44–5). In liquid modernity, crucially, interhuman ties are temporary and easily split (LF 44).[8] Thus, 'life' becomes 'a daily rehearsal of death ... performed by proxy', and indirect 'death experience' becomes a recurrent event. The radical other-ness distinguishing 'death experience' turns into a 'familiar' part of the everyday (LF 44). Upon every 'separation' follows the establishment of new 'bonds' (LF 45). The repeated '"metaphorical rehearsal" of death' *qua* '"irre-versible" end' is supposed to ensure that such terminations end up appearing 'revocable' to people (LF 49, see also 6). Incidentally, the above-mentioned TV 'tales' of eviction present comparable regular 'public rehearsals of death' with the purpose of 'banalizing the sight of dying' so as to render people immune to the fear of the end (LF 29). Yet ultimately, this deep-seated 'fear' will, in some 'form', remain a part of 'human life'[9] (LF 52). 'Threats', Bauman argues referring to Freud, come from different 'directions', but the 'destination' in each case is physical 'pain and suffering', that is, 'dress rehearsals' of death; and each of those 'sources' provides 'infinite supplies of fear' (LF 52–3).

CONCLUSION

For many years, Bauman's inquiries into contemporary social conditions revolved around the differences between solid and liquid modernity, which manifest themselves in a whole range of domains of society. Inextricable from those inquiries is the question of life in twenty-first-century society. Bauman formulates it as, *inter alia*, the questions of the liquid life, the con-suming life, and living with fear. Not least, it appears, because of the suffering and anxiety that continue to shape it, the human life of the present is a focal point of Bauman's work. In turn, these writings suggest that the liquid life cannot be understood separately from liquid social conditions – and thus that questions about human life today cannot but also be addressed to sociology.

Abbreviations

CL: *Consuming Life* (2007)

LF: *Liquid Fear* (2006)

LL: *Liquid Life* (2005)

LM: *Liquid Modernity* (2000)

Selected Further Reading

The following texts – a monograph and an edited volume – contain critical engagements with Bauman's work on liquid modernity, liquid life, and consumerism:

Davis, M. (2016) *Freedom and Consumerism: A Critique of Zygmunt Bauman's Sociology*. London: Routledge.

Jacobsen, M. H. and Poder, P. (eds) (2008) *The Sociology of Zygmunt Bauman: Challenges and Critique*. Aldershot: Ashgate.

For an engaging discussion of several themes raised in this chapter, see also Bauman, Z. (2003) *Liquid Love: On the Frailty of Human Bonds*. Cambridge: Polity Press.

Notes

1   Bauman does not unpack the term 'other-directed' in this context. He probably has in mind the difference between 'inner-directed' and 'other-directed' persons famously examined by David Riesman in *The Lonely Crowd* (1953).
2   For a discussion of Bauman's views on power, see for instance Campain (2008).
3   The ideal 'business organization' of the 'exterritorial elite', Bauman remarks with reference to Nigel Thrift, is now not 'solid' but 'fluid', so that it can always be quickly 'dismantled and reassembled' (LM 154).
4   According to Blackshaw, Bauman 'holds up a mirror to a culture whose stamp is the *market-mediated mode of life* ...' (Blackshaw 2008: 117).
5   For a more detailed, critical discussion of Bauman's reading of the two TV programmes, see Davis (2016: 96–100, see also 69–70, 94, 168).
6   Bauman also comments on the 'commercial' aspects (LF 143–4, see also 7–8, LL 69–70).
7   Briefly, for Bauman 'globalization' has hitherto been completely '*negative*': a 'globalization' primarily 'of trade and capital' and of 'crime and terrorism, all now disdaining territorial sovereignty and respecting no state boundary' (LF 96), without a simultaneous 'globalization ... of political and juridical institutions able to control them' (LF 135). See Davis (2016: 51, 65–71) for a discussion.
8   On this well-known argument of Bauman's, see above all his *Liquid Love* (2003; see also Davis 2016: 69–70, 163–5; Poder 2008: 106).
9   And it will, Bauman warns, continue to lend itself to being economically and politically 'manipulated and capitalized on' (LF 52).

6

Jean-François Lyotard: Living in Postmodernity

PART 1: SOCIETY AND THE GAMES OF LANGUAGE

The dimension of Jean-François Lyotard's *œuvre* that has had the deepest impact on sociology is doubtless his examination of postmodernity. In *The Postmodern Condition* from 1979, Lyotard notes that the term '*postmodern*' is used in sociology to capture present-day 'culture'. His famous book employs the term specifically to characterise 'the condition of knowledge', namely 'in the most highly developed societies' (PC xxiii; see also Malpas 2003: 15, 17; Williams 1998: 26). According to the 'working hypothesis' of *The Postmodern Condition*, 'the status of knowledge' is changing at a time when 'cultures' are arriving in the so-called 'postmodern', and 'societies' in the so-called 'postindustrial', era (PC 3; see also Malpas 2003: 18). Lyotard indicates in this context several reasons why *A Report on Knowledge* – the subtitle of that book – might have relevance for those seeking insight into contemporary social conditions (PC 3–6; Malpas 2003: 16–20). Importantly for the following discussion, Lyotard proposes that '[s]cientific knowledge is a kind of discourse' (PC 3), whilst a particular conception of language is indispensable to his conception of society.

Language Games

Outlining the 'Method' of his study, Lyotard refers to Ludwig Wittgenstein's investigations of 'language'. These concentrate 'on the effects of different modes of discourse' (PC 9–10; see Wittgenstein 1953: esp. § 23; see also

Malpas 2003: 20–2; Williams 1998: 27). Lyotard mentions the 'denotative' type of 'utterance' or 'statement' – his example being '"The university is sick ..."' – as one illustration of what he has in mind. An utterance of this type has a 'sender' emitting it, an 'addressee ... receiv[ing] it', and a 'referent'. It also has a series of effects. For instance, it puts 'the sender in the position of "knower"' and the recipient in that 'of having to give or refuse ... assent' (PC 9). It is possible similarly to identify other 'kinds of utterances', including the 'declaration', the 'question', the 'promise', and many more, each with its own 'effects' (PC 9–10, see also 16, 20–1).

Crucially, Lyotard proposes to conceive of an 'utterance' or statement 'as a "move" in a game' (PC 10; see also Malpas 2003: 21–3; Williams 1998: 30). He adopts the concept of 'language-games' from Wittgenstein (1953: § 23). According to Lyotard, Wittgenstein seeks to articulate that every 'categor[y] of utterance' must be determinable by 'rules' that pinpoint its respective 'properties' as well as possible 'uses'. These 'rules', Lyotard makes explicit, 'define' a 'game'; the slightest change to a single 'rule' changes the whole 'game'; and any '"move" or utterance' contravening those 'rules' is not part of that 'game' (PC 10; see also Malpas 2003: 21–3; Williams 1998: 27–30, 35).

Language Games and Social Relations

Lyotard's approach draws vital inspiration from philosophy, but it is also strongly shaped by sociology (see also PC 16–17). This is unsurprising. One cannot, he holds, 'know' the present 'state of knowledge' whilst remaining ignorant about 'the society within which it is situated' (PC 13). In turn, before one can deal with 'knowledge' within current social conditions specifically, it is necessary to decide on a 'methodological representation' of these conditions (PC 11), on the way in which 'society' is interrogated and can respond (PC 13).

What Lyotard proposes for his own overall methodology are, precisely, 'language games' (PC 15). In his remarks on these games, he formulates as a clear 'principle' for his inquiries 'that the observable social bond is composed of language "moves"' (PC 10–11; see also Malpas 2003: 23). In slightly different terms, 'language games ... combine to form the social bond' (PC 25). In his remarks on the latter, Lyotard stops short of asserting – albeit also of ruling out – that 'social relations' consist entirely of 'language games' (PC 15). He does, though, insist that such 'games' constitute 'the minimum relation' without which there can be no 'society' at all, and that in the present conditions 'language' is acquiring 'a new importance' (PC 15–16).

Lyotard – unlike Jean Baudrillard (1983) in his view – emphatically rejects the diagnosis of the current 'dissolution of the social bond and the disintegration of social aggregates [orig. *collectivités* (Lyotard 1979: 31)] into a mass of individual atoms ...' (PC 15). For every 'self', so Lyotard argues, '... is always located at a post through which ... messages pass'. In this sense, everyone is enmeshed 'in a fabric of relations ...'. As also already indicated, 'the messages' crisscrossing that self put it in the position 'of sender, addressee, or referent'

(PC 15; see also Malpas 2003: 23, 29). Lyotard emphasises that every self has some 'powe[r] over' those 'messages'; it is possible for the self to shift 'in relation to these language game effects', in relation to the position in which one has been put (PC 15).

Lyotard's remarks on language games reveal that his approach is based on a further tenet, namely, 'to speak is to fight, in the sense of playing' (PC 10; see also Williams 1998: 30). To repeat, as 'messages' travel across somebody – that is, during every '"move"' that somehow concerns her or him – this person is 'displaced'; she or he is changed in one way or another with regard to the ability to send, receive, and be a 'referent' of, further messages. Such '"moves"', Lyotard states, underscoring this 'agonistic' quality of language games, will 'provoke "countermoves"'. The issue for the players in this moment is by which type of 'countermove' one can reshape 'the balance of power' once more (PC 16). Consistently with his ascription of a major role in the social world to language games, Lyotard's 'idea of an agonistics of language' (PC 10; see also Williams 1998: 30) finds its complement in his description of 'society' as 'the sum total [orig. *l'ensemble* (Lyotard 1979: 46)] of partners in the general agonistics' (PC 25, see also 10).

Lyotard has observed that in modernity 'language games' tend to take 'the form of institutions …' (PF 25). A 'battle' such as a debate among 'friends' has 'rules' permitting maximum 'flexibility of utterance': the participants throw whatever they have – 'questions, requests, assertions' etc. – at each other. By contrast, every 'institution' needs 'constraints'. Within institutions, some 'things' must 'not be said', whilst others 'should be said', and in specific ways – for example, 'orders' in military or 'denotation' in educational institutions. However, Lyotard seeks to avoid a '"reifying" view of what is institutionalized' (PC 17). Reifying translates Lyotard's '"chosiste"' (1979: 35) here. In sociology, the term *'chosisme'*, literally thingism, is sometimes (e.g. Adorno 2000: 77, 81, 106, 175n26) used to refer to Émile Durkheim's 'rule' of sociology *'to consider social facts as things'* (Durkheim 1982: 60). For Lyotard, any institutional restrictions 'on potential language "moves"' emerge themselves from 'language strategies'; far from final, they are 'provisional' and changeable (PC 17).

System and Division

Lyotard has also inspected other 'representational models for society' (PC 11), which, whilst he has not adopted them, play a role in his thinking. One of them is 'society' *qua* 'functional whole' (PC 11). This 'model' is illustrated by the sociology of Talcott Parsons (1970), for instance, for whom 'society' constitutes 'a self-regulating system' (PC 11). That said, and although Lyotard brands it 'technocratic' and 'cynical', German systems theory seems to be a more persistent reference point in his work, as will become clearer. Briefly, from this theoretical perspective society is a 'system' that aims primarily for 'performativity', that is, for the best overall 'output' to 'input' ratio. Alterations to 'rules', 'innovations', and 'dysfunctions', including 'political revolutions', all amount merely to 'an internal readjustment', leading to an improvement of 'the system's "viability."' (PC 11). What Lyotard finds in several bodies of thought, including Parsonian social theory and Niklas Luhmann's systems theory, is the notion of 'society' as 'a unified totality' (PC 12).

Contrary to these, Marxist thought offers another model, namely, society 'is divided in two' (PC 11). Here, as is well known, 'the principle' is that 'of class struggle' (PC 11, 12). Importantly for Lyotard's investigations, the 'decision' to conceptualise the social world in terms of the first model or the second determines how one can conceptualise the 'role' or 'function' of 'knowledge' within that world (PC 13).[1] Lyotard himself, though, as may be expected, advances his inquiry primarily in terms of language games instead.

The Language Game of Science

As mentioned, Lyotard examines scientific knowledge as a discourse. From his perspective, 'science' consists of 'statements'. These are understood as '"moves" made by ... players' according to 'rules' (PC 26). Sketching the language 'game' of 'scientific ... research', Lyotard specifies that what is subject to 'regulat[ion]' is what makes a 'statement' acceptable 'as "scientific."' For instance, a 'sender' is meant to state 'the truth about the referent', that is, to be capable of both proving what is being said and rebutting all 'statements' to the contrary. Simultaneously, an 'addressee' is supposed to be able 'to give (or refuse)' their agreement with the assertion 'validly', thus also being 'a potential sender' (PC 23).

'Scientific knowledge', Lyotard points out, demands the separation of the 'language game' of 'denotation' from 'all others', which are to be 'excluded'. In this respect, the sole 'criterion' for an utterance's 'acceptability' is its 'truth-value' (PC 25; see also Connor 1989: 29). Every 'statement' must remain 'verifiable' by 'argumentation and proof'. An 'accepted' statement is, of course, always disputable. Yet every 'new statement ... contradict[ing]' an already accepted utterance about 'the same referent' is itself only acceptable if it fulfils those conditions, that is, 'refutes' that utterance by dint of 'arguments and proofs' (PC 26).

Discursive Species

It must be emphasised that for Lyotard '[k]nowledge [*savoir*]' is more than just 'learning [*connaissance*]', and learning more than just 'science' (PC 18, see also 7). 'Learning' comprises only 'statements ... denot[ing] ... objects', which one can say to be 'true or false' (PC 18). A '"learned"' person is defined as someone capable of 'a true statement about a referent' (PC 25). 'Science' is even more specific, including only 'denotative statements' whose 'objects' one can 'access ... in explicit conditions of observation' and which one can identify as part or not part of a 'language' that 'experts' accept as 'relevant' (PC 18). A 'scientist' is someone capable of 'verifiable or falsifiable statements about referents accessible to the experts' (PC 25).

'Knowledge', however, instead of simply being equated with 'denotative statements', is associated with a 'competence'. Moreover, it amounts to a wide-ranging 'competence', rather than to one concerning a single type of utterance. It enables a person to produce '"good" denotative', 'prescriptive', 'evaluative', and other kinds of statements; it enables '"good" performances' regarding various 'objects of discourse', regarding those 'to be ... decided on' or 'evaluated', but also those to be 'transformed' (PC 18). A '"good"' statement or 'performance' is one that meets certain 'criteria', for example, 'truth' or 'efficiency' (PC 19).

Lyotard draws a thorough distinction between, for instance, 'science' and 'narrative knowledge' (PC 25), which, he claims, have been in perpetual 'conflict' (PC 7, see also xxiii). This well-known distinction cannot be revisited here (see PC 19–23, 25–7; Connor 1989: 28–30; Malpas 2003: 20–1, 24–5; Williams 1998: 30). It is important to bear in mind, though, that, for Lyotard, the 'existence' of 'nonscientific (narrative) knowledge' is just as 'necessary' as that of scientific knowledge. Each consists of 'statements' *qua* '"moves" ... by ... players within ... rules'. But the very 'rules' of scientific differ from those of narrative knowledge. The '"moves"' considered '"good"' in the latter are of a different kind to moves deemed '"good"' in the former. One can neither 'judge' the former's 'validity' in terms of the latter nor the latter's in terms of the former (PC 26, see also xxiii; Williams 1998: 30). One can only 'gaze in wonderment at the diversity of discursive species ...' (PC 26; see also Connor 1989: 34).

Dispersal and Heteromorphy

An important attribute of 'science', explains Lyotard, is that it must provide 'legitimation' for 'the rules' that regulate the scientific 'game' (PC xxiii, see also 18, 27–31; Connor 1989: 28–30). In the Western world, 'legitimacy' is itself 'a referent' for 'inquiry' (PC 23). Consistently with earlier considerations, Lyotard argues that what applies to the language game applies to social relations: 'the institutions governing the social bond ... must be legitimated as well' (PC xxiv). Through 'legitimation' as Lyotard understands it 'a legislator' is given the authority to proclaim 'a law' – a law which demands that certain 'citizens' act in a particular way. In his work, though, 'legitimation' simultaneously means that someone is given the authority to state a 'rule' concerning utterances – 'to prescribe' specific 'conditions' of the sort already mentioned, for instance 'experimental verification', which 'a statement must fulfill' so that it is considered 'scientific' (PC 8; see also Williams 1998: 31).

Lyotard designates a 'science' as *'modern'* if it gives itself legitimacy in terms of 'a metadiscourse' that draws on a 'grand narrative' (PC xxiii; see also Malpas 2003: 24–5; Williams 1998: 27). He proceeds to detail 'a narrative of emancipation' and 'a speculative narrative' (PC 37), a 'more political' and a 'more philosophical' variant, which have been especially prominent in modernity (PC 31; see e.g. Connor 1989: 30–1; Malpas 2003: 24–7; Williams 1998: 32–3). What is more important for this discussion, though, is his diagnosis that in today's 'postindustrial society' and 'postmodern culture' both variants of the 'grand narrative' (PC 37) are met with 'incredulity' (PC xxiv; see also Connor 1989: 8–9, 31; Malpas 2003: 16, 24, 27–8; Williams 1998: 27–8, 32–5, 83). Notably, examining the difficulties accompanying certain 'legitimation' efforts leads to a recognition that scientific 'discourse' is 'a language game with its own rules', but without any 'special calling' to regulate any other 'game', such as the practical or aesthetic games. 'The game of science is ... put on a par with ... others'. Here, too, Lyotard simultaneously keeps a close eye on the social world. In further course, as 'language games' disperse, the 'social subject itself seems to dissolve'. Lyotard reiterates the 'linguistic' quality of the 'social bond'. Yet, crucially, this bond constitutes a weave in which 'an indeterminate number ... of language games', each following its own distinct 'rules', cross (PC 40; see also Connor 1989: 9, 31–2, 34; Malpas 2003: 29; Williams 1998: 5, 27–35, 62, 69–70, 79–83, 103–5).

These considerations are decisive for Lyotard's characterisation of postmodernity. He is unconvinced, namely, that one can define rules shared by 'all ... language games'. He doubts that a consensus – even 'a revisable consensus' – might comprise all the rules 'regulating' all the 'statements circulating in the social collectivity', that 'all speakers' reach a consensus on a set of 'rules ... valid for all language games' (PC 65, trsl. modified; see also Connor 1989: 34; Williams 1998: 27–8, 32–5, 83). Societies, writes Lyotard, comprise 'vast clouds of language material' (PC 64, see also xxiv). But their 'pragmatics' consist of an imbrication of 'networks of ... classes' of statements – 'denotative' ones, 'prescriptive' ones, 'evaluative' ones etc. – of different forms. For Lyotard, it is vital to recognise 'that language games are heteromorphous' and 'subject to heterogeneous ... rules' (PC 65, see also WIP 72–3; Connor 1989: 32, 34, 37–8; Malpas 2003: 21–2, 30; Williams 1998: 5, 27–35, 62, 69–70, 79–83, 103–5). A major issue in his discussion of postmodernity is how these conditions are and should be responded to, respectively.

The System's Decision Makers

Lyotard is critical of the response of today's 'decision makers' (PC xxiv). 'The ruling class', he points out, is, now and for the time being, that of the 'decision makers'. It has come to consist of 'corporate leaders, high-level administrators ... heads of the major professional ... organizations', and others, in place of 'the traditional political class' (PC 14). Crucially, the 'decision makers' are trying to administer the 'clouds of sociality' described above in accordance with 'a logic ... of maximum performance'. This logic 'implies that their elements are commensurable' (PC xxiv). A 'terror' is exercised to ensure that 'language games' take the same form (PC 66). The decision makers' endeavour is 'to manage' the social world in 'input/output matrices'. Ultimately, 'all ... games' are meant to answer to the standard of 'efficiency', which is to say, of 'optimizing the system's performance' (PC xxiv; see also Connor 1989: 32–3; Malpas 2003: 28, 30; Palumbo-Liu 2000: 202, 213n6; Williams 1998: 126–7).

The resonances with Lyotard's already mentioned reading of Luhmann's theory of society as a system are clear. An important point of Luhmann's, Lyotard adds, is that this 'system' needs to arrange for people's different 'aspirations' (PC 61) – or *expectations* (Lyotard 1979: 99, orig. English) – to be adjusted to the system's 'ends' (PC 61, see also 64). 'Administrative procedures', Luhmann is said to argue, can 'make individuals "want" what the system needs' for its own performativity (PC 62). Lyotard finds similar conceptions in the sociological works of David Riesman (1953) and Herbert Marcuse (2002), for example. What he appears to have in mind is the former's conception of the other-directed character and the latter's critique of the creation of false needs.

Inventions

Lyotard further develops his own perspective on the contemporary social world with reference to scientific research. According to Lyotard, striving for 'proof' is a pursuit of something 'unintelligible', striving for 'an argument' a quest 'for a "paradox"' and the creation of 'new rules' of the 'reasoning' game (PC 54; see also Connor 1989: 33–4). Each 'new statement', 'observation', or 'theory' unfailingly raises 'the question of legitimacy'. What is conspicuous about 'postmodern scientific knowledge', Lyotard maintains, is that it contains 'the discourse on the rules that validate it' within itself (PC 54). What is important is that this 'science ... suggests a model of legitimation' which is not that of the best 'performance', but rather that of 'difference' in the sense of 'paralogy' (PC 60; see also Malpas 2003: 31).

Lyotard reiterates two points in this context: scientific 'pragmatics' involves chiefly 'denotative' statements, and discussing these requires 'rules' – in other words, 'metaprescriptive' statements of the sort that determine 'moves' acceptable within 'language games' (PC 65). He concedes that debates about those rules enter a 'state' of 'consensus' (PC 65, see also 63; Williams 1998: 30). Crucially, though, consensus is not the 'end' of such debates; 'paralogy' is (PC 65–6). 'Paralogy' is understood as one – decisive – type of 'move ... in the pragmatics of knowledge'. Eventually, namely, a player will appear who disrupts 'the order of "reason"'. Lyotard assumes 'a power that destabilizes the capacity for explanation'. This power is behind each 'proposal of new rules of the scientific language game ...' (PC 61, trsl. modified, see also 63; Connor 1989: 33–4, 40–2; Malpas 2003: 31). In scientific 'pragmatics', Lyotard explains, a 'statement' is to be held on to as soon as it, on the one hand, contains something that diverges from the 'known' and, on the other, can be argued and proven. This 'differential or imaginative or paralogical activity' makes the 'metaprescriptives', the prevalent scientific '"presuppositions"', come to the fore and demands that the partners 'accept different ones' (PC 64–5; see also Connor 1989: 33–4; Malpas 2003: 30–3). This 'will generate ideas', generate 'new statements' (PC 65, see also 64) – 'dissension' gives rise to 'invention', says Lyotard (PC xxv; see also Connor 1989: 34, 39) – and that constitutes the sole 'legitimation' capable of rendering such a demand permissible (PC 65, see also 64).

On the basis of his insights, Lyotard comes to espouse a mode of thinking about the social world that is characterised by a clear set of components: the acknowledgement that 'language games' have different forms and the diagnosis of the diversity of these games' rules, as outlined earlier; and the twofold 'principle that any consensus on the rules defining a game ... *must* be local', that is, reached only by the particular game's current 'players', as well as temporary, that is, open to dissolution (PC 66; see also Connor 1989: 32, 34, 37–8; Malpas 2003: 30, 32; Williams 1998: 5, 27–35, 62, 69–70, 79–83, 103–5). Lyotard notes that such thinking is in tune with current developments in 'social interaction': in various 'domains', including, for instance, the 'international' sphere, politics, the world of work, or the 'family', 'permanent institutions' are being replaced by 'the temporary contract' (PC 66). Simultaneously, it jars with the thinking of the decision makers of the system.

PART 2: LIVING IN THE SYSTEM

The Postmodern Condition does not thematise life in postmodernity elaborately or very explicitly. Of note, though, '*knowledge*' as the wide-ranging 'competence' as which Lyotard has been shown to frame it in that book comprises, *inter alia*, '"knowing how to live ..." ... [... *savoir-vivre* ...]' (PC 18). A later, much less famous book of Lyotard's on postmodernity, a collection of 'notes' (PF vii) from the late 1980s and early 1990s entitled *Postmodern Fables* (PF)[2] (originally *Moralités Postmodernes* (1993)), does pose key 'questions' about the problem at the centre of that knowledge domain: 'how to live, and why?' (PF vii). In the present conditions, a vital question for those engaged in critical thinking and writing, *Postmodern Fables* seems to suggest, is how to live without solely or chiefly serving the system's improvement. The 'moral [orig. *moralité* (1993: 11)]' at the end of a 'fable', Lyotard points out, 'draws' from it a local and temporary 'bit of wisdom' (PF vii; see also Palumbo-Liu 2000: 204–5). Several of Lyotard's considerations have been inspired by his encounters in his own life as a thinker and writer as well as by his reception of works of art. There are, of course, differences between 'fables' and 'science' (PC 27, see also xxiii). But 'scientific knowledge' is not all there is to 'knowledge [orig. *savoir* (1979: 18)]' (PC 7, see also 18; Palumbo-Liu 2000: 205). 'The answers' to the questions posed, Lyotard admits, 'are deferred' (PF vii). What he doubts is that 'we know' what appears to be known today, namely 'that life is going every which way'. Instead, this is what people 'represent ... to' themselves. One can currently observe '[e]very which way of life' being 'flaunted' and 'enjoyed' – but, specifies Lyotard, they are flaunted and enjoyed 'for the love of [orig. *en amateur de* (1993: 11)] variety' (PF vii). The system itself, as will become clearer, promotes variety, yet inside a range delimited by rules. Lyotard's considerations point to what might be recalcitrant against the pressures of the system.

The System and Exploitation

If one turns to the 13th piece in *Postmodern Fables*, 'The intimacy of terror' from 1993,[3] for further clues about what Lyotard means by the system, one appears at first sight to be offered little: 'the system', he writes, '... is quite simply called the system' (PF 199). In fact, here and throughout the book Lyotard goes on to accentuate – albeit partly in terms familiar from *The Postmodern Condition* – properties of this system that the earlier, more widely known study does not illuminate particularly strongly.

Lyotard's notion of the system is not identical with a reiteration of Marx's theory of capitalist society. However, his references in more than one of the pieces in *Postmodern Fables* to Marx's conception of labour power, for instance, do reveal important aspects of the orientation of the system Lyotard has in mind. In 'Interesting?', Lyotard presents a dialogue between a woman, SHE, and a man, HE. The latter squarely equates 'what we are calling the system' with 'capitalism' (PF 63). It may revolve chiefly around 'seizing upon what one doesn't have, and making it "(sur)render."', HE suggests (PF 63). As Lyotard puts it in 'Unbeknownst', the 12th piece, and in more widely familiar terminology, Marx argues that 'the capitalist organization of being together' entails 'the exploitation of labor power' (PF 191). According to Marx's critique of capitalism, as is well known, the capitalist pays the worker a daily wage equal to the value of what is required for replenishing labour power for another day. The worker provides the capitalist with labour power for a day (Marx 1990: 270–93). The upshot of 'the capitalist organization' of social life as Marx understands it, writes Lyotard, is a 'sacrifice of pure creative power' (PF 191). For Marx holds that the capitalist's 'usage' of the labour power purchased yields 'more value than it consumes' (PF 64). That is to say, labour power 'consum[es] *less* energy (less value) than it produces as it goes into ... productive action ... , as it goes to work ...' (PF 191). In Marx's critical analysis, '[c]apital', Lyotard reasserts, 'deprive[s] the proletariat of the use of [labor] force', which is all the proletariat owns, with the purpose of acquiring 'the fruits of its strange power: creating more value than it consumes' (PF 72). This, adds Lyotard, constitutes '[a]n eminent case of "good productivity" ...' (PF 72) – in other words, greater output than input as a clear instance of good performativity, the principle of which has been said to guide the system as such.

The System's Openness

And yet, for Lyotard class struggle no longer poses as great a threat to the system as one might have once thought, and the political potential of social critique, too, needs to be carefully reconsidered. Lyotard clarifies this, in part at least, in his reflections in the fifth piece of *Postmodern Fables*. Here, he addresses the transformations that have shaped 'the historical situation' generally and the kind of critical endeavour he himself has been participating in specifically (PF 68). Lyotard begins by looking back on his time at *Socialisme ou barbarie* (*Socialism or Barbarism*), which he retrospectively describes as a 'sort of "Institute" of critical theory and practice' (PF 67, see also PC 13, 89n46; Palumbo-Liu 2000: 206). During the 1950s and 1960s, Lyotard recalls, he and his fellow members were working on a 'critical analysis of "late capitalism"', but also 'of supposedly "communist" society' (PF 71). The 'strategy' they were following was one of 'offense' (PF 69). They were engaged in 'situation analysis'. This involved examining 'events' perceived as crucial to 'the historical context at that time' for the purpose of attempting to grasp 'the contemporary world and its development'. Simultaneously, however, these inquiries were inextricable from 'a practical project' (PF 67). The aim that he and his colleagues were pursuing, Lyotard accentuates, was to find out through which 'intervention' they could 'help those subject to exploitation and alienation emancipate themselves' (PF 68). In this context, '[e]mancipation' meant nothing less than 'an alternative to reality' *tout court* (PF 69).

The 'interventions' put forward nowadays, argues Lyotard, are, by contrast, confined to the word: to 'petitions', 'texts', 'conferences', 'books', etc. Moreover, today's 'strategy' revolves around 'defense':

> We must constantly reaffirm the rights of minorities, women, children, gays, the South, the Third World, the poor, the rights of citizenship, the right to culture and education, the rights of animals and the environment, and I'll skip over the rest.

Importantly here, the 'rules' of what it is to be 'an intellectual' in the present day allow for and promote such activities (PF 68–9; see also Palumbo-Liu 2000: 202–3). 'Emancipation' understood in a particular way, Lyotard explains, has become something 'the system' itself tries to achieve, namely within certain of its discrete – for instance, the familial, sexual, racial, or educational – 'sectors' (PF 69).

Lyotard recognises that 'the system' encounters 'resistance' and 'obstacles' in this regard. Yet he maintains that they lead it to foster 'new enterprises' and 'become ... more open' (PF 69). Its operations nowadays include '*venture programs*' (PF 70, orig. English, see PF 3n1), which, more exploratory in their orientation, will increase its 'complexity and make room for more "flexible" institutions' (PF 70). Incidentally, this development seems to come as no surprise to Lyotard. Conducting his reflections in the autumn of 1990 (PF 74), he reads the end of twentieth-century Central and Eastern European communism as the most recent demonstration of the tendency of any 'system' that is 'more "open"' to be 'more performative' and of the proneness of any system that 'closes in on itself' either to fall victim to 'competitors' or to die of 'entropy' (PF 80). What appears to him to determine a system's success in its contest with others – a 'competition' to be inspected more closely in a moment – is that 'openness', that is, 'the "free play"' it protects in its 'mode of functioning' (PF 80). It is emancipation in this sense that is at issue here. To come back to the situation of the intellectual, it is assumed, Lyotard reiterates, that such 'emancipation' has become the responsibility 'of the system itself'. The latter appears to have considerable appetite for 'critiques'. Indeed, what critics critically identify is 'every failure of the system with regard to emancipation'. Thus, encouraging criticism helps the system meet its responsibility of emancipation (PF 70). Even 'before speaking or acting', and no matter what their 'intervention' is, his fellow thinkers and writers of today, suggests Lyotard, are as aware as he is 'that it will be taken into account by the system as a possible contribution to its perfection' (PF 204, see also PC 13; Palumbo-Liu 2000: 202–3, 213n7).

Lyotard draws further insight into the contemporary situation of political critique from two visits to the German Democratic Republic shortly before and shortly after the fall of the Berlin Wall. He reports that during his travels he encountered 'East German intellectuals ... concerned about ... elaborating a position' that might make it possible to criticise not only the 'totalitarianism' of Central and Eastern Europe but also 'Western liberalism' (PF 71). In the month of the reunification of Germany less than a year after that momentous night in November 1989, Lyotard notes the difficulty of envisaging how the sort of 'radical critique' that his 'East German colleagues' called for might be accomplished. Cornelius Castoriadis and Claude Lefort, founders of the *Socialisme ou barbarie* group with which Lyotard was once associated, have demonstrated that 'criticism' needs 'an open social and mental space'. Yet today it is precisely 'the system' itself that, requiring such an open space, 'alone ... guarantees' it (PF 74).

Intertwined with these considerations are Lyotard's own thinly disguised doubts about certain strands of the politics of the left today. What Marxism was once concerned with, he argues, was a diversity of 'working classes' – in other words, of 'communities of laborers' enchained in 'capitalist relations'. The objective of Marxism was the transformation of these classes into one 'proletariat', namely into one 'collective subject' that would be 'emancipated', 'conscious and autonomous'. As such, this subject was meant to be 'capable of emancipating all of humanity' (PF 72). However, in place of what was once an 'international workers' movement', Lyotard now identifies 'local institutions'. The purpose of each of these is not the transformation of different groups of workers into one collective subject, but 'defending the interests of this or that category of laborers'. 'Class struggles' of this sort do 'put up a resistance to the development of the system', Lyotard concedes

(PF 73). Yet this resistance is again to be understood in the sense of the afore-mentioned 'obstacles', which -the system requires so as 'to improve its performance' in the manner already indicated (PF 73, see also PC 13).

The System of Competition

These observations notwithstanding, the system's permissiveness should not be overestimated. *The Postmodern Condition*, as mentioned, emphasises the importance to the system of commensurability. 'The intimacy of terror' in *Postmodern Fables* underscores the importance of 'competition' as a further key property of the system (PF 199, though see also PC 48). Competition, Lyotard claims here, is the system's only 'means'. The system cannot allow 'peace'. Not only does it accept 'multiculturalism', but the system also 'arouses disparities', even 'solicits divergences' (PF 199; see also Connor 1989: 40–1; Goux and Wood 1998: 3–4). And yet his argument does not deviate dramati-cally from his earlier point in *The Postmodern Condition*. For the system, Lyotard specifies, does so only to the extent that there is 'consensus' – in other words 'agreement' about 'the rules of disagreement'. They state which 'ele-ments' and 'operations' are 'permitted'; complete 'freedom of strategy' reigns inside these boundaries (PF 199–200; see also Goux and Wood 1998: 3–4; Palumbo-Liu 2000: 200–2, 206).

Correspondingly, the system uses competition for a twofold purpose. On the one hand, through a 'competition' in which all 'operations' remain inside a range defined by a given set of rules, the system 'guarantees security'. Its 'constitution' is not open 'to radical upheaval' (PF 199–200). On the other hand, through competition the system ensures 'development'. From competi-tion emerge 'winning strategies', which it can then 'integrat[e]'. Thus, the 'constitution of the system' can always undergo 'revision' (PF 199–200, see also PC 15; Palumbo-Liu 2000: 201–2).

Lyotard, as already indicated above, and to add this only briefly, deploys the concept of competition also to characterise a different level of the con-temporary condition. The 'authority' of the current arrangement of 'the world', he argues, is supported by the widespread acceptance of a 'fact'. Humans, it is said, have been experimenting with various 'communitarian organizations' for thousands of years. A 'competition' is thought to have been in operation for just as long – here, namely, as the engine of a 'natural selection ... of the best performing' form of organisation as such (PF 201). The past hundred years or so specifically have witnessed the endeavours of different 'regimes' to enforce 'fascism, nazism, communism' as 'modes of community organization' (PF 70). Yet the latter were 'eliminated from the competition' (PF 70), whereas 'capitalist democracy', going by the 'name of system', is understood to have come out on top (PF 201). In Lyotard's use of the term, 'the system' means 'a triumphant liberal, imperialist capitalism' (Goux and Wood 1998: 4; see also PF 199). Capitalist democracy's 'superior-ity' is not disputed anymore (PF 201).

The System's Rules

In Lyotard's experience, the pressure on critics to restrain their moves can, in fact, be considerable. He maintains that this 'world in which we live' contains much still to 'be said[,] ... done, and ... proposed' (PF 203). He has even compiled a list – incomplete to boot, by his own admission – of issues requiring discussion and resolution. Several of its items – 'the status of immigrants and refugees', for instance, or 'the protection of minority cultures', or 'help for the sick and the old', or 'the right of women over their own bodies' (PF 202) – remain just as pressing two decades into the twenty-first century. Many who, like him, are engaged in thinking and writing, Lyotard continues, collaborate with one or another 'association' striving to help in solving 'difficulties' of that kind, contribute to 'debates', and even enter into 'combats' (PF 203). Crucially, though, issues such as those he has identified are to be tackled within 'the rules of the game, in consensus with the system' (PF 202).

That is to say, any 'attention' paid to 'thought and writing' today is attached to certain prerequisites (PF 204). Lyotard reads a 1980 piece by the historian Pierre Nora, which appears to have left a deep impression on him, as both a complaint about the works of certain French intellectuals and an assertion of certain of those prerequisites (PF 204–6, WIP 71). The objection, Lyotard recalls, was that different 'groups' – or rather 'sect[s]' – of intellectuals were engaged in 'a war of words', but without any effort 'to make themselves understood by each other or ... the public' (PF 205). What was being precluded 'in French criticism and philosophy', so the diagnosis went, was 'debate' (PF 204). The corresponding proposition, reports Lyotard – without naming Nora, but doubtless referring to him – in his essay from 1982 'Answering the question: What is postmodernism?', was to 'impos[e] on the intellectuals a common way of speaking' (WIP 71). This would enable the regeneration of 'the conditions for a fruitful exchange' (WIP 71). It was a request 'for some communicational consensus ... and a general code of exchanges ...' (WIP 73, see also PF 215). The current 'anarchy' was supposed to be turned into 'order', the intellectuals' 'domestic squabbles' domesticated under a Roman Peace (PF 205). Much, notes Lyotard, has indeed been done with the aim of enforcing 'dialogue and argument' among those 'aggressive and confused scriveners' (PF 205). In his view, Nora's proposition contains one of a host of recent demands that 'experimentation, in the arts and elsewhere', be terminated (WIP 71, see also 73). The 'color of the times', Lyotard observes, is 'slackening' accordingly (WIP 71).

The Marketplace of Singularities

Lyotard provides yet another perspective on the system's particular tolerance of variety in the first piece of *Postmodern Fables*. There, he tells of Marie, a Frenchwoman who has travelled to Japan to give a lecture and a seminar (PF 3–4, 10, 13). Marie relates her encounters and begins to reflect on her situation

more widely. She has observed that, whereas Immanuel Kant encouraged people to 'think for yourself',[4] nowadays doing so is considered 'not *politically
correct*'. All 'streams ... must converge', and the myriad 'colloquia, interviews,
seminars' are merely to assure everyone that all are 'saying the same thing'.
What is on all 'lips', highlights Marie, is 'alterity, multiculturalism' (PF 6,
politically correct orig. English, see PF 3n1; see also Palumbo-Liu 2000: 207).
'If you are a woman, and Irish, and still presentable, and some kind of professor in Brazil, and a lesbian, and writing non-academic books, then ... [c]ultural
capital is interested in you' (PF 6). Marie holds – her contention being quite
similar to Bauman's aforementioned problematisation of individuality – that
this constitutes a demand on everyone equally. Everyone should 'express' their
respective 'singularity' (PF 7).

What appears decisive, namely, is that 'cultural capitalism has found ...
the marketplace of singularities' (PF 7; see also Connor 1989: 40–1; Palumbo-
Liu 2000: 200–2, 205–7). Marie describes herself as a 'little stream' of '*cultural
capital*' (PF 3, *cultural capital* orig. English, see PF 3n1, see also PF 4). She is
someone 'they buy culture from' (PF 3). Simultaneously, Marie describes herself as a 'cultural labor force they can exploit' (PF 3), and who – like the
exploited labourer in Marx's critique of political economy (e.g. Marx 1990:
270–80) but also, for instance, in Adorno's more recent sociology (e.g. Adorno
2008: 96–9) – has signed a 'contract' to this effect (PF 3). She is, she says, a
'wage earner' as much as a 'craftsperson' (PF 3). With a vague echo of
Horkheimer and Adorno's (2002: 94–136) famous concept, Marie notes that
'the culture industry' of the late nineteenth century, which was centred on the
production and sale of standardised artefacts, left 'no future' for 'minorities'
and 'singularities'. Yet customers have become dissatisfied with 'snacking
always on the same images, the same ideas at the cultural fast-food outlets' (PF
11; see also Palumbo-Liu 2000: 200–2, 207). Marie's own challenge is to come
up with ever novel 'product[s]': 'to invent, read, imagine' (PF 3, see also 9, 12).
The crux nowadays is that 'new energy is always available' as well as 'manage-
able'; 'multiculturalism' has de facto become 'profitable' (PF 10–11; see also
Connor 1989: 40–1).

According to Marie, 'all the streams' are to enter – all 'singularities to
enrich' – 'the museum' (PF 7). The achievements of the past, from the Lascaux
caves to the Maginot Line to the writings of Agatha Christie, have already
been 'stored'. The task today is to do the same with all things 'contemporary',
the 'great works', of course, but also 'the ways of living' of the present, 'the
means of preparing fish', current 'slangs', and so forth (PF 8). Marie knows
that her lecture, too, will be heard with the question if her work is 'worth preserving' in mind (PF 9). Again, what is under consideration here is '[c]ultural
capital'; what she is witnessing, Marie is convinced, is 'the capitalization of all
cultures in the cultural bank' (PF 8). Marie insists on her identification of 'cultural institutions' with 'banks' proper in that the former are 'laboratories' rather
than mere 'repositories': their 'managers' have to 'put' the items stored in
these institutions 'to work', for instance, to exhibit, examine, or restore

them (PF 9–10), much like banks are expected not merely to hold on to, but to do something with, the capital entrusted to them.

The Question of Resistance

Yet Lyotard also offers perspectives on recalcitrance against such conditions. This recalcitrance can be noticed particularly, though by no means exclusively, in the sphere of art. In response to the question of what postmodernism is, Lyotard calls 'postmodern ... that which ... puts forward the unpresentable' (WIP 81; see also Connor 1989: 212; Malpas 2003: 49–50). Drawing on Kant's work, he sketches the situation where 'the imagination fails to present an object which might ... come to match a concept'. He illustrates this situation by noting that people harbour an 'Idea of the world ...' as 'totality of what is' yet no one can 'show an example of it' (WIP 78; see also Malpas 2003: 46–7; Williams 1998: 21–3, 88). Lyotard locates 'the postmodern' inside 'the modern'. The objective of 'modern painting', for instance, is '[t]o make visible that there is something which can be conceived' but not 'seen' or 'made visible' (WIP 78–9; see also Malpas 2003: 45–50).

'The postmodern' can nonetheless be distinguished. Lyotard specifies it as 'that which ... puts forward the unpresentable *in presentation itself* ...'. Vital to the postmodern, in other words, is the quest 'for new presentations' so as to create 'a stronger sense of the unpresentable' (WIP 81, emphasis added; see also Connor 1989: 212; Malpas 2003: 47–50; Williams 1998: 23, 108–13). The 'postmodern artist or writer', says Lyotard, '... are working without rules ...'. The product of their work, like that of a philosopher's work, is 'not in principle governed by ... rules' that have already been set. Nor can one 'judg[e] ...' such works 'by applying' to them 'categories' that are already known. Rather, the piece of art or writing is still in the process of 'looking for' the 'rules' that might respectively govern it (WIP 81; see also Malpas 2003: 45–50; Williams 1998: 22–3, 109–13). Lyotard identifies a similar process in the realm of 'knowledge', where '"progress"' can mean either 'a new move' in a language game and merely inside 'the established rules' or an 'invention of new rules', which entails 'a change to a new game' (PC 43, see also 53). This demarcation of the truly postmodern is vital for the question of recalcitrance.

In 'The intimacy of terror', Lyotard proceeds to question whether certain works of philosophy, literature, art, and music – Edmund Husserl's phenomenology, Franz Kafka's *The Castle*, Pablo Picasso's *Young Ladies of Avignon*, or Pierre Boulez's *Répons*, to name a few – can ever be a subject matter for 'debate' (PF 206). These 'works', he notes, are not products of 'the system'. What is decisive is that they bear a 'solitude', a 'retreat', and an 'excess beyond all possible discourse'. A certain 'measurelessness' distinguishes them (PF 206–7). As 'cultural objects' such works are relatively 'accessible to the community', yet they cannot be reduced to the existing 'usages or mentalities' of that community (PF 207). Echoing *The Postmodern Condition*'s thematisation of science, Lyotard adds that the emergence of science's 'inventions' is just as 'wondrous' – namely inexplicable through, and frequently 'resisted by', their contemporaneous 'state of knowledge' (PF 207). Marie, to return to her fable briefly, is aware that the lecture she is about to give to her audience in Japan will not be understood. She is also aware that what would be demanded of her is clarity, and clarity would mean contextualisation of what she is saying in relation to already existing and known works (PF 6).

Here, though, Lyotard's focus remains on art. In a famous note by Charles Baudelaire,[5] Lyotard makes out '[p]oetic hysteria' as it 'confesses' to '... cultivat[ing] its retreat with joy and terror' (PF 209). Art, literature, but also thinking, Lyotard explains, 'hysterically cultivate' a relationship with an 'inhuman stranger' that resides inside the person. Indeed, it is necessary to 'trace' that relationship in 'colors, sounds' or 'words' (PF 214). Those engaged in 'writing, painting, or composing' will work with '[w]ords, sounds, colors', which are, emphasises Lyotard, always 'already organized by the rhetorics' that have been 'inherited', and which will have a certain 'eloquence' (PF 215). In the tracing of that relationship with the inner stranger, in turn, words, sounds, and colours are to be brought 'back to *their* silence' (PF 214). 'Poetic hysteria', asserts Lyotard referring to Baudelaire again, promptly terminates 'the circuit of repetitions' (PF 209, see also 215). Thus emerge instances of genuine recalcitrance against the demand for commensurability and also against the demand for mere variety within a range delimited by given rules.

This issue also surfaces from the above-mentioned dialogue on 'the interesting' between the unnamed woman and the unnamed man, which Lyotard presents in the fourth of the *Postmodern Fables* (PF 49). Towards the end of the exchange, the question what 'the interesting' might be for an 'artist', a 'scholar', or an 'engineer' is raised (PF 60). Referring, as does *The Postmodern Condition* on several occasions, to Wittgenstein, SHE describes a situation in which a person in receipt of 'some tennis balls and ... rules about how to play with them' encounters another person who is also playing with tennis balls. Instead of playing tennis, however, the latter handles them in a manner the former fails to comprehend (PF 62). She claims that 'data', the 'given', from 'physical effects' to 'cosmic phenomena' to 'the color of a landscape' and so forth, are similarly encountered as though they were 'signs', but 'in an unknown language' (PF 61). Finally, SHE points to 'something or someone' within herself 'who is ... speaking', but in a 'language' different to hers (PF 62).

In what seems like a direct response to the question Lyotard poses in the *Fables'* 'Preface' – to its first part, 'how to live ... ?', anyway (PF vii) – SHE urges that the person encountering another who handles tennis balls in an incomprehensible fashion nonetheless absolutely not 'stop playing with' the latter (PF 62). Nor, SHE holds, can the 'clandestine host' within her 'be ignored'. Rather, her advice for each situation is: first, to posit 'a hypothesis about that other language' and about its rules; and, second, to experiment with – indeed 'to invent' – 'responses' in accordance with those 'supposed rules' and with the other's 'enigmatic messages' (PF 62). Again, great artworks serve as illustrations. Paul Cézanne, SHE argues, has 'com[e] to "speak" Mount Sainte-Victoire in little chromatic strokes' (PF 62–3). What the 'interesting' is, in her view and, so she appears to claim, from the viewpoint of artists, scholars, and engineers, 'is to try to speak the language of another that you don't understand' (PF 61, see also 63). The moves Lyotard sketches here against different backdrops show recalcitrance against being related to the already familiar; they do not remain within the limits set by already established rules. As such, they show resistance to the more stubborn pressures of the system.

CONCLUSION

In a system with an appetite for critical interventions because they can help make it better, the political potential of social critique is in question. This would certainly sharpen the conundrum of how to live without only or mainly operating for the system's improvement, especially from the critic's perspective. Yet the system's 'decision makers' consecrating 'our lives' to 'the growth of power' also treat language games with a view to their commensurability (PC xxiv; see also Connor 1989: 32–3). Indeed, the system thrives on competition, encouraging variety within a range delimited by rules. Occasionally, the pressures on those engaged in thinking and writing to conduct moves in a manner that is debatable because it is relatable to what is already there is considerable. Finally, in these conditions even singularities have come to circulate in the marketplace. What Lyotard calls 'innovation' will contain little by way of clues for resisting these conditions: innovation 'is under the command of the system, or at least used by it to improve its efficiency'. 'Paralogy', distinct from innovation (though the 'one' de facto often turns 'into the other') (PC 61), constitutes a more promising point of reference; but it is not the only one.[6] In his remarks on Baudelaire, Lyotard locates the poet among 'the first ... to confront the stupidity of the system' (PF 208). Specifically, Baudelaire confronted 'the stupid world' of nineteenth-century capitalism (PF 209). Lyotard picks up on the concept – from Marx's (1990: 138–63) analysis of that world, of course – of 'money' as 'the general equivalent for all commodities' (PF 209). Consistent with Marx's concept of labour power, Lyotard's notion of commodities includes not only 'goods' but also 'bodies ... and souls' (PF 209). Unfolding 'under the poet's horrified eyes', says Lyotard, was the 'world of total exchangeability under the rule of money'. Today's 'system', he continues, is, in at least one important respect, but an advanced stage in the development of that world. It is 'the extension ... of the same routine of exchange' into the – for Lyotard decisive – dimension of 'language'. In 'interlocution, interactiveness, ... and debate', he insists, 'words are exchanged for words as use value is exchanged for use value' (PF 209, see also 12; Williams 1998: 126–7). In their solitude and measurelessness, not contained within existing rules, the works of art mentioned above show recalcitrance against such conditions.

Abbreviations

PC: *The Postmodern Condition* (1984b)

PF: *Postmodern Fables* (1997)

WIP: 'Answering the question: What is postmodernism?' (1984a)

Selected Further Reading

An inclusive discussion of Lyotard's work, including his conception of postmodernity, is provided by Williams, J. (1998) *Lyotard: Towards a Postmodern Philosophy*. Cambridge: Polity Press.

Malpas, S. (2003) *Jean-François Lyotard*. London: Routledge also provides further discussion of themes raised in the chapter above.

For an edited volume containing engagement with Lyotard in relation to education, see Dhillon, P. and Standish, P. (eds) (2000) *Lyotard: Just Education*. London: Routledge.

Notes

1   See in this context Lyotard's (PC 12) remarks on Max Horkheimer's (1972) seminal distinction between traditional and critical theory.
2   For a critical discussion of the fable in Lyotard, see Palumbo-Liu (2000: 204–13).
3   An alternative translation is available as 'Terror on the run' (Lyotard 1998). The latter was consulted, but this discussion refers to 'The intimacy of terror'. Readers aiming for an in-depth engagement with the piece and unable to access the French original are advised to consult both translations.
4   Marie is probably referring to Kant's (1991) 'An answer to the question: "What is enlightenment?"' from 1784, the title of which may also have inspired that of Lyotard's aforementioned early 1980s essay 'Answering the question: What is postmodernism?' (WIP).
5   '"I cultivated my hysteria with joy and terror. Now, I've always got this vertigo, and today January 23, 1862, I felt before me *the breeze of imbecility flapping its wing*"' (Baudelaire in PF 208; see also Baudelaire 1950: 205).
6   For a critical discussion, which, however, predates most of *Postmodern Fables*, see Connor (1989: 40–3). See also remarks by Malpas (2003: 30–3) and Williams (1998: 23, 111–12).

7

Michel Foucault: Power over Life

PART 1: POWER

Around the turn of the nineteenth century, remarks Michel Foucault, it was becoming customary 'for kings to lose their heads' (PP 20). George III of the United Kingdom, however, had not been 'decapitated' by the guillotine, but by the insanity that had 'seized hold of the king's head' (PP 21). In 1800, Pinel described to French readers how their neighbours' mad monarch had been treated (PP 19–20). In what Foucault, drawing on Pinel, calls a 'ceremony' of 'dethronement' (PP 20–1), the king was stripped of '"all trappings of royalty"' and told plainly that he was not '"sovereign"' anymore (Pinel in PP 20). Locked in '"a room … covered with matting"' (PP 20), he could no longer issue commands to anyone and was 'reduce[d] … to his body' (PP 21). When he furiously smeared a doctor who was visiting him with faeces (Pinel in PP 20, see also PP 22–5), the 'insurrectional gesture' (PP 25) was met by the 'restrained … force' of a quiet servant (PP 23), who calmly undressed the lunatic, cleaned him up (PP 25), and had to ensure his docility (PP 22, see also 20). Foucault observes in this 'scene' a manifestation of a decisive development in the formation of contemporary social conditions: the recession of one form of power, the power of 'sovereignty' (PP 22), and 'the emergence and definitive installation' of another form, 'disciplinary power' (PP 41, see also 26–7). Foucault places the question of power at the centre of the study of social conditions. Every society's 'social body', he argues, is fundamentally shaped by power relationships (SD 24).

Sovereign Power

The relationship between a sovereign and a subject, says Foucault, corresponded with the power mechanisms of 'feudal-type societies' (SD 35).

Of medieval origin, the theory of sovereignty is principally concerned with the workings of power in the 'feudal monarchy'. It also helped legitimise the 'great monarchical administrations' (SD 34). Sovereign power remained operative as late as 'post-feudal, pre-industrial government' (PP 27) and still operates in certain guises in spheres of contemporary society (e.g. PP 79, SD 36–40). Yet Foucault mentions sovereign power chiefly in order to distinguish from it those forms of power that truly characterise the social conditions of the present.

The theory of sovereignty, argues Foucault, centres on 'the monarch and the monarchy' (SD 34). The medieval monarchic institutions of power were established upon multiple intertwined, conflict-ridden power relations, such as those of suzerainty and vassalage, promising to establish order within them. Crucially, the monarchy's power mechanisms developed the form – which actually masked some of their operations – of an overarching juridical edifice of right and law (HS1 86–8; see also Sheridan 1990: 182). This edifice was constructed around the king and to justify and serve 'royal power' (SD 25, see also BP 7–8). It needed to be shown 'that the monarch was indeed the living body of sovereignty, and that his power, even when absolute, was perfectly in keeping with a basic right' (SD 26). In this modality, power could be said to be held or possessed by someone – a king, for example (PP 21–2, DP 192).

The power of sovereignty operated on a bounded territory and its produce (SD 36, STP 11). The conquest of new and defence of conquered land were major concerns (STP 64, see also 65, 91–2). Yet whilst the notion of 'sovereignty over an unpopulated territory' was by no means deemed outlandish (STP 11), sovereign power was de facto 'exercised ... on a territory ... and ... the subjects ... inhabit[ing] it' (STP 96, see also 11). More precisely, it involved a relationship between the sovereign's will and the wills of subjects, whereby the sovereign issued laws and regulations that mediated his will and dictated what subjects, who were supposed to obey, had to do (STP 65, 70, see also 98; Sheridan 1990: 141).

Sovereign power, Foucault specifies further, constituted a relationship of power that connected the sovereign and subjects through 'deduction' and 'expenditure' (PP 42). The expenditures of the sovereign included, for instance, gifts to subjects or services, notably protection (PP 42, see also BP 66). However, expenditure was generally smaller than deduction (PP 42) and is, Foucault seems to think, less important for describing sovereign power. For sovereign power functioned primarily as a 'subtraction mechanism'. It 'was ... a right of seizure'. What distinguished the sovereignty relation in the main was the sovereign's seizing a share of the wealth, products, time, and services of the subjects through levies (HS1 136, see also 89, PP 42, 46, SD 35–6; Lemke 2011: 35; Sheridan 1990: 191–2).

Although the theory of sovereignty revolves around the king, Foucault notes that in 'feudal-type societies' the sovereignty relation characterised the exercise of power 'from the highest to the lowest levels' (SD 35). That said, the various sovereignty relationships, for example, between suzerain and feoffee, lord and serf, or priest and laity, formed no 'unitary hierarchical table with subordinate and superordinate elements'; these relations were not classifica-tory; there was 'no common measure' (PP 43, cf. 52). The 'elements' of sovereignty relations, Foucault emphasises, were non-equivalent: a sovereignty relation could operate between 'a suzerain ... and a family, a community, or the inhabitants of ... a region', that is, 'human multiplicities'; yet 'sovereignty may also bear on something other than ... human multiplicities', 'on land, a road, an instrument of production', and their 'users' (PP 44). What is decisive in this context for tracing the trajectory of Foucault's analyses of power is his contention that in sovereignty relations 'the subject-element' was usually not 'an individual body' (PP 44, see also 46n, 55). Sovereignty relations operated on 'multiplicities' such as 'families' or 'users' (PP 44). Alternatively, they operated on 'fragments ... of somatic singularity': it was specifically as 'son of X' or as 'bourgeois of this town', for instance, that someone might be 'sovereign' or 'subject' in sovereignty relationships, and one could 'be both subject and sov-ereign in different aspects' (PP 44).

By contrast, 'individualization' could be witnessed 'towards the top'. At the peak of the sovereign power configuration, Foucault argues, albeit with qualifications, 'the king in his individuality, with his king's body', could be located (PP 45, see also DP 192–3; Sheridan 1990: 155–6). This 'single, indi-vidual point' had the role of arbitrator between the various sovereignty relations: what was required was 'something like a sovereign who, in his own body, is the point on which all these multiple, different, and irreconcilable relationships converge' (PP 45, see also 82).[1]

Power Relationships

The monarchy, Foucault diagnoses in 1976, is haunting contemporary analy-ses of power: right, law, will, state, and sovereignty remain major concerns. However, increasingly prevalent new processes of power (HS1 88–9) demand that power be reconceptualised (HS1 102, see also SD 34; Sheridan 1990: 182–3). Foucault famously proposes to sidestep questions of sovereignty and obedience (SD 27) in favour of exploring 'a multiple and mobile field of force relations' (HS1 102, see also 97; Sheridan 1990: 139, 183, 186, 218).

Force relations

At the core of Foucault's opposition to extant conceptualisations of power is his disagreement with the idea of power as a right which, like a commodity, can be owned, contractually surrendered, and appropriated by some but not others (SD 13–14, 29, HS1 94; Sheridan 1990: 139, 184–5, 218). Power, he contends, is force in operation between points; it 'functions' (SD 29); 'it exists only in action' (SD 14); it is the reciprocal '"... exercise of an unbalanced force"' (Davidson 2006: xv, citing PP 14; see also Sheridan 1990: 139, 184, 218). Power is a *relationship* of unequal force between points (HS1 93–5, SD 15; Davidson 2006: xvi; Sheridan 1990: 139, 184, 218). This means that all power also involves the exercise of 'resistance'. Power relations cannot exist without 'points of resistance' that 'play the role of adversary, target, support, or handle' (HS1 95–6; see also Davidson 2006: xxiin9; Sheridan 1990: 139, 184–5).

Force relations, Foucault instructs, must be analysed in their 'multiplicity' (HS1 92; Davidson 2006: xv–xvi; see also Sheridan 1990: 139, 183, 186, 218). In fact, given the indelibility of resistance, power must be seen as a range of incessant 'struggles and confrontations' (Davidson 2006: xv; HS1 92; Sheridan 1990: 183). Indeed, Foucault doubts that one headspring feeds all revolting and rebelling in society, insisting instead on the 'plurality of resistances' (HS1 96; see also Sheridan 1990: 139–40, 184–5).

Relations of force, Foucault points out, can draw 'support' from each other, coming together as a 'chain' (HS1 92) or as 'local systems of subjugation' (SD 34), whereas mutual discrepancies may keep them apart (HS1 92). Similarly, the 'focuses of resistance are spread over time and space at varying densities', sometimes 'mobilizing' people and generating social 'cleavages' (HS1 96; see also Sheridan 1990: 139–40, 185). Finally, force relationships may be 'coded' or consolidated (HS1 93) in keeping with 'the logic' (HS1 97) or 'more general lines' of wider 'strategies' (Davidson 2006: xv; see also Sheridan 1990: 184–6). The 'design' or 'crystallization' of such 'strategies' can be found in the 'state apparatus', for instance, or in different 'social hegemonies'. From this perspective, neither states nor instances of social 'domination' of some over others are pre-given, but are among the ultimate 'forms power takes' (HS1 92–3, see also 96–7; Sheridan 1990: 218–19). From the same vantage point Foucault argues that revolutions can occur thanks to 'the strategic codification of … points of resistance' (HS1 96; see also Sheridan 1990: 139–40, 185).

Investigating power

Foucault therefore suggests to examine first of all the most minuscule workings of power (SD 30) and to investigate it 'in its most regional' domains (SD 27). It can then be established how the 'procedures' playing out in these domains are 'used', 'invested', and 'annexed' by ever more encompassing 'mechanisms' and, finally, by 'forms of overall domination' (SD 30–1, see also HS1 94); how local 'tactics' begin to link up with each other and together draw the contours of larger apparatuses (HS1 95; see also Sheridan 1990: 184–6). The 'school apparatus' of a society, for instance, is best understood in respect of extensive 'strategies' traversing, utilising, and interlinking much smaller 'mechanisms' and 'local tactics of domination', which in turn interlink tiny relations of subjugation such as those between children and grownups, offspring and parents, or families and administrations (SD 45–6).

In his analyses, Foucault seeks to avoid all attempts to reduce power. Notably, he challenges the Marxist view that the economy constitutes power's 'historical raison d'être' and that power's purpose is basically to maintain the existing 'relations of production' and 'class domination' (SD 13–14, see also HS1 94; Sheridan 1990: 219). Power relationships are certainly closely intertwined with economic – but also other, for instance sexual – relationships, yet they are 'effects' as well as 'conditions' of 'divisions, inequalities', or 'differentiations' in other relations (HS1 94, see also SD 14; Sheridan 1990: 184, 219).

Foucault, as is well known, highlights the inseparability of power and knowledge. The exercise and mechanisms of power depend on, and are strengthened by, the operation of discourses of truth (SD 24, 33–4, HS1 101; Sheridan 1990: 131, 138, 165, 169–70, 186, 220). For instance, power can work on sexuality thanks to 'techniques' for knowing and 'procedures' of speaking and writing about sexuality (HS1 98, see also 97; Sheridan 1990: 165–6, 169–70, 185).[2] Conversely, power fashions the devices for knowledge production, for example, techniques of observation, documentation, and inquiry (SD 33). In fact, power generates 'statements', 'negations', 'discourses', and 'theories' themselves (PP 13, also cited in Davidson 2006: xviii; see also HS1 101; Sheridan 1990: 131, 138, 165–6, 169–70, 185–6, 220). Moreover, it 'institutionalizes', 'professionalizes', and 'rewards' the pursuit of 'truth' (SD 25). And as far as sexuality is concerned, it was only insofar as 'power had established it as a possible object' that it could become a field of inquiry (HS1 98, see also 97; Sheridan 1990: 165–6, 169–70, 185).

This point about sexuality illustrates a more far-reaching argument. What power works upon, Foucault insists, does not precede its operations but is produced by it (see e.g. Davidson 2003: xix–xx). The individual, in particular, is by no means a basic entity which subsequently comes under the purview of power or is crushed by it. Instead, it is 'power' that 'allows bodies, gestures, discourses, and desires to be identified and constituted as something individual ... The individual is ... a power-effect' (SD 29–30, see also 28; Sheridan 1990: 140, 152, 154–6, 165). Thus, analyses of power should not seek a foothold in components that pre-exist power relations, but proceed from an 'actual or effective relationship of domination' and investigate how it 'determines the elements to which it is applied' (SD 45). The problem of disciplinary power already strongly reverberates here.

Disciplinary Power

Much of Foucault's work on power is dedicated to disciplinary power. Utterly 'incompatible with relations of sovereignty' (SD 35), discipline became a major modality of power in Western societies in the 1600s and 1700s (DP 137, SD 35). 'It was', says Foucault, 'one of the basic tools for the establishment of industrial capitalism and the corresponding type of society' (SD 36).[3] It is, he holds, among the most widespread forms of the exercise of power today (PP 40, 79).

Discipline's target

Sovereign power was exercised on legal subjects in a territory and their produce. Disciplinary power grabs hold of bodies rather than products (PP 40, 46, AN 193, DP 136; Sheridan 1990: 138–9, 148–9, 192, 217, 219). Whereas 'vassalage', for example, '... bore less on the operations of the body than on the products of labour' (DP 137), discipline, Foucault emphasises, is a 'modality by which ... power ... reaches the level of bodies' (PP 40; see also Lagrange 2006: 361–2). More precisely, disciplinary power acts on the individual body (STP 12, PP 40, 46; Lemke 2011: 36; Sheridan 1990: 192, 217, 219).

Disciplinary power works chiefly upon 'bodies and what they do' (SD 35). Indeed, whereas the sovereign seized but a part of the subjects' work and time (PP 46, HS1 136), discipline aims for a comprehensive 'hold' on the individual's actions, including words, and habits (PP 40, 46, see also DP 138): on the individual's 'time in its totality' (PP 46).

In this context, the body is not approached as an indivisible 'unity', though. Disciplinary power disassembles it, reconfigures it, and operates on its components: movements, gestures, behaviours, attitudes etc. (DP 137–8; see also Lagrange 2006: 361–2; Sheridan: 1990: 149, 217). The body is treated 'at the level of the mechanism' (DP 137). Power's grab for the body coincided with the conception of 'Man-the-Machine' (DP 136; see also Lemke 2011: 36; Sheridan 1990: 148–9, 192–3).

What disciplinary power ultimately targets are the body's forces: its aptitudes, capabilities, skills, and energies. This procedure has two aspects. Discipline enhances the body's forces – for instance, training certain of its capacities – in order to make the body more useful. At the same time, it weakens the body's forces – restraining certain of its energies – and makes it more docile (AN 193–4, DP 137–8; Lemke 2011: 36; Sheridan 1990: 139, 148–52, 192, 219). '[D]isciplinary coercion establishes in the body the constricting link between an increased aptitude and an increased domination' (DP 138).

Disciplinary operations

Where disciplinary power is exercised, the body – its habits, parts, and potential – is seen as deeply mouldable (DP 135–6). Nonetheless, for Foucault 'power need not be violent' (Davidson 2003: xx; see also Sheridan 1990: 139). One crucial mechanism of disciplinary power is 'constant surveillance' (SD 36): individuals are permanently under supervision (PP 47; Lemke 2011: 36; Sheridan 1990: 152–3). Surveillance is tied to the production of written records of people's every word and deed (PP 48–9). The 'police discipline' emerging in the 1700s illustrates this (PP 50). The police received the task of always and everywhere observing – without becoming visible itself – everything that was happening, done, and said down to the details and of documenting them in 'reports and registers' (DP 213–14, see also PP 50–1).

Foucault outlines a whole set of broad operations of power on the body, each of which is supported by several disciplinary 'techniques' (DP 139, 141). The 'distribution of individuals in space' (DP 141; see also Sheridan 1990: 150), for instance, involves the technique, among others, of defining *functional sites*' (DP 143). In the late 1700s, factories were divided into spaces for discrete operations of the production process and the corresponding sections of the workforce. These spaces were then respectively partitioned into identical individual workplaces. This facilitated the observation of each worker and their comparison in view of their activities and ability, whilst 'each variable' of the workforce, such as 'promptness' or 'skill', could be 'assessed ... and related to the individual who was its particular agent' (DP 145).

Controlling activity in time is supported – again by way of example – by an 'instrumental coding of the body' or '*body-object articulation*' technique. Discipline prescribes exactly how a series of body parts and a series of parts of an object are to connect through several 'simple gestures', before arranging these connections in a temporal sequence (DP 152–3; see also Sheridan 1990: 151). The role of 'disciplinary power', then, is not 'deduction', appropriating a product, but 'synthesis', constructing 'a body-weapon, body-tool, body-machine complex' (DP 153).

Foucault also underscores discipline's training function. One of the means of disciplinary training is 'normalizing judgement' (DP 170; see also Sheridan 1990: 148–55). Operant, for instance, in schools or workshops, this tactic involves micro-punishments such as 'minor deprivations' or 'petty humilia-tions'. These are dished out for activities and behaviours such as 'negligence' or 'impoliteness', which, whilst not necessarily breaking any laws, fail to 'measure up to' rules determined by prescriptive 'regulations' or 'observable ... regularit[ies]' (DP 178–9; see also Sheridan 1990: 153–4). 'To punish', cru-cially, 'is to exercise': behaviour which falls short entails obligatory repetitive training in good behaviour so that behaviour is corrected according to the rule (DP 179–80). Simultaneously, correct behaviour is rewarded to make those whose behaviour departs desire conformity. Behaviours are thereby precisely distributed between various opposing poles of 'good and evil', every person receives a 'punitive balance-sheet', and 'individuals' are finely 'differentiat[ed]' (DP 180–1; see also Sheridan 1990: 154).

In addition to correcting, micro-punishment also prevents. The discipli-nary workshop, an area of close 'supervision', penalises 'anything that might involve distraction', such as loud singing or sharing lewd stories during work (PP 51). This is to create 'continuous punitive pressure' on 'potential behavior', generate aversion to offending, and thus enable discipline to 'intervene' in advance of 'the actual manifestation of the behavior', before bodies can do or say what they are not supposed to do or say (PP 51–2).

It is important to underline that for Foucault the individual on which disciplinary power operates in various ways is not given in advance. Rather, disciplinary power deals with 'multiplicities' and turns them into individuals. 'The individual is ... a particular way of dividing up the multiplicity for a disci-pline' (STP 12; see also Lemke 2011: 37–8). By attaching the 'subject-function' to the 'somatic singularity' – to the body's actions, words, movements, and forces – through surveillance, documentation, and other procedures, disciplinary power creates the individual (PP 55–6, see also 49–50; Sheridan 1990: 140, 152, 154–6, 165). It is discipline which, by dint of operations, techniques, and train-ing methods such as those illustrated above, manufactures bodies into individuality with its specific properties (DP 167, 170, 192, see also 194, 217). Thus, in contradistinction to sovereign power, 'the disciplinary system entails ... individualization at the base' (PP 55, see also DP 192–3; Sheridan 1990: 154–6).

Security and Government

Foucault distinguishes discipline from a further major type of power, 'the apparatus (*dispositif*) of security' (STP 6). Security is younger than disciplinary power, having emerged roughly in the mid-1700s, and differs from it (e.g. STP 55–6, 64, 66; Lemke 2011: 37, 47). Foucault asks if security, too, increasingly characterises the operations of power in contemporary society (STP 10–11; Senellart 2009: 378).[4]

Security and population

The development of security apparatuses, Foucault argues, is connected to the appearance of a particular 'idea' and 'reality' of 'population' (STP 11, see also 67; Lemke 2011: 37; Senellart 2009: 379). Here it is 'the population' that constitutes the 'pertinent level' of power operations (STP 66, see also 42). To this population, in turn, is attributed a certain '"naturalness"' (STP 70; see also Lemke 2011: 45).

Its 'naturalness' emerges, firstly, as the regularity of numerous population phenomena, for instance, as the constant ratios of various illnesses' casualties each year (STP 74). Moreover, the population is seen as naturally affected by a range of 'variables', especially the 'means of subsistence', but also climate, material environment, conventions, and many others (STP 70–1, see also 345, 366). These 'factors' are not 'all natural'; they can potentially be modified to an extent (STP 366; see also Lemke 2011: 46–7). Thirdly, it is held that each 'individual acts out of desire', which cannot be changed. 'Desire' is the sole driving force of the actions of the population (STP 72). And the 'play' of people's desires will ensure advantageous outcomes for the population as a whole (STP 73). Notably, the 'game of the interest of competing private individuals who each seek maximum advantage for themselves' will yield 'the most favorable economic situation' for the population (STP 346).

The onset of this political concern with the population, argues Foucault, constituted 'the entry of a "nature" into the field of techniques of power'. Securitising power does not, however, involve a sovereign's imposition of laws from on high demanding 'obedience' against nature, but the application of 'reflected procedures of government within this nature, with the help of it, and with regard to it' (STP 75). Indeed, given the population's dependence on so many 'variables', it is hard to transform it directly 'by decree' (STP 71; see also Lemke 2011: 47). 'If one says to a population "do this," ... there is quite simply no guarantee that it can do it' (STP 71). Instead, one envisages influencing a population indirectly by acting upon the various 'remote factors' that are known to affect it (STP 71–2). Eighteenth-century town planning projects illustrate security's orientation towards organising spaces so as to steer the interactions of their natural elements, for example rivers, and artificial elements that function like natural ones, for example clusters of houses, with the nature of the population within them (STP 21–3).

Rather than centring on legal 'prohibition' or disciplinary 'prescription', security, Foucault continues, chiefly 'works on the basis of' and 'within reality'. Through conducting 'analyses' and configuring 'arrangements', it seeks to make reality's elements 'work in relation to each other'. Its operations thus remain within 'the interplay of reality with itself' (STP 47–8, see also 344; Lemke 2011: 47). Whereas disciplinary power aims to control every detail, 'security ... "lets things happen ..."' to some extent (STP 45). It ensures that 'reality' proceeds along its proper path correspondingly with its own 'laws, principles, and mechanisms' (STP 48). Security 'relies' on 'natural processes' for achieving particular results in the population (STP 45). The potential of desire suggests that government ought to 'stimulat[e] and encourag[e]' (STP 73; see also Lemke 2011: 47) 'desire' and allow it to 'play' freely so it can generate 'the general interest of the population' (STP 73). Notably, if the 'private interest[s]' of 'competing' individuals are permitted to function of their own accord, the actions of each individual will help ensure the 'good of all' (STP 346).

Government and liberalism

His considerations of population and security lead Foucault to a more persistent discussion of government (STP 76, 88; Lemke 2011: 44–5; Senellart 2009: 379). The appearance of 'the problem of population', especially through statistical demonstrations of its 'regularities' and 'effects', facilitated the development of an explicit 'art of government' (STP 103–4; see also Lemke 2011: 45–6). The purpose of such government is to enhance the population's situation, its wealth, health, longevity etc. (STP 105).

The sphere in which politics thus intervenes is conceptualised as processes and mechanisms with a certain 'naturalness' – 'the naturalness of society' (STP 349; see also Lemke 2011: 45–7). The population, specifically, 'has its own laws of transformation' and is 'characterized by the law of the mechanics of interests' (STP 351–2). This naturalness entails that government does not operate primarily through prohibitions and orders, but maintains 'respect' for those 'natural processes': to govern means to be mindful of them, to 'work with them', 'to arouse', 'facilitate', and '*laisser faire*' to safeguard the functioning of 'the necessary and natural regulations' (STP 352–3; see also Lemke 2011: 46–7). Government deploys means that are intrinsic to the population itself (STP 105), from '"campaigns"' to alter its views and habits (STP 366) to 'techniques' whose operations people may not even notice, focusing particularly on their interests (STP 105). Moreover, those 'natural phenomena' are considered scientifically knowable, and 'scientific knowledge' of them is deemed a prerequisite of 'good government' (STP 350; see also Lemke 2011: 46–7). Successful, 'rationally reflected' government depends on 'observations and knowledge' of the population (STP 106). Government thus understood does not, then, centre on a sovereign's rule through the imposition of laws on subjects (STP 115–16), but constitutes rather a 'management' – involving 'apparatuses of security' (STP 107–8) – of 'the mass of the population' (STP 110; see also Senellart 2009: 379).

In this context, Foucault unpacks his well-known concept of '"governmentality"' (STP 108; Senellart 2009: 379–80). He uses this 'ugly word' (STP 115) to designate *inter alia* the trajectory towards the primacy of government over sovereign and disciplinary power as well as precisely the combination of 'institutions, procedures', and 'analyses' that enables the workings of this 'power' on the population that involves 'apparatuses of security' and 'political economy as its major form of knowledge' (STP 108; see also Senellart 2009: 388). Ours, insists Foucault in 1978, is 'the era of a governmentality discovered in the eighteenth century' (STP 109).[5]

This problem of government, finally, is also at the centre of liberalism.[6] Foucault explores liberalism 'as a principle and method of the rationalization of the exercise of government' (BP 318, see also 321; Lemke 2011: 45). The exact 'question of liberalism' is that of 'frugal government' (BP 29, see also 321).[7] Of major importance here is the notion that the market operates according to 'natural mechanisms', and that if these mechanisms are left to operate, they will allow the 'true price', which 'fluctuates' around a product's 'value', to form. Market mechanisms and their revelation of the 'natural price' make it possible to distinguish 'correct' from 'erroneous' government action:

> ... inasmuch as it enables production, need, supply, demand, value, and price, etcetera, to be linked together through exchange, the market constitutes ... a site of verification-falsification for governmental practice. (BP 31–2; see also Lemke 2011: 46–7; Senellart 2009: 383–4)

Moreover, 'frugal government' is subject to 'internal' limits (BP 37). A particularly persistent mode of defining these limits (BP 43) was developed by 'English radicalism' (BP 40). Government is set 'desirable' as well as factual restrictions based on examinations of its aims, its objects, and which governmental practices would be 'useful' (BP 40; see also Lemke 2011: 46). In the Western world after 1800, Foucault emphasises, 'individual and collective utility ... will be the major criteria for working out the limits of the powers of public authorities ...' (BP 43–4; see also Senellart 2009: 384). What underpins 'exchange' and 'utility' in turn is 'interest' (BP 44). Ultimately, it is 'interests' that 'constitute politics'; the power of government may be exercised exclusively where 'interests' render something 'of interest' to people (BP 45).

PART 2: POWER OVER LIFE

Whilst Foucault concedes that several of the juridical monarchy's 'forms' still exist, he maintains that the 'new mechanisms of power' are more – and ever more – influential today. Crucially, the new 'mechanisms are', certainly 'in part, those that, beginning in the eighteenth century, took charge of men's existence, men as living bodies' (HS1 89; see also Lemke 2011: 33–6; Sheridan 1990: 182–3, 191–3). In fact, 'existence' in this passage is meant to translate the original's 'la vie' (Foucault 1976: 117). In the work of Foucault, who argues that 'in any society … mu[lt]iple relations of power traverse, characterize, and constitute the social body' (SD 24; see also Sheridan 1990: 139), the problem of life in contemporary social conditions is that of life and power. Once again, he distinguishes the area of his investigations from the context of sovereignty.

Right of Death

Sovereign power, Foucault has been shown to argue, was generally understood in terms of right. Importantly here, the 'classical theory of sovereignty' ascribed to the sovereign 'a right of life and death' (SD 240; see also Sheridan 1990: 191). That is to say, neither subjects' lives nor their deaths were 'natural or immediate phenomena … outside the field of power', but could themselves 'become rights only as a result of the will of the sovereign'. Yet the sovereign's 'right of life and death', Foucault emphasises, was actually mainly a 'right to kill'. The sovereign could not make people live as he could make them die (SD 240). His 'right … formulated as the "power of life and death" was in reality the right to *take* life or *let* live'. Foucault therefore suspects that this right must be linked to the aforementioned mechanism of 'deduction' in the sovereign power relationship. Sovereign power was the 'right' to subtract slices of people's wealth, parts of their time, 'and ultimately life itself' (HS1 136, see also 89, SD 240–1; Lemke 2011: 35–6, 38–9; Sheridan 1990: 191–2).

Albeit formally a derivative of Roman antiquity's 'absolute' right of the father to take the lives of his progeny and slaves, the 'right of life and death' in 'its modern form' was 'relative and limited' (HS1 135–6; see also Lemke 2011: 35). Sovereign power, as already said, involved passing laws that mediated the sovereign's will and were supposed to be obeyed. Defensive wars aside, only when a subject rebelled, breaking the sovereign's laws, could the sovereign have the perpetrator killed (HS1 135). The law, Foucault adds in turn, always carries a weapon: anyone contravening it is, in response, certainly 'as a last resort', threatened with execution (HS1 144).

The theory of sovereignty envisaged 'rules' as products of the sovereign's volition (SD 38) and, Foucault specifies, based power on his corporeal being (SD 36). This resonates with the idea of individualisation at the summit of the sovereign power configuration. The subject's relationship with the sovereign was 'personal' (BP 45). Thus, 'a crime' – apart from constituting 'voluntary harm done to another' and 'society' – was a strike against the sovereign's 'will' codified in his laws as well as against the sovereign's 'rights', 'strength', and 'physical body' (AN 82, see also DP 47; Sheridan 1990: 141), against 'the sovereign in the very body of his power' (BP 46, see also 50n16). The distinction between those obeying and disobeying his laws and will simultaneously demarcated his foes (HS1 144, see also DP 50; Lemke 2011: 38–9).[8] By the same token, punishment contained the sovereign's own intervention on the offender's body (BP 45; see also Sheridan 1990: 140–1), his 'personal vendetta' (AN 82). The 'death penalty' was among his retorts to people who had assaulted 'his will, his law, or his person' (HS1 137–8, see also BP 50n16, DP 48; Sheridan 1990: 141).

A key function of punishing in this context was the 'reconstitution of power in its integrity' (AN 83, see also DP 48–9). Punishment had to assert power's inherent supremacy – the supremacy of the sovereign's 'right' as well as of his 'physical strength' (DP 49). Punitive 'excess' needed to outdo ostentatiously, in 'a sort of joust' between punishment and crime, the 'excess' of the latter (AN 83). The penal ritual was meant to terrorise; its terror could be experienced in public torture and execution (DP 49, AN 83).

Controlling Life

However, what had been strengthened by the 1800s in contrast to the right of death was 'power's hold over life' (SD 239; see also Lemke 2011: 33–6; Sheridan 1990: 191–3): a 'power to "make" live and "let" die' in contrast to 'the right to take life or let live' (SD 241, see also HS1 138; Lemke 2011: 36). Formulated in the broadest terms, 'political power' had taken charge of 'administering life'. Foucault traces two modes, distinct but connected, in which this type of power has been developing (HS1 139, see also SD 249; Lemke 2011: 35–8; Sheridan 1990: 192–3). Some of his theoretical considerations on power were outlined above. Yet much of his work is dedicated to analysing its manifestations in specific settings, for instance in the field of health and illness.[9]

Disciplining life

Since the 1600s, argues Foucault, disciplinary power has been functioning as the first form of 'power over life'. The objectives of this *anatomo-politics of the human body* have been mentioned: targeting the 'performances' of the body 'machine', training its capacities, enhancing 'its usefulness and ... docility' (HS1 139, see also SD 241–3, 249–50; Lemke 2011: 36; Sheridan 1990: 139, 148–52, 192, 219). Discipline chiefly established itself in – though it has not remained confined to – institutions like schools or workshops (SD 250; Lemke 2011: 37). Foucault's analysis of the operation of disciplinary power on the sick provides one illustration of its operation as power over life.

In the Middle Ages and beyond, he points out, the demarcation of people stricken with leprosy from the rest of their group entailed 'a rule of no contact'

(AN 43, see also DP 199; Davidson 2003: xxi). In fact, lepers were expelled from the group and its spaces to a 'vague' outer sphere (AN 43; see also Davidson 2003: xxi), where they merged into an undifferentiated 'mass' (DP 198). Moreover, these outcasts were subjected to juridico-political 'disqualification' (AN 43; Davidson 2003: xxi). Their expulsions were marked by funerary rituals: every leper was 'declared dead' and their belongings 'passed on' (AN 43). In this cleansing of the group (AN 44, DP 198), the power of deduction and death still quakes palpably (see also AN 48).

It is hard to overstate the importance of these considerations for Foucault's studies of power: Western societies, he argues, have known but 'two major models for the control of individuals', 'the exclusion of lepers' and, in stark contrast to it, 'the inclusion of plague victims' (AN 44; see also Davidson 2003: xx–xxii). When the plague befell a late seventeenth-century town, it was immediately sealed off (AN 44–5, DP 195). Yet neither was the space thus demarcated allowed to remain 'vague' (AN 45), nor were its inhabitants left to amalgamate into an undifferentiated mass. As is characteristic of disciplinary power (DP 143), the plague-ridden town was rigorously partitioned down to single streets (AN 45, DP 195). Each inhabitant was identified individually by name and told to stay in her or his house (AN 45–6, DP 195–7). Instead of being kept at a distance, the people of the 'plague town' were placed under close, all-encompassing, incessant 'surveillance'; regular visitations to all the houses, during which each resident 'had to present himself at the window', for example, enabled inspectors to conduct a whole 'review … of the living and the dead' (AN 45–6, see also DP 195–7; Davidson 2003: xxi). Every detail – 'deaths, illnesses, complaints, irregularities' – was documented and its record passed on to those deciding on 'medical treatment' (DP 196). Power did not simply distinguish 'two types or groups' anymore, but individualised, establishing a range of delicate 'differences between individuals who are ill and those who are not' (AN 46, see also DP 197–8; Davidson 2003: xxi). The aim of these operations, finally, was not to cleanse the group, but 'to maximize the health, life, longevity, and strength of individuals' (AN 46). Disciplinary power was functioning with the objective of making live.

Foucault associates the recession of the former in favour of the latter 'model' with the recession, in the 1600s and 1700s, of a 'negative', deductive in favour of a 'positive', productive power (AN 48; Davidson 2003: xx–xxii). Power's productive orientation manifested itself in several ways in the plague town – in the ambition to generate health and life, of course (AN 46), but also, for instance, in the 'accumulation of observations' and the 'formation' and 'growth of knowledge', which, in turn, supported the proliferation of power 'effects' (AN 48; see also Davidson 2003: xxi).

Normalisation in discipline

What is more, the setting of the plague town reveals a tendency of disciplinary power, briefly touched upon above, which is crucial for power over life according to Foucault: the tendency to normalise (AN 49; see also Davidson 2003: xxi–xxv; Lemke 2011: 39). The operations of disciplinary power, he observes, often involve the definition of a 'norm' in the form of 'an optimal model' with regard to a specific outcome, for example, 'the best movement for loading one's rifle' (STP 57; see also Lemke 2011: 47) or, precisely, a 'norm of health' (AN 47). The uninterrupted investigation of the plague town, he argues, had the aim of figuring out the extent of each individual's 'conform[ity] to the rule, to the defined norm of health' (AN 47). In fact, a key component of disciplinary normalisation is the comparison of individuals – their attributes, conduct, and performances – in view of a norm. This is closely interlinked with the 'differentiation' between them. On the basis of such operations, disciplinary power constructs hierarchies, 'in terms of value', of 'the abilities, the level, the "nature" of individuals' (DP 182–3, see also 193; Lemke 2011: 47; Sheridan 1990: 154). The schemes for grading and ranking individuals in the school and the military – 'hierarch[ies] of values and success' – constitute prime examples (PP 52). At the same time, discipline exerts 'pressure', even 'constraint', on individuals to measure up to the same norm (DP 182–3). Its various 'training' methods are among its principal means to bring about people's conformance with the 'model' (STP 57; see also Lemke 2011: 47). In this sense, Foucault points out with reference to Georges Canguilhem, norms are not devices of expulsion, but related to the 'qualification' of individuals and to 'intervention' for their 'transformation' and 'correction' (AN 50; see also Davidson 2003: xxi).

However, whilst all those who thereby turn out to be capable of such conformity count as 'normal', those who turn out to be unable to adapt are categorised as 'abnormal' (STP 57, see also 63; Lemke 2011: 47). Thus, disciplinary power does draw an 'external' boundary, namely the boundary separating the sphere of 'the abnormal' from the arena of individual 'differences' (DP 183). Every disciplinary apparatus, Foucault argues, has borders that demarcate a remainder of 'unclassifiable' and 'inassimilable' people: the 'feeble-minded' who cannot be taught in schools, for instance, or the 'mentally ill', the 'residue of all residues', who cannot be assimilated according to any of the disciplinary schemata (PP 53–4). That said, finally, disciplinary power always also crosses this line, devising ever further mechanisms for dealing with 'the irreducible', too, and for 'reestablishing' norms with respect even to them, as the various 'schools for the feeble-minded' illustrate (PP 54). The procedures of division and exclusion did not, then, simply disappear at some point; it is just that by the 1800s the dwellers of the zones thus created – for example, the mad of the asylum – had become targets of disciplinary operations (DP 199).

Regulating life

The second form of life power identified by Foucault has been developing since the mid-1700s as *'regulatory controls'*. This *'bio-politics of the population'* revolves around managing the 'species body' and 'the biological processes' unfolding on and in it (HS1 139): birth and death rates, for instance (SD 243), or population health, and 'all the conditions that can cause these to vary' (HS1 139, see also SD 249–50; Lemke 2011: 36–7; Sheridan 1990: 171–2, 191–3). Disciplinary and regulatory power, emphasises Foucault, 'are not mutually exclusive' (SD 250): they can operate simultaneously (SD 250–2), and regulation has been utilising, 'by sort of infiltrating', the disciplines (SD 242; see also Lemke 2011: 37–8). Nonetheless, they must be distinguished. Regulatory power generally operates from the 'State level', although it can be located in 'sub-State' – for example, medical – 'institutions', too (SD 250; see also Lemke 2011: 37–8). More importantly, whereas disciplinary procedures seek to disassemble the 'multiplicity of men ... into individual bodies', so that they can be better supervised, drilled, 'used', and possibly 'punished', the new '"biopolitics"' engages with that multiplicity insofar as it constitutes 'a global mass' (SD 242–3), the 'body' of the 'population', which is conceived 'as a biological problem' (SD 245, see also 249; Lemke 2011: 37–8). Regulation involves endeavours to secure 'knowledge' and 'control' of problems such as 'the illnesses prevalent in a population' and draining its 'strength', as illustrated by the institutional organisation of healthcare and the campaigns to instruct the population in hygiene in the late eighteenth century (SD 243–4; see also Lemke 2011: 37–8). Moreover, regulation includes attempts to deal with the impact of the natural as well as human-made 'environment' or 'milieu' on population life (SD 244–5). Notwithstanding the resonances between Foucault's outline of regulation and his conception of security (see SD 246, 249, STP 24n5, 49), there are differences between them, too. That said, Foucault's discussion of how security mechanisms function in relation to illness does seem to help illustrate not only how security more specifically understood, but also how the modality of power concerning the population at issue here, operates as power over life.

In the 1700s, Foucault remarks, smallpox was both the 'most widely endemic' illness and prone to 'sudden ... epidemic outbursts'. Characteristic methods for tackling it were variolisation and, later, vaccination (STP 58). Foucault draws attention to a transformation of the understanding of disease in this context. The conception of an 'overall relationship between a disease and a place' gave way to numerical analysis and the representation of the 'distribution of cases in a population' (STP 60). This enabled the calculation of the 'risk' of falling ill for every member of a specific demographic, for example, a two in three risk of catching smallpox for every newborn (STP 60–1). The computation of increased risk of morbidity for people in some demographics compared to others allowed for the identification of 'danger'; being a small child, for instance, was seen to be 'dangerous'. The term 'crisis', finally, was given to a fulminant growth in numbers involving a 'spread' of disease in a certain location – a spread that bore 'the risk, through contagion ..., of multiplying cases that multiply other cases' (STP 61). The concern with population phenomena characteristic of security, focused, as it was here, on biological processes in the population, is typical also of the perspective of regulatory power over life.

For Foucault the approach to smallpox of that period is instructive not only with regard to the outlook of power but also with regard to its exercise. Vaccination and particularly variolisation, he highlights, did not merely mean preventing the disease, but involved inoculating people to trigger a slight form of smallpox and, by dint of this slight form, to avoid 'other possible attacks' (STP 59). Comparing this approach with contemporaneous strategies for dealing with grain scarcity, Foucault designates it as 'a typical mechanism of security' (STP 59, see also 30–49, 341–7). For unlike 'juridical-disciplinary regulations' concentrated on prevention, securitising strategies, as mentioned, centred on 'finding support in the reality of the phenomenon' and getting it to interact with other components to avoid the unwanted phenomenon. Foucault is convinced that their parallels and similarities with securitising strategies of that period contributed to the acceptance of variolisation and vaccination as viable approaches (STP 59).

Normalisation in security

The securitising approach to smallpox illustrates how power operated on population life as well as revealing an important transformation – which Foucault, however, only sketches – in the 'procedures of normalization' (STP 49). Normalisation in the disciplinary context began by 'positing a model' as the 'norm', proceeded to attempts to make individuals 'conform' to it, and culminated in the distinction between those able and unable to as 'normal' and 'abnormal' (STP 57, see also 63; Lemke 2011: 47). By contrast, security apparatuses began by ascertaining what was de facto 'normal', including whole varieties of 'normality'. For example, in the 1700s it was widely accepted that the smallpox death rate in the overall population was about one in eight, whilst the rate among small children was much higher. From the 'more favorable' of the 'distributions' thus charted, a 'norm' was then derived (STP 62–3; see also Lemke 2011: 47). Normalisation in the context of security comprised all the endeavours to align the least favourable, 'deviant normalities' with 'the normal, general curve' (STP 62). In the disciplinary procedure, 'the norm' is 'primary' and (ab)normality defined in view of it (STP 57), whereas in the procedure of security, normality is primary 'and the norm ... deduced from it' (STP 63). Hence, Foucault retrospectively proposes to speak of disciplinary 'normation' (STP 57) in contradistinction to security's 'normalization' (STP 63).

The 'norm', Foucault holds, finally, 'circulates between' both modalities of power over life mentioned above: it is capable of aiding the disciplining of 'a body' as well as the regulation of 'a population' (SD 253). Moreover, 'normalization' is more important for the functioning of power over human life than the law (HS1 89). This power does not simply distinguish those obeying the law from the disobedient, who will be punished and even threatened with death. Instead, it revolves around 'measur[ing]', 'apprais[ing]', and 'hierarchiz[ing]' with regard to norms and around corresponding strategies for 'correcti[on]' and 'regulat[ion]'. Due to the extension of power over life, the role of norms and normalising procedures is becoming ever more – that of the law per se ever less – relevant for understanding how power operates today (HS1 144, see also 89; Lemke 2011: 38–9; Sheridan 1990: 192–3).

CONCLUSION

For Foucault, examinations of current social conditions must centre on the problem of power. Disciplinary power as well as security and government have become more, sovereign power somewhat less, important to such examinations. Foucault's work also suggests that the problem of power over life has become crucial to investigations of contemporary society. In fact, this may well turn out to be one of his work's most influential intimations about what sociology should be dealing with – the sociological literature on biopolitics is substantial and growing. What Foucault's argumentation implies equally strongly, though this is less often emphasised, is that, as a consequence of the development of that power, sociological inquiry will remain an absolutely indispensable endeavour for at least as long as questions of life matter in any way at all:

> ... power ... has, thanks to the play of technologies of discipline ... and technologies of regulation ..., succeeded in covering the whole surface that lies between the organic and the biological, between body and population.
>
> We are ... in a power that has taken control of both the body and life or ... of life in general – with the body as one pole and the population as the other. (SD 253; see also Lemke 2011: 38; Sheridan 1990: 192)

If power has taken charge of life in its entirety, if nothing of life lies outside its target field, then all life is now social life.

Abbreviations

AN: *Abnormal* (2003)

BP: *The Birth of Biopolitics* (2010)

DP: *Discipline and Punish* (1991)

HS1: *History of Sexuality 1* (1981)

PP: *Psychiatric Power* (2006)

SD: *'Society Must Be Defended'* (2004)

STP: *Security, Territory, Population* (2009)

Selected Further Reading

See Sheridan, A. (1990) *Michel Foucault: The Will to Truth*. London: Routledge, for discussions of Foucault's conception of power, and Lemke, T. (2011) *Biopolitics: An Advanced Introduction*. New York: New York University Press, for a solid introduction to the theme of biopolitics in the work of Foucault and a series of other thinkers.

The journal *Foucault Studies* contains a range of scholarly articles on many aspects of Foucault's work and can be found here: https://rauli.cbs.dk/index. php/foucault-studies/index

Notes

1 The family, Foucault mentions, is a domain of sovereign power (PP 79, cf. 115–16, 124–5, DP 215–16). Among the attributes of its power configuration that identify it as sovereign power is 'maximum individualization' at the summit: 'the father, as bearer of the name, and insofar as he exercises power in his name, is the most intense pole of individualization' (PP 80).
2 Equally, discourse can be an obstacle to power, 'expos[ing]' it and offering 'a point of resistance' (HS1 101; see also Sheridan 1990: 186).
3 Foucault points out that disciplinary mechanisms had been formed centuries earlier and gradually spreading since then (PP 40–1, 63–70), before progressively pervading Western societies – in complex processes he describes in some detail – from the seventeenth and eighteenth centuries onwards (PP 70–3, 79, 93, DP 209–28).
4 For more detail on the following key concepts of population, security, government, and governmentality than can be offered here, see Gudmand-Høyer and Lopdrup Hjorth (2009: 99–109, 124–30).
5 Senellart (2009: 388–9) summarises how this concept develops in Foucault's subsequent work.
6 For more detail on the following – and further – aspects of Foucault's reading of liberalism, see Gudmand-Høyer and Lopdrup Hjorth (2009: 110–15).
7 'Liberalism', argues Foucault, entails that 'one should always suspect that one governs too much' (BP 319; see also Lemke 2011: 46). Foucault's related considerations of *homo œconomicus* and civil society cannot be discussed here (see BP 270–313; Senellart 2009: 385).
8 'There was a fragment of regicide in the smallest crime' (AN 82, see also DP 53–4).
9 For a brief overview of the following considerations, see STP 9–11.

8

Jean Baudrillard: Terror, Death, Exchange

PART 1: THE SOCIAL RELATIONS OF LIFE AND DEATH

For the purpose of the particular analyses, previous chapters of this book discussed the respective sociologist's conception of contemporary social conditions before proceeding to discuss their investigations of the problem of life in those conditions. Jean Baudrillard's *œuvre* does not render these analytical steps easily separable. His considerations of the social world are too closely intertwined with his considerations of life and, especially, death. Whilst from Baudrillard's perspective life and death are never not matters of social relations, his most penetrating and striking inquiry into social relations engages throughout with the social relations of life and death. Of central importance to his critical examination of contemporary social conditions is his conception of societies centred on symbolic exchange, including, crucially, exchanges with the dead and the exchange of death. Baudrillard distinguishes such formations from capitalist society, a social order or system in which life and death are mercilessly real, 'death power' operates, and lifetime is frantically accumulated.

Symbolic Exchange

Baudrillard associates what he calls 'the *symbolic*' chiefly with whom he calls 'the primitives' (SED 131). 'The symbolic', he emphasises many years after introducing it into his work, does not mean the same as '"imaginary"', but, for him, 'is *symbolic exchange* as anthropology understands it' (PW 15, emphasis added). Baudrillard distinguishes his notion of 'symbolic exchange' sharply from 'commodity exchange', which is dominant in capitalism (PW 73). When he deployed the former 'concept', he recounts, he sought to launch 'a political critique of our society'. He sought to do so with reference to a notion that some may call 'utopian'; but this notion, he insists, 'has been a living concept in many other cultures' (PW 15).[1] Whilst 'symbolic exchange' at first concerned the 'economic' sphere, that is, 'goods[,] as in potlatch', it was 'the symbolic exchange of death' that eventually became a major theme of Baudrillard's *œuvre* (PW 21).[2]

Exchanging with the dead

In his earlier work, notably in *Symbolic Exchange and Death*, Baudrillard discusses symbolic exchange indeed in explicitly anthropological and overtly sociological terms. It is also here that he discusses symbolic exchange most elaborately with regard to life and death. In other cultures, unlike in our society, 'exchange', he argues, 'does not stop when life comes to an end'. For '[s]ymbolic exchange' continues not only among 'the living', but also with 'the dead', with rocks, with animals (SED 134; see also Butterfield 2002; Genosko 1998: 20–1, 31; Pawlett 2007: 57, 59). Baudrillard speaks of 'an absolute law' (SED 134). During an initiation rite of the Sara people in Chad reported by the ethnologist Robert Jaulin (1967), which plays a privileged role in Baudrillard's thinking in this context (see esp. Genosko 1998: 29, 31–3), 'young initiates … are given and returned' between 'the living adults and the dead ancestors' (SED 134). First, 'the ancestral group "swallows …" … [the] young initiation candidates'. The candidates, crucially, thus 'die "*symbolically*" in order to be reborn… [T]he grand priests … put … the initiates … to death, … the latter are … consumed by their ancestors'. Subsequently,

> the earth gives birth to them as their mother had given birth to them. After having been 'killed', the initiates are left in the hands of their initiatory, 'cultural' parents, who instruct them, care for them and train them (initiatory birth).

The candidates' 'death' triggers a continuous 'play of responses' in which – and this is key – death and life can be ritually given and taken away, so that 'death can no longer establish itself as end …' (SED 131–2, see also 135–7; Genosko 1998: 31–2, 2006; Pawlett 2007: 60).

Indeed, according to Baudrillard these groups conduct exchanges with the dead such that the dead themselves exist as partners in exchange. In the above ritual, the 'death' of the young initiates 'becomes the stakes of a reciprocal-antagonistic exchange between the ancestors and the living'; it installs 'a social relation' which connects the living and the ancestors and in which they are 'partners' (SED 131; see also Genosko 1998: 20–1, 31, 2006; Tierney 1997: 63).

'Initiation lies at the basis of alliances amongst the living and the dead' (SED 134). Jaulin (1967: 245) describes a further occasion on which a husband, through an offering of a portion of meat, 'gives his wife to a dead member of the family', so that the dead man becomes alive again (SED 131). Through 'the nourishment [*la nourriture*], this dead man is included in the life of the group' (SED 131, trsl. modified).[3] In groups such as the Sara, 'the dead are there, different but lifelike [*vivants*] and partners of the living [*vivants*] in multiple exchanges' (SED 127–8, trsl. modified, see also 141–2; Butterfield 2002).[4] Baudrillard also draws upon Maurice Leenhardt's study of the Kanak people here (for more detailed remarks, see Pawlett 2007: 57–8). They, notes Baudrillard (citing Leenhardt, in fact; see Baudrillard 1976: 207n2), do 'not mistake the idea of death for that of nothingness' (SED 189n12).[5] In groups such as the Sara, a dead person can, insofar as the members of the group exchange with her or him, become a partner within the group and thus exist.[6]

Against nature

Whilst Baudrillard does not aim to explain practices of this kind, his work contains a hint at their context. In 'natural death', in 'decomposition', the 'flesh', he argues, stops being 'a sign', the dead body is losing 'its social force of signification' (SED 180; see also Pawlett 2007: 61). One can perhaps most readily imagine this process when thinking of a decomposing face's loss of countenance or the corpse's loss of posture. In Pawlett's formulation, 'putrefaction' is here but 'a formless squalor of signs signifying nothing' (2007: 61). During this precarious period, a 'group' comes to experience 'the terror of its own symbolic decomposition', of its impending inability to exchange signs, converse, and maintain its internal relationships (SED 180). In response to this terrifying experience, the group engages in 'thanatopraxis' (SED 181; Pawlett 2007: 61). This word, which has no entry in the *Oxford English Dictionary*, translates Baudrillard's 'thanatopraxie' (Baudrillard 1976: 274). *Larousse* defines 'thanatopraxie' as a '[m]ethod that permits to delay as long as possible the decomposition of the corpse by embalmment techniques' (s.v.). Leenhardt, notes Pawlett, reports that the Kanak people in fact 'hasten the decomposition of the corpse by the sprinkling of water over it, and obscure the signs of decomposition by embalming' (Pawlett 2007: 61). What is important is Baudrillard's suggestion that every social formation's 'thanatopraxis' can be connected to its urge to deflect the 'loss of signs that befalls the dead' (SED 181; Pawlett 2007: 61). In savage societies specifically, the living 'showe[r] the dead with signs'. This is to ensure their speedy move on to 'the *status* [*statut*] of death', to give 'the dead their difference' (SED 181, trsl. modified, emphasis added; see also Pawlett 2007: 61–2). The dead are thus retrieved from nature and decay, placed into a social position, and enabled once more 'to become partners and exchange their signs' (SED 181; see also Pawlett 2007: 62). The group's ability to converse and connect remains intact. Baudrillard also points to Palermo's famous catacombs, whose passageways are populated with 'disinterred corpses, meticulously fossilised ..., with skin, hair and nails' (SED 181). The bodies, he remarks, are clad – some in basic 'wrap', others 'in costume' – and hold a whole variety 'of attitudes – sardonic, languid, heads bent, fierce or timid' (SED 181–2). In the past, family and friends frequently visited this place 'to see their dead, ... acknowledge them, show them to their children ...' (SED 182; see also Tierney 1997: 63). Their 'society', too, was still able to converse, indeed 'associat[e] with [*frayer avec*]' its 'dead' (SED 182, trsl. modified).

Baudrillard's considerations are also clarified by his contention that the groups at issue here 'have no biological concept of death'. For these people, he holds, 'the biological fact' of 'death, birth or disease' – whatsoever 'comes from nature' and, for the members of modern society, has 'the privilege of necessity and objectivity' – is meaningless. It is that which 'cannot be symbolically exchanged'. The savages regard these as 'defunct, cosmic energies' that their collective could not master 'through exchange'. But those people, Baudrillard emphasises, 'know that death ... is a *social relation*, that its definition is social'. They see death's genuine 'materiality ... in its *form*, which is always the form of a social relation' (SED 131, see also 137; Genosko 1998: 31, 2006; Pawlett 2007: 60; Tierney 1997: 63). The initiation ritual is the installation of 'an exchange ... where there had been only a brute fact'. A 'natural' and 'irreversible death' is, Baudrillard argues, left behind for 'a death that is *given* and *received*' in exchange rituals and hence – and this is decisive – 'reversible in the social exchange, "soluble" in exchange' (SED 132, see also 147; Butterfield 2002; Genosko 1998: 29; Pawlett 2007: 60–1, 2016: 74; Wilcox 2003). Simultaneously, as those rites show, 'birth and death' cease to be in 'opposition': birth and death 'can ... be *exchanged*' for one another 'under the forms [*sous les espèces*] of symbolic reversibility' (SED 132, trsl. modified, see also 147; Pawlett 2007: 60, 62; Tierney 1997: 63).[7] In the realm of symbolic exchange, Baudrillard finds 'the reversibility of life and death'; here, death and life 'are, strictly speaking, exchanged' (PW 15–16, see also SED 159).[8]

It is worth raising two further issues in this context, although they require further clarification below. First, this 'act of exchange', this '*social relation*', that Baudrillard understands by the 'symbolic' does away with 'separated terms': with the separation between birth and death, which, as mentioned, can be ritually endowed and exchanged for each other, but also with the separation between '*soul and ... body*', for instance, or with that between '*man and nature*'. Thus, argues Baudrillard, 'the symbolic operation' finishes with '*the real*'; in other words, 'the two terms lose their reality principle' (SED 133, trsl. modified; see also Butterfield 2002; Genosko 1998: 28–9, 2006; Pawlett 2007: 60–2, 143, 2016: 35–6, 129, 133–4).

Second, Baudrillard problematises the concept of 'value' in this context. Value, he holds, moves in one direction following 'a system of equivalence'. The very notion of value, in turn, depends upon 'opposed terms between which a dialectic can then be established'. But 'in symbolic exchange the terms are reversible' – notably 'life and death', which 'are exchanged' for each other. The 'terms' are not 'separate' and do not enter into a 'dialectic', so 'the idea of value is cast into question' (PW 15). Baudrillard also comments on 'the exchange of goods' here, specifically on 'potlatch'. Potlatch involves 'a … circulation of goods … exonerated from the idea of value, a … circulation which includes … the squandering of things, but must never stop' (PW 16). What is characteristic of 'potlatch' is 'the sacrifice of value', which is tantamount to its 'negation' (PW 18). Both Baudrillard's point about reality and his point about value require elucidation with reference to his assessment of life and death in capitalism.

Life and Death in Capitalism

According to Baudrillard, a key difference between savage societies and modern, capitalist society is that the dead have been pushed ever 'further away from the group of the living'. Initially, they were shifted from the 'intimacy' of the household to 'the cemetery', which, however, was still located at the core 'of the village or town'. Within 'the new towns or the contemporary metropolises', by contrast, people make no 'provisions for the dead' anymore at all – not 'in physical space', not 'in mental space' (SED 126, trsl. modified; see also Gensoko 1998: 27; Pawlett 2007: 57). Graves expire nowadays, and the deceased are talked about ever less (SED 182). Unlike in previous societies, 'today', Baudrillard explains, '*it is not normal to be dead*'. Hence, unlike previous societies, 'we no longer know what to do with them'. What the dead are shown through being thus extradited is that they 'are no longer … worthy partners in exchange'. The dead have been excluded from 'the group's symbolic circulation'. 'From savage societies to modern societies', Baudrillard contends, 'the evolution is irreversible: little by little, *the dead cease to exist*' (SED 126, trsl. modified, see also 127–8, 142; Butterfield 2002; Genosko 1998: 20–1, 27; Pawlett 2007: 56–7, 2016: 69–70; Tierney 1997: 63–5).

Unlike primitive societies, modern society has 'de-socialised death'. That is to say, modernity supports 'the illusion of a *biological* materiality of death' (SED 131, emphasis added in accordance with the French original; see also Genosko 1998: 28–9). Today, all measures are taken to ensure a death of natural causes *qua* 'impersonal expiry of the body'. Of course, since, following the severance of all ties with the dead, 'we no longer know how to inscribe [death] into a symbolic ritual of exchange', it is unsurprising that we 'experience our death as a "real" fatality inscribed in our body' (SED 166, trsl. modified; see also Pawlett 2007: 58–9). But thanks to the aura of objectivity it is now granted, 'the physical materiality of death' downright 'paralyses us' (SED 131). The 'biological death', 'objective and punctual', is 'irreversib[le]' – though this is, Baudrillard claims, 'a modern fact of science' and 'specific to our culture' (SED 158). Today, one finds 'no reversibility' anymore, neither in respect of 'life' nor in respect of 'death'. Instead, the latter is the former's 'opposite' (PW 16; see also Butterfield 2002; Pawlett 2007: 56, 58–9, 62, 2016: 69–70; Tierney 1997: 65–7). Whereas in primitive societies, 'the *splitting* of birth and death' was 'conjure[d] away' by rituals in which they were exchanged for one another, now 'life ... is split in this way' (SED 132, trsl. modified). Thus, Baudrillard adds, 'life', too, turns into a 'biological irreversibility' in that it is destined 'to decline with the body' (SED 132). Baudrillard presents a configuration of several critical themes around these separations between birth and death and between life and death.

Reality and value

One of his most far-reaching assertions is that 'the separation of birth and death' constitutes the only basis of the very '*reality* of birth' (SED 133, trsl. modified). Likewise, 'the *reality* of life itself derives solely from the disjunction of life and death' (SED 133), and it is also this 'disjunction' that lies 'at the origin of the *reality* of death' (SED 147). Likewise, the 'reality' – the '"objectivity"', the '"materiality"' – 'of nature ... derives solely from the separation of man and nature ...'. Baudrillard speaks of the '*effect of the real*' and understands it as nothing but 'the structural effect of the disjunction between two terms'; and he conceives of 'our famous reality principle' as nothing but the 'generalisation of this disjunctive code to all levels' (SED 133; see also Butterfield 2002; Genosko 1998: 28, 2006; Pawlett 2007: 58–61). By contrast, where one term can be socially exchanged for another that is not its equivalent, such as death for life, the reality – the non-negotiable '"thing-ness"' (Pawlett 2016: 36, see also 133–4) – of both is in question. The life/death separation, Baudrillard emphasises, is the original model of 'all the disjunctions' underpinning the various 'structures of the real' (SED 133; see also Genosko 1998: 28; Pawlett 2007: 56).

Moreover, Baudrillard describes the current 'system' as one 'of values': in this system 'what is positive is on the side of life, what is negative is on the side of death'; in it, life and death are not reversible; in it, 'death' constitutes the 'opposite' and 'the end of life' (PW 16, see also SED 147; Butterfield 2002; Pawlett 2007: 56, 58–9, 62, 2016: 69, 106; Tierney 1997: 65–7). It is, Baudrillard specifies again, the life no longer exchanged for death, the 'life' from which 'death' has been 'removed [ôtée]', the '*residual* life', that 'can', henceforth, 'be read in the operational terms of calculation and value' (SED 130, trsl. modified). Within the modern capitalist 'system', not only does 'life' have '"reality"', it is also, in fact, 'live[d] ... as a positive value' (SED 133; see also Wilcox 2003).

Death power

In comparatively brief passages roughly contemporaneous with Foucault's development of his distinction between the right of death and biopower (*biopouvoir*) (Foucault 1976) (see Chapter 7 of this book), Baudrillard outlines what he, giving it this English name, calls '*Death Power*' (SED 129; 1976: 200). The initial 'point of emergence of social control', Baudrillard claims, can be located in the breaking apart of 'the union of the living and the dead' and thus in the interruption of 'the exchange of life and death'. In other words, it can be located in the extraction of 'life from death' and in the imposition of 'a prohibition on death and the dead'. 'Power' installs itself exactly on this barrier separating death from life. The power of 'the castes of priests', in particular, fed on their 'exclusive control over relations with the dead' (SED 130, trsl. modified; see also Genosko 1998: 27–8; Pawlett 2007: 56–8) and on their monopoly upon 'manag[ing] ... the imaginary sphere of death' (SED 144, see also 127–9). But ultimately, says Baudrillard, all 'power' is founded 'on the manipulation and administration of death' (SED 130; see also Pawlett 2007: 64; Tierney 1997: 64). 'The power of the State' of modernity simply rests on its 'management *of life as the objective afterlife* [Baudrillard plays on the French term *survie* here, which also translates as *survival*]' (SED 144).

Economy of life

Finally, Baudrillard outlines the theme of political economy in this context. According to Baudrillard, 'the Church' initially implemented 'a *political economy of individual salvation*', which would eventually turn on 'the accumulation of works and merits', in particular. In this arrangement, 'the Kingdom' came to be situated beyond 'death', whilst death was now faced by each person alone, rather than communally. From the 1500s onwards, Baudrillard elaborates, Protestantism, for instance through dismantling 'collective ceremonials', was advancing the isolated person's 'anguish of death' (SED 145). More importantly perhaps, Protestantism, as Baudrillard adds with reference to Max Weber's (2001) famous sociological analysis of the protestant ethic, set in motion an 'immense modern enterprise of staving off death: the ethics of accumulation and material production, sacralisation through investment, labour, and profit, which one commonly calls the "spirit of capitalism" ...'. From 'this salvation-machine ...', Baudrillard concedes, 'intra-worldly ascesis is little by little withdrawn in the interests of worldly and productive accumulation'. Yet 'the aim' remains the same: 'the protection against death' (SED 145–6, trsl. modified; see also Palwett 2016: 69).

Traditional 'communities' having been dissolved, 'death', continues Baudrillard, is not 'divided' (SED 146) or shared – 'se partage' (1976: 224) – anymore. Death begins to reflect the properties of 'material goods' (SED 146). These goods, however, 'circulate ever less, as in previous exchanges, between inseparable partners' (SED 146, trsl. modified). Instead, they circulate 'increasingly', as is characteristic of capitalism, 'under the sign of a general equivalent', that is, ultimately, money. And just like, in capitalism, everybody stands 'alone before the general equivalent', everybody stands 'alone before death' (SED 146). Soon, the urge to eliminate 'death' by way of 'accumulation' – by accumulating value, notably 'time as value', and thus by pushing 'death' to the end 'of a linear infinity of value' – begins to operate as an essential component in the engine 'of the rationality of political economy' (SED 146–7; see also Butterfield 2002; Tierney 1997: 68).

> Even those who no longer believe in a personal eternity believe in the infinity of time as they do in a species-capital of double-compound interests. It is the infinity of capital that passes into the infinity of time, the eternity of a productive system which no longer knows the reversibility of gift-exchange, but only the irreversibility of quantitative growth. (SED 146, trsl. modified)[9]

Baudrillard sees similarly stark commonalities between the function of Christianity's 'ascesis' and the 'paradoxical logic' of contemporary 'security'. In ascesis, an 'accumulation of suffering and penitence' was to constitute 'a protective sarcophagus against hell'. Today's obsession with 'security' involves 'an anticipation of death in life itself'; life proceeds as though in a 'sarcophagus' behind 'protection' after 'protection', 'defence' after 'defence', as death lurks behind every corner of life (SED 178). Life turns into a 'book-keeping ... on survival', an accountancy of time gained, which has replaced 'the radical compatibility of life and death' under symbolic exchange (SED 178–9). With the termination of 'the *ambivalence* of life and death', of the latter's 'symbolic *reversibility*', not only does life turn into value, as already mentioned, but also begins 'a process of accumulation of life as *value*' (SED 147, emphasis added on reversibility in accordance with the French original).

Today, 'death' is unidimensional, merely 'the end of the biological journey', as though, sighs Baudrillard, 'a tyre' were deflating. Life is now a 'quantity'; 'death' is 'nothing' (SED 163–4; see also Pawlett 2007: 58, 63). A dead person has nothing left 'to exchange'. They simply vanish from the scene (SED 164).

The Breach of Suicide

According to Baudrillard, it is only when 'life' becomes 'life-capital', that is, becomes 'a quantitative evaluation', as 'living' turns into 'accumulation', that 'a biomedical science and technology' of life extension emerge. Crucially, this new ability to make 'the limits of life' retreat gives rise to the conception of a '"natural" death'. Here, a natural death means simultaneously a '"normal"' death, a death arriving '"at life's proper term"', a 'death ... subject to science' – to its capabilities at the present moment in time – and a death destined, ultimately, 'to be exterminated by science'. As though every individual had a '"normal expectancy" of life' and a '"contract of life"', each ought to be able to get to the end of his or her 'biological "capital"', to enjoy life "to the end" without violence or premature death' (SED 162, trsl. modified; see also Butterfield 2002; Pawlett 2007: 62–3; Tierney 1997: 67–8, 70, 76n19). Increasingly, 'society', deploying its scientific and technological means, is 'responsible' for every person's 'death'. But living to their 'natural death' is equally 'a *duty*' of every individual. Any death deviant from this 'natural' and simultaneously socially controlled death constitutes 'a *social* scandal' (SED 162; see also Pawlett 2007: 55, 64, 66, 2016: 70, 128). Whereas the savages' arrangements were such that death was 'given and received', in other words 'socialised through exchange', current arrangements are such 'that death is never done to anybody by *some-one* else, but only by "nature"' under social surveillance (SED 166, see also 1976: 253).

What is thus of vital importance is that people's lives and deaths not be 'freely theirs'. In fact, death should not be prone 'to biological chance' either. All 'life and death' is to come under 'social control'. This objective reveals itself, for instance, in the maintenance, assisted by very expensive health technologies, 'of life as value'. But it is also manifest in the 'economic choice' to let a certain percentage of sufferers from a particular illness die (SED 174, trsl. modified; see also Genosko 2006; Pawlett 2007: 55, 64, 66; Tierney 1997: 68–9, 71–2). To illustrate his point, Baudrillard also cites an ad for seatbelts (SED 177) with the telling phrase '"Bouclez-la"' (Baudrillard 1976: 269), whose double meaning is similar to that of the English instruction '"Belt up"' (SED 177). 'Security', he argues, 'is another form of social control'. People must be deprived 'of the last possibility of *giving* themselves their own death' (SED 177).

In this context, Baudrillard draws attention to suicide.[10] In a passage written many years after *Symbolic Exchange and Death*, he describes 'suicide' as nothing less than 'the only political act worthy of the name' (IELP 131). *Symbolic Exchange and Death* offers several considerations in support of this contention. Insofar as any 'system' is comprehensively beaten simply by the inability to achieve 'total perfection', that is, as soon as the least thing eludes 'its rationality', every 'suicide' causes a tiny yet 'inexpiable breach' in a system of social death regulation. In short, 'in a highly integrated system', 'every suicide becomes subversive' (SED 175–6; see also Genosko 2006; Pawlett 2007: 64–5; Tierney 1997: 70–1).

Today, Baudrillard adds, every person constitutes 'a parcel of capital'. According to the contemporary 'law of value', people have no 'right to remove any capital or value' (SED 175). Consequently, they have 'no right' to self-destruction (SED 175–6). The 'suicide', who obliterates the bundle of 'capital' she or he disposes of, thereby 'revolts', namely against that very 'orthodoxy of value': taking one's life 'in a society saturated by the law of value' poses 'a challenge to its fundamental rule' (SED 176; see also Genosko 2006; Pawlett 2007: 65).

The contemporary 'system', Baudrillard sums up, 'exhorts one to live [*somme de vivre*] and capitalise life'. It is a tightly 'regulated' sphere – a sphere, he remarks, 'of realised death'. In it, the sole 'temptation is to normalise everything by destruction'. And to Baudrillard 'resistance' is becoming noticeable. This resistance is directed against the precept 'of accumulation, production and conservation' of the human being, wherein she or he is facing her or his already 'programmed death'. Suicide thus becomes a form of 'death ... played off against death' (SED 177, trsl. modified; see also Pawlett 2007: 65–6).

Baudrillard's formulations regarding the political, subversive quality of suicide would yet prove highly prescient.

PART 2: THE SOCIAL RELATIONS OF TERRORISM

Contemporary capitalism, Baudrillard diagnoses, supports vast endeavours of 'archiving the entire world' (SED 185, trsl. modified). The aim of these endeavours, he claims, is the world's being 'discovered by some future civilisation' (SED 185). In Baudrillard's view, 'political economy' itself is established with the intention of being 'recognised as immortal' by a society yet to come (SED 185–6). In fact, he points to 'the hieroglyphic schemes' of Paris's La Défense district and, not long after its 1973 opening, New York's World Trade Center – alongside the media's 'great informational schemes', for instance – to suggest that today's 'humanity' is already 'an object of contemplation to itself' (SED 186).[11] The entire 'system of political economy' is now a 'finality without end', an 'aesthetic vertigo of productivity'; and 'with its gigantic towers, its satellites, its giant computers …', the system 'double[s] itself as signs' (SED 186). Understandably, the attack on the World Trade Center in 2001 immediately drew Baudrillard's sustained attention. For Baudrillard, contemporary terrorism is – and September 11, in particular, was – a conspicuous scene in which not only the problem of life and death but the problem of the social relations of life and death can be analysed further.

Towering Twins

In the aftermath of 9/11, during a philosophical discussion concerning the Manhattan atrocities, Baudrillard presented a 'Requiem for the Twin Towers' of the World Trade Center (ST 35–48). The piece draws heavily on – almost replicating – several formulations published a quarter-century earlier in *Symbolic Exchange and Death*.[12] The latter book reports Baudrillard's observation that New York City has, by dint of its architecture, always 'retraced … the contemporary form of the system of capital' (SED 69, trsl. modified, see also ST 40). When capitalism was still 'competitive', it was delineated by a skyline drawn by 'great buildings … confront[ing] each other in a *competitive* verticality' (SED 69, see also ST 38). Generally, every skyscraper has been exceeded by another, thus constituting an 'original moment of a system continually surpassing itself' (SED 70; see also Genosko 2006). In the 1970s, however, structures began to 'stand next to one another, without challenging each other any longer, like the columns of a statistical graph' (SED 69, trsl. modified). They embody a social 'system' that has become 'digital and countable', in which 'competition' has given way to 'networks and monopoly' (ST 38–9, see also SED 69). The Twin Towers, in particular, were 'identical', which '*signifies* the end of all competition' and 'of every original reference' (SED 69, see also ST 39; Genosko 2006). Each tower was its twin's 'model';

disregarding all other structures, they did not 'compare themselves to' and 'challenge' those others anymore (SED 70, see also ST 39–40). The towers indicated that a 'strategy of the model' rather than one 'of competition' would be dominant at the system's core (SED 70). What was hit in New York on that cloudless September morning in 2001, says Baudrillard, was 'the brain … of the system' (ST 41).

The Twin Towers, Baudrillard points out, were not only a material, but also, and more importantly, 'a symbolic object' (ST 43) – 'symbolic in the weak sense', to be sure, yet 'symbolic' still (ST 43n3). They symbolised 'financial power and global economic liberalism'. They 'were the emblem of [global] power' (ST 43–4, see also 47) and, 'in their very twinness', the consummate 'embodiments' of a world 'order' that, by the turn of the millennium, had become 'definitive' (ST 6; see also Butterfield 2002; Genosko 2006; Pawlett 2007: 144–5, 2016: 130). The hijackers, Baudrillard holds, pointed the aeroplanes specifically at 'the symbolic object' (ST 44). They demolished a highly 'prestigious' edifice – in fact, as he will shortly be shown to argue, 'a whole (Western) value-system and a world order' were wrecked along with it (ST 37; see also Pawlett 2007: 143–5, 2016: 129–30).

Globalisation and Terrorism

To make this explicit, Baudrillard sees the devastation of the World Trade Center on 9/11 as part of a 'violent protest against' the 'violence of globalization' (ST 41; see also Merrin 2005: 104, 112). 'Current terrorism …', he emphasises, 'is contemporaneous with globalization' (ST 87; see also Merrin 2005: 103–4, 111–12). The West has been fond of presenting specifically modern 'Western' creations – for instance 'human rights' or 'freedoms' or 'democracy' – as 'universal', as in harmony with 'all cultures and their difference' (PX 11–12, see also SO 155, ST 87–8). For a time, those values were proclaimed 'as mediating values' and, Baudrillard acknowledges, were somewhat successful at 'integrating singularities, as differences, into a universal culture of difference' (ST 91, see also PX 14, SO 158; Merrin 2005: 104).[13] However, the 'promotion' of a 'value … to universality' is perilous: 'universalization' has come to involve an 'indefinite extension' of 'values' that entails their 'neutralization'; the 'expansion' of 'human rights' or 'democracy' matches 'their weakest definition', warns Baudrillard (PX 12, see also SO 156, ST 88–9, 97–8).

From his perspective, it is actually 'the market' – the constant movement of capital and 'promiscuity of … all products' – as well as 'the promiscuity of all signs and … values' that are being 'globalized' (PX 12, see also SO 156, ST 89–90). The 'universal values' are increasingly illegitimate (ST 91, see also PX 14, SO 158). A now victorious 'globalization' removes 'values' as well as 'differences' (ST 91, see also PX 14, SO 158; Merrin 2005: 104).[14] Thus putatively 'universal values' are not able to fulfil their integrative role anymore. In the end, an omnipotent 'global technostructure' on the one hand confronts 'singularities' – which have been 'returned to the wild' – on the other (ST 91, see also PX 14, SO 158–9; Merrin 2005: 104). Indeed, the occident of today seeks to impose the 'law of equivalence' upon the various 'cultures' (ST 97). Global capitalism 'hounds out any form of … singularity' (ST 94; see also Merrin 2005: 104, 112). For such 'singular forms', the sole options are 're-enter … or … disappear' (ST 97).[15] Vis-à-vis globalisation's simultaneously 'homogenizing' and 'dissolving power', in turn, 'heterogeneous forces' are rebelling around the world (ST 94, see also PX 15, SO 159; Butterfield 2002; Merrin 2005: 103–4, 111–12). Baudrillard sees here 'a rejection' of both 'the global technostructure' and 'the mental structure of equivalence of all cultures' (ST 95, see also PX 13–14, SO 157–8).[16] In fact, he deems 'singularities' able to frustrate 'the system' and its 'single-track thinking'. They can be 'subtle', for instance in 'art', but also 'violent', as, precisely, in the case of 'terrorism' (ST 96). Terrorism wreaks vengeance for 'all the singular cultures' that have vanished so the 'single global power' could be installed (ST 97, see also 9; Merrin 2005: 103; Pawlett 2007: 144, 2016: 130).

Humiliation and Terrorism

Yet Baudrillard unequivocally rejects any notion of 'a clash of civilizations or religions' (ST 11, see also 73, 97; Merrin 2005: 103; Pawlett 2007: 144, 2016: 130). For one thing, one might, he says, rather 'speak of … the Fourth' – and, to be exact, the first truly worldwide – 'World War' (ST 11). The near all-encompassing 'single world order' is forced to tackle 'antagonistic forces', rebellious 'singularities', everywhere, including in its very midst (ST 12; see also Merrin 2005: 103–4, 112). Baudrillard insists that no 'world order' could avoid such conflicts: 'if Islam dominated the world, terrorism would rise against Islam' (ST 12). For another thing, this 'confrontation', whereby an equalising 'universal culture' and phenomena that still preserve elements of 'irreducible alterity' come to blows, is, he argues, 'almost anthropological' (ST 97). The latter adjective deserves underlining, for it simultaneously points to a dimension of globalisation and terrorism from which a further issue already thematised in *Symbolic Exchange and Death* resurfaces.

In *Passwords*, which was published shortly before the Manhattan attacks, Baudrillard calls into question the anthropological approach to 'potlatch', the narrow focus on its operation 'in primitive societies', and the idea that 'we are totally in market societies'. Suggesting that contemporary social relations, too, might call for an anthropological perspective, he confesses his readiness 'to believe … that … things are decided', now as ever, in the realm of 'symbolic exchange'. What Baudrillard emphasises here is that the specific 'form' of the 'challenge, of one-upmanship, of potlatch' continues to be 'fundamental' (PW 17–18; see also Merrin 2005: 104–5; Pawlett 2007: 55, 145, 2016: 131).

Correspondingly, Baudrillard holds that the antagonism that came to a head on 9/11 cannot be grasped without paying close attention to the problem of 'symbolic obligation' (ST 100). For in Baudrillard's eyes 'terrorism rests' to a great extent 'on the despair of the humiliated and insulted' (ST 104). Everyone else's 'hatred of the West', he claims, is fuelled not by 'deprivation and exploitation' but by the 'humiliation' they have suffered. They have suffered this humiliation, crucially, as the West has 'given' them 'everything', and they cannot return it (ST 100, see also 6; Merrin 2005: 104–5; Pawlett 2007: 140). And not only they: Baudrillard considers ours a similar position of 'always receiving' – possibly anything at all – 'through a technical system of generalized exchange and general gratification' (ST 102; see also Genosko 1998: 22–4; Merrin 2005: 105). Whereas the 'God' or 'nature' of previous societies could be presented with something in return, notably through 'sacrifice', in 'our culture' any 'counter-gift' has become 'impossible'. Making 'reciprocation' impossible – and this, again, is decisive – constitutes the foundation 'of all domination'. For Baudrillard, a 'unilateral gift' amounts to 'an act of power' (ST 101–2; see also Genosko 1998: 22–4, 2006; Pawlett 2007: 66). Experiencing such 'saturation' and 'protected', our Western 'existence' is simultaneously 'captive' (ST 103). An 'abreaction' to it, be it as 'open violence', including terrorist acts, be it as the 'self-hatred and remorse' we feel, is, Baudrillard claims, unavoidable (ST 103; see also Merrin 2005: 105). Everybody is averse 'to *any* definitive power' (ST 6, emphasis added) – 'they *did it*, but we *wished for* it' (ST 5; see also Butterfield 2002; Merrin 2005: 103; Pawlett 2007: 143–4, 2016: 34, 106–7, 129–30).

Terrorism and Its Ramifications

In Baudrillard's view, on September 11 the global system was not merely attacked, but hit hard. He points to several reasons for this. First of all, to the extent that 'the system' constitutes a 'single network', inflicting damage at even just one 'point' amounts to harming the whole system. Thus, a small number of 'suicide attackers', by striking but two sites, '… unleashed a global catastrophic process' (ST 8). More specifically, and crucially, they did so 'thanks to the absolute weapon of death, enhanced by technological efficiency' (ST 8; see also Merrin 2005: 103–4; Pawlett 2007: 143–4, 2016: 129–30). On the one hand, notes Baudrillard, 'the terrorists' have access to, and are using, 'weapons that are the system's own' (ST 20), such as 'stock-market speculation' and various technologies, to attack it (ST 19, see also 23, 27; Genosko 2006). On the other hand, what ultimately lends the attackers their 'superiority' is their successful deployment of those 'modern resources' together with a further, 'highly symbolic weapon', namely 'their own deaths' (ST 20–1; see also Butterfield 2002; Merrin 2005: 103–4; Pawlett 2007: 143–4, 2016: 129–30). Baudrillard, as is well known, had pinpointed the scandalous, subversive, rebellious quality of suicide as early as the 1970s (see e.g. Genosko 1998: 6, 21, 2006; Pawlett 2007: 64–6; see also above). The 9/11 attackers, using 'their own deaths' both 'offensive[ly]' (ST 16) and in conjunction with the weaponry of 'the system' under attack, rendered their suicides truly damaging (ST 20–1; see also Merrin 2005: 103–4).[17] Amidst Baudrillard's considerations of this attack and its ramifications, his spotlight on the symbolic sphere is once more vital.

Terrorism's symbolic relationship

Nothing is more damaging 'for global power', Baudrillard holds, than being 'humiliated'. Yet this is just what happened. Whilst the West had been humiliating the rest of the world throughout the late twentieth century, global power 'was humiliated' at the beginning of the twenty-first – and in a very similar fashion: the hijackers 'inflicted something on it ... that it cannot return'. Here, 'global power was defeated symbolically' (ST 101; see also Merrin 2005: 105–6; Pawlett 2007: 146). The 'excess of power' of the 'system', Baudrillard concedes, 'poses an insoluble challenge', but 'the terrorists respond with a definitive act ... not susceptible of exchange' either (ST 9). The New York attacks were a 'symbolic challenge' (ST 12; see also Butterfield 2002; Merrin 2005: 103–4, 106, 163n2; Wilcox 2003).

The objective behind terrorism, elaborates Baudrillard, is 'to radicalize the world by sacrifice' (ST 10). It is decisive within the terrorist act that the attackers throw 'their own deaths' at the 'system' to attack it. This 'system', as already indicated with reference to *Symbolic Exchange and Death*, adheres to 'an ideal of zero deaths'. This entails, of course, that attacks such as those in 2001 are intolerable to it (ST 16; see also Genosko 2006; Merrin 2005: 103–4; Pawlett 2007: 136–7, 2016: 106–7, 127–8). And indeed, the West is deploying 'means of deterrence and destruction' in response – although, since the West's adversaries are manifestly '"... as eager to die as the Americans are to live ..."', these measures appear trivial (ST 16).

Yet Baudrillard also draws attention to a further and, it seems, graver problem. The hijackers successfully moved the confrontation 'into the symbolic sphere'. What was important on the morning of 9/11 was the incursion not simply 'of death in real time ... but ... of ... a death which [was] symbolic and sacrificial'. Baudrillard goes as far as to suggest that on that day 'the system' was challenged or provoked 'by a gift'. Within the symbolic realm, crucially, a strict 'rule' applies, namely a rule 'of challenge, reversion and outbidding'. As a consequence of this, the only possible response by 'the system' is reciprocation, which is to say, 'its own death and ... collapse'. On Baudrillard's reading, the 'terrorist hypothesis' is precisely this: 'the system ... will commit suicide in response to the multiple challenges posed by deaths and suicides' (ST 16–17; see also Butterfield 2002; Genosko 1998: 6, 12–13, 22–3, 25–7, 2006; Merrin 2005: 103–4; Pawlett 2007: 64–6, 145, 2016: 36–7, 106–7, 130–1; Wilcox 2003).

However, in capitalist society, to repeat, 'death' is basically 'forbidden' (ST 94). The 'system' absolutely 'cannot exert' the 'symbolic violence ... of its own death' (ST 18). According to Western society's 'values', the terrorists' introduction of their 'own death into the game' constitutes 'cheating' (ST 23, see also 19). The West pursues a '"zero-death" strategy', that of a '"clean" technological war', which is no suitable response (ST 21; see also Genosko 2006; Merrin 2005: 83–4, 106–7, 112). Having obliterated this 'from its own culture', global power has not the slightest notion of 'the terrain of the symbolic challenge and death' anymore and can no longer act on that level (ST 15; see also Merrin 2005: 103–4; Pawlett 2007: 145–6, 2016: 130–1; Wilcox 2003). When, in the aftermath of 9/11, the United States were commencing military operations in Afghanistan, Baudrillard sensed that their goal would be simply to 'liquidat[e]' an 'invisible' 'target' (ST 26; see also Butterfield 2002; Merrin 2005: 83–5, 103–4; Pawlett 2007: 142–3, 146). Yet the terrorists' attacks, which require their 'death', do not follow an exclusively 'destructive logic'; they rather form part of a 'challenge', a 'duel', a 'personal' relationship with the opponent: the 'power' that 'humiliated you ... must be humiliated' – must 'be made to lose face' – in turn (ST 25–6; see also Genosko 2006; Pawlett 2007: 142–4, 2016: 130). In the end, the West's answer to the terrorists' 'challenge' remained inferior. Neither 'bombing' the opponent 'to smithereens' nor caging them 'like a dog at Guantánamo', Baudrillard insists, will do. The West was bitterly 'humiliated' and fell short of 'humiliating the other' in response (ST 101; see also Butterfield 2002; Merrin 2005: 106–7).

The system's escalation

Still, 'the system and power' cannot extricate themselves from the 'symbolic obligation', and it is with this obligation that Baudrillard associates 'the only *chance* of their catastrophe' (ST 18, trsl. modified, emphasis added; see also Genosko 1998: 22–3, 2006; Merrin 2005: 26; Pawlett 2007: 64–5, 145, 2016: 37, 107, 131; Wilcox 2003).[18] In a remark in his late 1970s essay '... Or, the end of the social', Baudrillard describes the 'position' of a 'protagonist of defiance' (SM 70) or of the challenge – 'défi' in the original (1982a: 73) – as 'suicidal' (SM 70). By dint of 'the destruction of value', namely her or his 'own', the protagonist compels the recipient of the challenge to issue 'a never equivalent, ever escalating response' (SM 70; see also Pawlett 2007: 135–6, 2016: 44). In his closely related considerations of the German Autumn of 1977 – the hijacking of the Lufthansa airliner *Landshut*, which ended in Mogadishu with the pilot and most of the hijackers dead, and the deaths of members of the Red Army Faction at Stammheim prison shortly afterwards – Baudrillard describes 'the death of the terrorists (or of the hostages)' as an 'abolition of value' (SM 120). This brief text supports key components of his analysis of 9/11 (ST). Referring to the latter event, Baudrillard identifies a 'vertiginous cycle' in which the 'exchange of death' is 'impossible' (ST 18, see also SM 122). Within it, argues Baudrillard, as Merrin (2005: 104, see also 163n2; Wilcox 2003), too, has highlighted, the terrorists' 'death', though a minute 'point', generates a massive 'suction ... Around this tiny point the whole system of the real and of power [*la puissance*] gathers' (ST 18, see also SM 120). It contracts or cramps momentarily (ST 18; SM 120), then activates 'all its anti-bodies' (SM 120), and, crucially, ultimately 'perishes by its own hyperefficiency'. The terrorists seek to provoke 'an excess of reality, and have the system collapse' underneath (ST 18, see also SM 120; Merrin 2005: 163n2; Wilcox 2003).

According to Baudrillard, Merrin continues, the terrorists' assault 'provokes a hyperreaction and reversal of the system, leading it to introduce the same repressive security measures as fundamentalist societies' (2005: 104, see also 163n2). Still drawing on his considerations of the terrorist activities of 1977 (SM 113–23), Baudrillard accentuates that after 9/11 one can observe the 'repression of terrorism ru[n] along the same unpredictable spiral as the terrorist act'. For Baudrillard, such 'unleashing of reversibility' constitutes the terrorists' 'true victory' (ST 31, trsl. modified, see also SM 115–16; Merrin 2005: 163n2; Pawlett 2007: 136–7). It can be seen in several of their attack's 'ramifications': in various recessions (ST 31; see also Wilcox 2003) and, most strikingly to Baudrillard, 'in the slump' (ST 32) – 'récession' in the original text (Baudrillard 2001) – 'in the value-system, ... the ... ideology of freedom, of free circulation'; that is, in the slump in the very ideology of which the West, as mentioned, has been availing itself for influencing 'the rest of the world'. What can be witnessed after September 11 is the realisation of 'liberal globalization' as, conversely, the institution of 'total control', the 'terror' of security, the 'maximum' level 'of constraints and restrictions' (ST 32; see also Butterfield 2002).

Collapsing Twins

In his 'Requiem' for the World Trade Center structures, Baudrillard once more reports his observation that New York's architecture has been delineating 'the present form of the system and ... its ... developments' with remarkable precision (ST 40). This observation leads him to read the Twin Towers' 'collapse' as an early indication of the eventual 'disappearance ... of the world system' such structures have embodied (ST 40–1). As he has just been shown to argue, on September 11 that system was, for various reasons, struck severely. Notably, shortly after the attack Baudrillard was already able to highlight the ensuing slump in the ideology of free circulation. As he reiterates in 'Hypotheses on terrorism' (ST 51–83), the attackers' triumph is their having aroused an 'obsession with security' in the Western world that amounts but to 'a veiled form of perpetual terror' (ST 81; see also Merrin 2005: 104, 163n2; Pawlett 2016: 107).

Simultaneously, the propositions in 'Requiem' resonate also with another point addressed earlier. Baudrillard treats the Twin Towers' 'collapse' as 'the major symbolic event'. It is evidence of the 'fragility of global power' (ST 43). In Baudrillard's eyes, as Genosko (2006), in particular, has emphasised, the towers in fact 'collapse[d] themselves'; their collapse 'resembles a suicide' (ST 43, see also 7–8; Merrin 2005: 103; Pawlett 2007: 145, 2016: 131). It was as if, Baudrillard specifies, the 'system, by its *internal* fragility', partook in 'its own liquidation', in 'terrorism' (ST 45, emphasis added, see also 7–8; Genosko 2006). In 'Hypotheses', Baudrillard provides the diagnosis of

> a society's obscure predisposition to contribute to its own doom – as illustrated by the high-level dissensions between the CIA and FBI which, by reciprocally neutralizing information, gave the terrorists the unprecedented chance to succeed. (ST 79)

Moreover, and consistent with one of the aforementioned claims, 'Hypotheses' not only classes the attackers' 'strategy of ... overturning power' among the consequences of the 'unacceptability of that global power', but also accentuates that both 'Islamist' extremists and others ('we') alike meet the 'global order' with 'rejection' (ST 73–4). According to 'Requiem' again, when 'the power of power' grows, so, inevitably, does 'the will to destroy it': the closer a 'system' comes to being all-powerful, 'the stronger' will be 'the rejection' – but also, and crucially, the '*internal* rejection' – it is met with (ST 45, emphasis added, see also 5–7; Genosko 2006; Merrin 2005: 103–4, 111–12).

CONCLUSION

In Baudrillard's sociological work, considerations of the social world are intertwined – possibly more closely than in any other *œuvre* discussed in this book – with considerations of life and death. This is true of his conception of societies centred on symbolic exchange relations, in which life and death are reversible and exchangeable, as well as of his critique of the capitalist system, in which life is accumulated and death staved off. In 1987, Baudrillard admitted that his distinction between these two formations disclosed a certain 'nostalgia for a symbolic order ... born out of the deep of primitive societies' (EC 80). Some of his writing may well convey nostalgia, but Baudrillard does not associate symbolic exchange exclusively with archaic or tribal societies:[19] his essays regarding the Manhattan attacks unequivocally identify expressions of the problematic of the social relations of life and death, including, crucially, the problematic of symbolic exchange, in the social relations that foment, in the acts that constitute, and in the processes that are triggered by contemporary terrorism (see also e.g. Butterfield 2002; Genosko 2006; Merrin 2005: 100–1, 113; Pawlett 2007: 55, 143–6, 2016: 33, 67, 126–31; Wilcox 2003). These phenomena still pester the global order over a decade after Baudrillard's death. Not only in this sense will his sociological inquiries into the social relations of life and death – his analyses of symbolic exchange relations no less than his account of the capitalist system – keep provoking and challenging sociologists in their critical examinations of social life in the twenty-first century.

Abbreviations

EC: *The Ecstasy of Communication* (1988)

F: *Fragments: Conversations with François L'Yvonnet* (2004)

IELP: *The Intelligence of Evil, or, The Lucidity Pact* (2013)

PW: *Passwords* (2003a)

PX: *Paroxysm: Interviews with Philippe Petit* (1998)

SED: *Symbolic Exchange and Death* (1993)

SM: *In the Shadow of the Silent Majorities or, the End of the Social and Other Essays* (1983)

SO: *Screened Out* (2002b)

ST: *The Spirit of Terrorism and Other Essays* (2003b)

Selected Further Reading

For a thorough and accessible discussion of many of the key domains of Baudrillard's social thought, including his conception of symbolic exchange and his analyses of terrorism, see Pawlett, W. (2007) *Jean Baudrillard: Against Banality*. London: Routledge.

An engaging discussion of Baudrillard's thinking with specific attention to the media is provided by Merrin, W. (2005) *Baudrillard and the Media: A Critical Introduction*. Cambridge: Polity Press.

The International Journal of Baudrillard Studies contains a wealth of articles on many aspects of Baudrillard's work. It can be accessed here: https://www2.ubishops.ca/baudrillardstudies

Notes

1 A few years before Baudrillard conducted these reflections, Tierney had asserted – somewhat less equivocally – that Baudrillard 'offers' the 'claims about symbolic exchange' in his 1970s work 'as a sort of counter-myth to the story ... moderns have been telling themselves about death ...', 'as a utopian alternative to modernity's more rigidly demarcated stance toward death', but 'not ... as historical truths', and that their 'value ... lies' more 'in their ability to reveal and challenge certain features of modernity that have gone unnoticed' and less 'in their historical veracity' (Tierney 1997: 64, see also 69, 75n16; Butterfield 2002; Wilcox 2003).

2 For wider discussions of Baudrillard's notion of symbolic exchange, see for example Pawlett (2007: 66–9, 2016: 32–7). On the influence of Baudrillard's reception of Marcel Mauss's (2002) examination of potlatch and gift exchange on that notion, see Genosko (1998: 25–7); Pawlett (2007: 49–55).

3   According to Jaulin, the 'value' of the 'nourishment ... is, like the hunger of the dead man, symbolic of participation in the exchanges of consumption goods and thus of inclusion in the life of the group ...' (Jaulin 1967: 244).

4   When '[c]annibals ...', in turn, 'eat their own dead', they do so, Baudrillard claims, '... to pay homage' to the dead. Thereby, they seek to avoid that the dead, 'left to the biological order of rotting [la pourriture], ... escape from the social order and turn against the group ... This devouring is a social act, a *symbolic* act, that aims to maintain a tissue of bonds with the dead man ...' (SED 138, trsl. modified).

5   In the realm of 'the symbolic', where 'life and death are reversible' – as in the above rituals, for instance – 'death/nothingness does not exist ...' (SED 159, trsl. modified).

6   The flipside of this, continues the note citing Leenhardt (see Baudrillard 1976: 207n2), is that 'an idea similar to our "nothingness"' might be discernible from the Kanak word '*sèri*', which 'indicates the situation of the bewitched ... man ... abandoned by his ancestors ...', someone 'in perdition, out of society', who 'feels himself non-existent ...' (SED 189n12). In Mauss's (1979) essay on the idea of death in Australia and New Zealand, Baudrillard finds the comparable observation that in such societies death in this sense is, precisely, 'being removed from the [être ôté au] cycle of symbolic exchanges' (SED 134, trsl. modified).

7   Baudrillard describes 'initiation' as a 'symbolic hyperevent', in which 'birth and death lose their status as fatal events, as necessity ...' (SED 137). A 'sacrifice', too, designates, for the savages, the rejection 'of natural and biological succession, an intervention of an initiatory order, a controlled and socially governed ... anti-natural violence' (SED 165; see also Pawlett 2007: 63).

8   Baudrillard proposes ultimately to 'extend ... symbolic exchange to [the] broader ... level of forms. So the animal form, the human form, the divine form are exchanged according to a rule of metamorphoses in which each ceases to be confined to its definition, with the human opposed to the inhuman, etc.' (PW 16).

9   But 'communism', Baudrillard adds, also seeks to end 'death', and '... in accordance with the same fantastic schema of an eternity of accumulation and of productive forces' (SED 147, trsl. modified).

10 Baudrillard places particular emphasis on 'suicide in prison', which he deems 'an act of *subverting* [détournement] institutional death and turning it against the system that imposes it': the suicide 'invert[s] the authorities' and 'condemns society' (SED 175; see also Genosko 2006; Pawlett 2007: 65, 2016: 37; Tierney 1997: 70–1).

11 Here, Baudrillard develops Walter Benjamin's famous remarks from the 1930s on '*the aestheticizing of politics, as practiced by fascism*' (Benjamin 2003: 270). Benjamin's ideas have been important for Baudrillard's work (see e.g. F 6).

12 A number of commentators have highlighted similarities between Baudrillard's earlier writings, including earlier considerations of terrorism, and his writings on the 9/11 attacks (e.g. Butterfield 2002; Genosko 2006; Merrin 2005: 102–3, 163n2; Pawlett 2007: 134, 143, 145, 2016: 129; Wilcox 2003). On those earlier considerations, see, for example, Butterfield (2002); Pawlett (2007: 134–8, 2016: 126–9); Wilcox (2003).

13 'Singularities', Sandford suggests, means 'unique or unusual identities or approaches' in this context (in Baudrillard 2002a). Baudrillard counts 'species, individuals and cultures' among them (ST 9).

14 Following the fall of the Iron Curtain, the West, Baudrillard argued in the 1990s, was sending Eastern Europe Western 'technologies and markets'; 'the global' had won at the cost of 'the disappearance of the universal' *qua* 'value system' (PX 10).

15 Writing shortly after the US–UK invasion of Afghanistan, Baudrillard added that such 'wars ... aim ... to normalize savagery, to knock all territories into alignment[,]... to quell any refractory zone, to colonize and tame all the wild spaces, whether in geographical space or in the realm of the mind' (ST 98; see also Merrin 2005: 106, 111–12).

16 In the 1990s, Baudrillard proposed that the Balkan War be seen in the context 'of globalization' (PX 18). The 'violence' in Bosnia could be understood as a manifestation of a 'surge of vital energy, like hatred, against a "cleansing" in all fields at the global level', as a 'revolt against the world order' (PX 17–18). From this angle, 'the exacerbation of national, linguistic and religious sentiment, or of a sense of identity, is a form of singular resistance' (PX 18).

17 By contrast, as 'the Palestinian suicide attacks' had illustrated over the years, when terrorists launch exclusively 'their own deaths' at 'the system', 'they ... disappear ... quickly in a useless sacrifice' (ST 20–1).

18 Genosko proposes 'to read Baudrillard's account of 9/11 in the mode of the "as though/if"': 'the twin towers collapsed by themselves as though in a response in kind to the challenge of the suicide planes'; 'it was as if they were fulfilling an obligation to return something' (Genosko 2006). Whilst such a reading cannot be attempted here, it appears that reading the following considerations of Baudrillard's in that fashion could be possible. As might become clearer in a moment, this seems to be the case particularly in view of Genosko's spotlight on a passage from *Symbolic Exchange and Death* (SED 37). In that passage, Baudrillard 'claim[s] ...', according to Genosko, 'that the so-called "system ..."... turns on itself like a scorpion when faced with the challenge of death in the form of the counter-gift. Scorpions,' Genosko notes, 'do not, however, commit suicide but, on occasion, in a frenzy of stinging, fatally immolate themselves. In other words they are not fulfilling an obligation, even though Baudrillard used this example to make precisely the opposite claim' (Genosko 2006, see also 1998: 22–3, 46–7).

19 On the question of nostalgia, see also Merrin (2005: 18, 42); Tierney (1997: 62–3, 75n10, 75n14).

9

Emerging Sociological Themes and Concerns

The preceding eight chapters have discussed a range of very different socio-theoretical *œuvres*. It would be difficult to ascertain conceptions, arguments, or elements of analyses common to all eight thinkers. By contrast, it is possible to recognise sociological themes and concerns – dealt with in various ways, of course – shared by some of the thinkers in focus. This is the case both in respect of their endeavours to examine and critically interrogate social relations, contexts, and conditions and in respect of their investigations of specific phenomena associated with living in the contemporary social world. On the basis of the foregoing discussions, some – not all – of these themes and concerns can be, if only briefly, highlighted.

PART 1: THEORISING THE CONTEMPORARY SOCIAL WORLD

Social Conditions

One question raised by some of the socio-theoretical bodies of work under discussion here is whether the social conditions of the present should be characterised as a modern or as a postmodern society. One can discern at least three different responses from those writings: the contention that contemporary society is in a radical or second phase of modernity; the view that the current social – or at least cultural – conditions are postmodern; and the suspicion that the very notion of modernity must be problematised. The different interpretations of the radically modern, postmodern, or non-modern conditions reveal much about the respective theorist's understanding of the social world of today as such and aim to contribute to sociology's wider endeavours to grasp and explain that world.

According to Giddens, present-day social conditions ought not to be described as postmodern. However, he does observe 'the emergence of ways of life and forms of social organisation' that differ from those facilitated by 'modern institutions' (CM 52). Giddens argues that people living in contemporary society are living in a radicalised, extreme version of modernity. This form of modernity, he holds, is future-oriented, reflexive, and global (CM, RW). One of the key challenges for Giddens is how people harness the problems associated with radical modernity, for example, climate change (BLR, TW). Bauman, in his writings on liquid modernity, also focuses his analysis on modern conditions. Yet he provides a detailed portrayal of two different modernities, a portrayal centred on his distinction between 'solids' and 'liquids' (LM 1–2). As shown, Bauman draws this distinction with regard to many domains of the social world. Individualisation, modernisation, and transformations in the time and space dimensions of society occupy core positions in his thinking (LM, LL).

That said, Bauman's concept of liquid modernity is comparable to the conception of postmodern society. The concept of postmodernity is, of course, deployed in Lyotard's analysis of the contemporary condition. This analysis revolves around a specific notion of language games and draws heavily on observations of developments in twentieth-century science (PC). The assertion that 'language games' are 'heteromorphous' and that the agreement on any game's 'rules' is temporally 'limited' chimes, as he himself points out, with the insight that 'the temporary contract' is increasingly commonplace in various areas of 'social interaction' (PC 66). This insight, in turn, is reconcilable with Bauman's assessment – which is, however, much more overtly critical than Lyotard's diagnosis – of social relations in liquid modernity, for instance, with his identification of those relations that are creating growing 'uncertainty' for the individual at work (LM 147; see also Campain 2008: 202–3; Poder 2008: 106).

While Giddens and Bauman scrutinise what they describe as a radical stage of, and as a liquid, modernity, Latour seeks to offer an alternative approach to the theorisation of modernity per se. Latour does not suggest – as modernists do – that the contemporary condition is a second or radical modernity. Rather he seeks to problematise the very idea that we have ever been modern (WHNBM). According to Latour, 'modernity is often defined in terms of humanism'. However, he also argues that this 'overlooks the simultaneous birth of "nonhumanity"' (WHNBM 13). The very notion of the modern is, for Latour, contradictory. Instead of occupying a radical or second modernity, we are, he states, currently entering a non-modern world 'without ever having really left it' (WHNBM 130). Haraway also argues that 'the modern' will not be 'superceded or infiltrated by the postmodern' (PM 77). Along with Latour she maintains that to believe in the existence of 'something called the modern' has always been 'a mistake'. According to Haraway, we have never been at the start or end of things; rather we are always right 'in the middle' (PM 77).

Inequality and Capital

Attempts to understand social and economic inequality are of major signifi-cance for socio-theoretical interrogations of contemporary society. The discussions of inequality in several of the works explored above thematise forms of capital. As mentioned earlier, according to Bourdieu, it is capital that 'makes the games of society – not least, the economic game – something other than simple games of chance' (FC 46). In his analysis of solid and liquid modernity, Bauman problematises the current relationship between capital and labour. In solid modernity, he argues, 'labour' 'depended' on 'capital', but capital also on labour: they were permanently bound to one another (LM 145; see also Poder 2008: 101). In liquid modernity, the 'fulfilment' of the 'capacity' to work still hinges on an investment of capital (LM 121), but the 'reproduc-tion and growth' of the latter no longer strictly on a long-term 'engagement with labour' in any specific location. Thus, those 'ties' are ever weaker (LM 149; see also Campain 2008: 202–3; Davis 2016: 66–7; Poder 2008: 106). This analysis of society, which includes, as shown, further considerations of contemporary power relationships and politics, is evidently strongly shaped by Marx's critique of political economy. Although Lyotard is highly sceptical of the potential political impetus of the class struggle – or rather, of class 'struggles' (PF 73) – today, Marx's scrutiny of the class relationship has influenced his con-ception of the system, too: the system follows the principle of '"good productivity"', an 'eminent case' of which is the 'exploitation' of labour power – the wages expended being lower than the 'value' gained – at the hands of 'capital' (PF 72).

The sociological contribution of some of the theorists whose works were discussed in this book lies not only in elucidating the role of economic capital but also in conceptualising other types of capital and incorporating these conceptions into their analyses. Bourdieu, for example, conceptualises different forms of capital, which he identifies as economic, cultural, and social, and which, when legitimated, are converted into symbolic capital and power. For Bourdieu, the distribution of cultural and economic capital is the main source of class differen-tiation in society (FC, D; Skeggs 1997: 8). Bourdieu extends his analysis to include a focus on embodied capital. The embodied nature of capital appears to underpin much of Bourdieu's work – from inheritance of cultural capital to the biological occupation of particular social and physical spaces. For Bourdieu 'embodied capital' is 'external wealth' that is then 'converted into an integral part of the person, into a habitus'. Embodied capital cannot be transmitted immedi-ately (unlike money, for example) and is often acquired unconsciously (FC 48).

Baudrillard's critical examination of contemporary society accentuates the living's suspension of symbolic exchange relationships with the dead. On the one hand, Baudrillard suggests that the multifaceted structures of social 'discrimination' of capitalist societies can be linked to the severance of social relations with, to the expulsion from society's 'symbolic circulation' of, 'the dead' (SED 126; see also e.g. Genosko 1998: 27; Pawlett 2007: 56–7, 2016: 69–70; Tierney 1997: 63–5). On the other hand, he has been shown to argue that in these conditions 'life' has become 'value' (SED 133), 'a quantitative evaluation', indeed 'life-capital' (SED 162). Human existence has become 'accumulation', and this is the setting that has given rise to the scientific and technological means of life extension (SED 162; see also 147; Butterfield 2002; Pawlett 2007: 55–9, 62–4; Tierney 1997: 65–72; Wilcox 2003). The rapid expansion of the biomedical sciences over recent decades has meant that the notion of embodied or biological capital is becoming increasingly important to contemporary sociological discussions on inequality (Webster 2007). Both Baudrillard's and Bourdieu's account were prescient in this regard.

Power

Power – its distribution, exercise, and operation – is a key topic in much contemporary sociology. Out of all the theoretical works explored in the preceding chapters, it is Foucault's *œuvre* that places the strongest emphasis on power for conceptualising social conditions. His approach to power is distinct from many prior sociological frameworks, though. This is partly because Foucault argues that power cannot be owned and that it is not something that can be acquired only by some members of, or groups in, society (SD 13–14, 29, HS1 94; Sheridan 1990: 139, 184–5, 218). To repeat, power is a relationship of unequal force, and power relations cannot exist without resistance (HS1 93–6, SD 15; Davidson 2006: xvi, xxiin9; Sheridan 1990: 139, 184–5, 218). Moreover, Foucault refuses to embed power in other dimensions of the social world. Whilst power relationships are entangled with, for example, economic relationships, they are the result of 'differentiations' in such other kinds of relationships but also their 'conditions' (HS1 94; see also SD 14; Sheridan 1990: 184, 219). Foucault's analyses of power are supported by a comprehensive set of concepts, notably by the concepts of disciplinary power, security, regulation, and government, but also by the concept of sovereign power, against which those are demarcated.

However, power is an important theme also in other writings discussed above. Drawing on Foucault's research on disciplinary power, Bauman traces a transformation in the power relationships between, *inter alia*, 'capital and labour': the period of their '*mutual engagement*' and direct 'confrontation' is coming to a close, as advances in technology are beginning to allow those who have power to exercise power without having to be in the same locality as the targets of that power (LM 10–11; see also Campain 2008: 202–3). Understood in yet another way, power is also an important dimension of the agonistic language games – in which speaking *qua* moves and countermoves amounts to fighting – at the heart of Lyotard's conception of the social (PC 10–11, 15–16; Malpas 2003: 20–3; Williams 1998: 27–30). Absolutely nobody, Lyotard insists, 'is ever entirely powerless over the messages that traverse and position' them (PC 15).

Social Relations

The concept of the social is usually positioned at the core of the discipline of sociology. Developing a conception of social relations has been central to many socio-theoretical endeavours to analyse the contemporary social world. Several of the theorists whose works were explored above problematise and extend sociology's understandings of the social. Both Latour's and Haraway's notions of the social are informed by science and technology studies. One of the distinguishing features of Haraway's social theory is her accentuation of the role of non-human actants and agents, namely animals and technology. According to Haraway, when discussing the concept of the social, social theorists tend to refer to the study of social relations and history. She, however, seeks to move away from locating the social solely in the context of human social relations (Gane and Haraway 2006: esp. 142–3). What Haraway seeks to make clear through the development of the concept of the cyborg is that one cannot attempt to theorise contemporary social conditions without grasping the relationships between humans and other, non-human forms. Latour, too, seeks to contribute an alternative socio-theoretical view to the concept of the social (RAS). Rather than seeking to use the concept of the social for developing social explanations, he focuses instead on exploring networks and associations, including those involving both humans and non-humans (RAS; de Vries 2016: 88).

Lyotard, in turn, argues that it is a conception of their linguistic dimension that – although this dimension may not exhaust the social – ought to be at the core of any attempt to analyse social relations and interactions. Once such a conception has been achieved, it becomes possible both: to rebut the claim that social relationships are disintegrating and collectivities are becoming but 'a mass of individual atoms thrown into the absurdity of Brownian motion' (PC 15), a view that has never sat particularly easily with many sociologists; and to trace current transformations of social relationships themselves, an endeavour that has been vital to the sociological discipline. What Foucault prioritises in his study of the social – also without asserting that these exhaust the social – are, as mentioned, relationships of 'power'. They crisscross in, and decisively shape, the social world (SD 24; Sheridan 1990: 139).

When discussing social relations between people, most of the socio-theoretical writings explored here and much sociology *tout court* tend to focus these discussions on relationships between the living. Through his work on symbolic exchange, Baudrillard emphatically diverges from this tendency. Sociology's understanding of social relations, he suggests, must be underpinned by a conception of the relationships between the living and the dead. In some cultures, '[s]ymbolic exchange' continues even 'when life' no longer does; that is to say, it operates not only among 'the living', but also between the latter and 'the dead' (SED 134; see also Butterfield 2002; Genosko 1998: 20–1, 31; Pawlett 2007: 57, 59). A key contribution of Baudrillard's to existing sociological perspectives of social relationships lies in this conception of symbolic exchange and of relations across the boundary of life and death. His remarks on societies centred on symbolic exchange, including exchanges *with the dead* and the exchange *of death*, may primarily evoke images of premodern social conditions. But they are, as has been underscored, of central importance to Baudrillard's critical delimitation and interrogation of contemporary social conditions, of capitalist society (see e.g. PW 15; Tierney 1997: 64, 69).

Social Change

Sociology often seeks to contribute to political debates about social transformation. Several of the theorists whose writings have been in focus above provide striking perspectives on the problem of social change. Haraway does so, for example, through the development of her concept of the cyborg, which, she argues, can be a source of inequality as well as a facilitator of social change. As mentioned earlier, the notion of the cyborg – with its possible mix of human/technology/animal – has the potential to challenge various 'dualisms' that have permeated 'Western traditions' (e.g. 'mind/body, culture/ nature, male/female') (CM 177). These dualisms, according to Haraway, have been key to the oppression of minority ethnic groups, women, nature, workers, animals etc. – to the 'domination of all constituted as others, whose task is to mirror the self' (CM 177). For Haraway, high-tech culture has the potential to challenge these dualisms in new ways (CM 177).

In contrast, Giddens develops what he calls a radical politics of the centre to address the problems posed by radical modernity (BLR, PCC, TW). A framework of radical politics should, according to Giddens, be guided by utopian realism, a critical theory 'without guarantees' (CM 155). This framework should, he says, relate to 'the four overarching dimensions of modernity' and be focused on countering poverty, environment degradation, arbitrary power, and violence (BLR 246).

Latour, in turn, seeks to break with what he refers to as the dominant 'emancipatory master narrative'. By questioning what it means to be modern, he seeks to tell a different story about our past, present, and potential future. He argues that if what it means to be modern is rethought, then the role of oppressed 'others' in history must be recast, too. They must be seen instead 'as companions in a long history that has collected humans and nonhumans in various assemblages and at various scales' (www.bruno-latour.fr/node/328). By reinterpreting the past in this way, he suggests that one would also need to rethink our future, thus potentially altering the course of change.

In the works of Baudrillard and Lyotard, the political question of social transformation is inextricable from the concept of the system. For Baudrillard, the capitalist system remains vulnerable to acts of defiance both tiny and massive. In particular, 'suicides' are 'political', and even one person's self-destruction can constitute a serious 'breach'. One of the reasons for this is that within 'a system' the failure to regulate even just a minute detail amounts to 'total defeat' (SED 175; see also Genosko 2006; Pawlett 2007: 64–6; Tierney 1997: 70–1). In his essays on 9/11, Baudrillard puts forward a multifaceted set of arguments to show, firstly, that the global system itself has created an environment conducive to such events, and, secondly, that such events can – as the New York attacks did – create deep and lasting damage to the system (ST). An important political conundrum highlighted by Lyotard's writings on postmodernity ensues from the fact that 'the system' – 'an alternative' to which, if not 'a "pure"' one (PC 66), would be at issue – has use for critical interventions, including those of intellectuals, and even for disturbances, including class struggles (PF 67–74; Palumbo–Liu 2000). Lyotard, as shown, searches for clues in contemporary science and art, but also in the kind of thinking and writing he is engaged in, for ways of resisting the more stubborn pressures of the system. Neither in the social world Baudrillard depicts nor in the society at the centre of Lyotard's attention do more conventional strategies for social change, for instance those attaching to democratic institutions or even those attaching to class conflict, seem to hold a great deal of political significance.

PART 2: LIVING IN SOCIETY

The stark differences between the conceptions and analyses of the social world of the present day in the bodies of sociological thought explored in this book are evident. Yet several sociological concerns, albeit approached in different ways, are shared by some of the sociologists whose works have been discussed. Among those are the questions of whether the contemporary conditions are best characterised as modern, postmodern, or not at all modern, how this society can be understood and critically interrogated in view of longstanding problems such as inequality and the exercise of power, how social relationships are to be conceptualised, and where the potential for, and barriers to, social change lie. Further, it is possible to highlight – though once more only selectively and briefly – concerns that some of the eight thinkers have in common – although, again, they tackle these in different ways – with regard to their investigations of specific phenomena associated with life and people's lives in the current social conditions.

Pluralities

Several of the theorists stress the need to develop a methodological approach that can account for and capture the plurality of perspectives and values present in contemporary social life. Of course, each theorist puts such arguments forward in their own respective manner. In his work on social suffering (WOTW), Bourdieu, for example, underscores the importance of juxtaposing different 'points of view' (the space for points of view) in research in order to illuminate what happens when different perspectives of the world 'confront each other' (WOTW 3). By adopting an approach that allows space for different points of view, Bourdieu seeks to capture all forms of suffering in contemporary social life. This may include extreme forms of suffering on an individual or collective basis as well as what he refers to as *'positional suffering'*, which, as mentioned earlier, is often taken as the 'point of reference for criticism' (WOTW 4).

Latour also seeks to show that there is not 'one "outside world"', but rather 'a plurality' of 'worlds' that relate directly to the key 'institutions' that frame people's 'lives' (Muecke 2012). A comparative anthropological approach needs to be developed, according to Latour, which is based on establishing 'common ground'. This approach however also 'requires an instrument to make the differences among collectives emerge anew' (www.bruno-latour.fr/node/328). This must then frame the way problems in contemporary social life, such as the ecological crisis, are dealt with. In her work on partial perspectives, Haraway also argues that in order to offer 'a better account of the world', we must recognise the 'irreducible difference and radical multiplicity of local knowledges' (SK 579; see also Clough and Schneider 2001: 342). This focus on situated knowledges frames her approach to specific phenomena in social life, namely immunology.

These calls for acknowledging plurality in present-day social life also resonate with the work of Lyotard. He encourages the 'recognition of the heteromorphous nature of language games' and of the 'heterogeneous' nature of their 'rules' (PC 65–6). The system's 'decision makers' wish to treat the 'language games' taking place in society as 'commensurable' nonetheless (PC xxiv). One strand of Lyotard's investigations in response to the question 'how to live, and why?' (PF vii) concerns ways of resisting commensurability and exchangeability as a critical intellectual in one's own language game moves.

Suffering and Terror

It scarcely needs pointing out that suffering is a major characteristic of contemporary social life. It is also a substantive focal point in a number of inquiries into social life discussed above. Each of the theorists in question, however, illuminates and examines a different aspect of suffering, and these investigations reflect the theorist's own particular analyses of the contemporary social world. Bourdieu, for example, prioritises and explores the relativity of suffering. He draws on ethnographic data to analyse the ways in which suffering is part of daily life for many people (from the individual to the population level), focusing on a range of sociologically pertinent issues, including poor housing and unemployment, social and symbolic forms of exclusion, intergenerational and interethnic conflict, and urban dystopia (Couldry 2005: 355). Bourdieu continues to explore the transmission of cultural and social capital in his work on suffering in the context of the family and education and social and physical space.

Bauman problematises the liquid life partly because it involves continued suffering. Life is characterised by perpetual 'non-satisfaction' associated with living in the market (LL 80). But more problematically, it is also pestered by 'liquid modern fears' (LF 21). Bauman is able to contextualise non-satisfaction and liquid modern fears in the specific social relations and contexts that constitute liquid modernity. At the same time, he is able to remain critical, not only of those social conditions, but also of people's responses to, and attempts to act against, non-satisfaction and fear.

In his work on terrorism, Baudrillard establishes explicit links between suffering and globalisation. Whilst he does not seek 'to deny' the 'suffering and death' of the 'victims' of the devastation of the World Trade Center on 9/11 (ST 24), he seeks, on the one hand, to emphasise that these attacks were part of a 'violent protest against' the 'violence of globalization' (ST 41; see also Merrin 2005: 104, 112). On the other hand, he suggests that 'terrorism' is vitally fuelled by 'the despair' of those who have been 'humiliated and insulted' (ST 104) by being at the receiving end of the West's, the system's, stream of products without any possibility of reciprocation (ST 100–2; Genosko 2006; Merrin 2005: 104–5; Pawlett 2007: 66, 140). The social relations in which terrorist attacks are sparked, the attacks themselves, and their ramifications cannot, Baudrillard thinks, be understood without an understanding of how relationships of the gift, the challenge, and symbolic exchange manifest themselves today.

Life and the Ecological Crisis

Climate change has for several years been central to a global political agenda. As numerous scholars have argued, a continued warming of the world's temperature has the potential to 'transform human and animal life as it has been known' (Urry 2009: 87). Both Giddens's and Latour's analyses of contemporary social life address the problem of climate change and the current ecological crisis. Giddens's work on climate change incorporates components of his writings on radical modernity as well as of his writings on politics. As discussed earlier, his investigation centres on what he calls 'Giddens's paradox'. He argues that as many of the dangers posed by climate change are not visible in everyday life, people are often not compelled to do anything about them (PCC 2). 'Giddens's paradox', he holds, 'affects almost every aspect of current reactions to climate change'. It is why climate change is an issue that is often at the back of people's minds (PCC 2). While Giddens outlines the problem of climate change in his work on radical modernity (CM), he starts to map out a strategy to deal with environmental decay in his more politically focused texts (BLR, TW), which he then elaborates on more fully in his writing on climate change (PCC). Although some have argued that Giddens's work on climate change is less academic than his earlier conceptual work (James and Steger 2014), the message that he articulates in his book on climate change is consistent with his writings on radical modernity. He is keen to stress that the world we occupy now is one 'where hazards created by ourselves are as, or more, threatening than those that come from the outside' (RW 34).

Latour also takes the current ecological crisis as the background to his comparative anthropology, arguing at the start of AIME (8) that we need to choose between modernising and ecologising. In *Politics of Nature* (PON), Latour argues for new perspectives on 'political ecology' (de Vries 2016: 194), outlining 'the principles of the politics that he thinks will be needed' (de Vries 2016: 198).

In AIME, Latour seeks to develop 'a platform for the diplomatic exchanges that will be necessary, if ... ecological catastrophe [is] to be avoided' (de Vries 2016: 199). AIME does clearly extend Latour's work on actor network theory, shifting his focus from networks to modes of existence. The main purpose of the text, however, is to revisit the main questions he posed in WHNBM in order 'to offer the Moderns a clearer view of themselves' and other people (de Vries 2016: 199). According to Latour, once the moderns start reflecting on their own position, it then becomes 'possible to think of comparative anthropology as a diplomatic enterprise'. This is because 'the former Moderns ... are no longer cheating about who they are ... and what they want to achieve' (www.bruno-latour.fr/node/328).

Life, Death, Bodies, and Power

Finally, several investigations of social life discussed in the preceding chapters unearth close connections between phenomena of life and living and the exercise and operation of power. Foucault's work has been decisive in this context. According to his famous conception, disciplinary power operates upon the individual 'body', notably its actions – broken down further into components such as movements or behaviours – and 'forces'; it is to serve to render the body docile and productive at the same time. The 'regulations of the population', by contrast, concentrate on 'the mechanics of life' within and 'biological processes' on 'the species body' (HS1 139; see also Lemke 2011: 33–8; Sheridan 1990: 139, 148–52, 171–2, 191–3, 219). Foucault distinguishes discipline, regulation, and security from the sovereign's right of death. He illustrates different modalities of power with reference to their manifestations in the treatment of the ill at different moments in European history: the latter right with reference to the treatment of lepers in the Middle Ages, the disciplines of the body with reference to the approach to plague victims in the 1600s, and security with reference to the approach to smallpox in the 1700s.

Foucault's studies have fundamentally shaped the ongoing analysis of biopolitics in the social sciences (e.g. Lemke 2011). Haraway, too, has developed a position on biopolitics, namely in her essay on the immune system (BPB; see also Munnik 1997: 112–14). This is implicit in the development of the concept of the cyborg in her manifesto and in her introduction to the term material-semiotic in her work on partial perspectives. However, Haraway uses her work on the immune system to illustrate that position more fully. Just as Foucault does, Haraway focuses on 'the body as a specific object of biopower'; however, she does this from what she calls a 'material semiotic' perspective, through which she 'deconstruct[s] the unitary character' of the body (Esposito 2011: 146). In contrast to Foucault, Haraway 'approaches the body' through a focus on its deconstruction and multiplication, which is prompted by the 'proliferation of technology' (Esposito 2011: 146). She continues to acknowledge the 'relations of power into which the management of the living being is inscribed' (Esposito 2011: 146). Simultaneously she also draws attention to the ways in which the connections between 'life' and other spheres such as the social or political are being 'radically redefined'. For Haraway, it is the increasing 'proliferation of technology' that is driving this change (Esposito 2011: 146). For other theorists, such as Giddens, the increasing proliferation of technology is just one part of a broader juggernaut of modernity, which is responsible for radically altering contemporary social life as we know it.

Many sociological analyses of power focus on power as it is exercised in relation to the living and life. This includes Foucault's analyses. He distinguishes from his concept of power as right of death several further concepts of power, such as those of discipline, security, and regulation, that he deems more pertinent to examining the key developments in its operation in the past three to four centuries. Baudrillard has been shown to extend the sociological understanding of power by virtue of his notion of death power (SED 129). What he emphasises is that 'social control' has arisen from the severance of the relationships of 'the living' with 'the dead', and that, in the end, all forms of power, including all 'power' over the living, are grounded in the control over the management 'of death' (SED 130; see also Genosko 1998: 27–8; Pawlett 2007: 56–8, 64; Tierney 1997: 64).

10

Conclusion

The conceptions of and arguments about social relations, contexts, and conditions explored in the preceding chapters, and the eight thinkers' attempts to analyse present-day society that those conceptions and arguments support, have made decisive contributions and posed serious challenges to sociology's project of understanding and critically scrutinising the contemporary social world. The foregoing studies have sought to highlight that each theorist's conceptions of and inquiries into wider social conditions are also intertwined with their own endeavours to analyse how those conditions shape, are manifested or expressed in, and receive influence from more particular phenomena. Being aware of – indeed unsettled by – most of these phenomena per se does not hinge on prior exposure to sociological research. Many, such as non-satisfaction or fear, are frequently part of immediate experience; others, such as climate change or terrorist attacks, can be heard and read about daily. What each theorist's work demonstrates is the potential of a specifically sociological engagement with such phenomena to provide critical insights that would not otherwise be available. The focus in this context has been on key components of the eight thinkers' investigations and analyses of phenomena that are in one way or another associated with the problem of living, of people's lives, of human life in contemporary social relations and conditions. Their critical interrogations illustrate what it can mean when sociologists explicitly or implicitly work with the idea that people live in society. They will continue to offer much to the sociological study of social life.

References

Adorno, T. W. (2000) *Introduction to Sociology*. Stanford, CA: Stanford University Press.

Adorno, T. W. (2008) *Philosophische Elemente einer Theorie der Gesellschaft. Nachgelassene Schriften IV: Vorlesungen, Band 12*. Frankfurt am Main: Suhrkamp.

Baudelaire, C. (1950) *My Heart Laid Bare and Other Prose Writings*. London: George Weidenfeld & Nicolson.

Baudrillard, J. (1976) *L'Échange Symbolique et la Mort*. Paris: Éditions Gallimard.

Baudrillard, J. (1982a) À *L'Ombre des Majorités Silencieuses ou la Fin du Social (suivi de) L'Extase du Socialisme*. Paris: Denoël/Gonthier.

Baudrillard, J. (1982b) *Der Symbolische Tausch und der Tod*. Munich: Matthes & Seitz.

Baudrillard, J. (1983) *In the Shadow of the Silent Majorities or, the End of the Social and Other Essays*. New York: Semiotext(e).

Baudrillard, J. (1988) *The Ecstasy of Communication*. New York: Semiotext(e).

Baudrillard, J. (1993) *Symbolic Exchange and Death*. London: Sage.

Baudrillard, J. (1998) *Paroxysm: Interviews with Philippe Petit*. London: Verso.

Baudrillard, J. (2001) 'L'Esprit du terrorisme'. *Le Monde*, 3 November 2001.

Baudrillard, J. (2002a) 'The despair of having everything'. *Le Monde Diplomatique*, November 2002.

Baudrillard, J. (2002b) *Screened Out*. London: Verso.

Baudrillard, J. (2003a) *Passwords*. London: Verso.

Baudrillard, J. (2003b) *The Spirit of Terrorism and Other Essays*. London: Verso.

Baudrillard, J. (2004) *Fragments: Conversations with François L'Yvonnet*. London: Routledge.

Baudrillard, J. (2013) *The Intelligence of Evil, or, The Lucidity Pact*. London: Bloomsbury.

Bauman, Z. (2000) *Liquid Modernity*. Cambridge: Polity Press.

Bauman, Z. (2003) *Liquid Love: On the Frailty of Human Bonds*. Cambridge: Polity Press.

Bauman, Z. (2005) *Liquid Life*. Cambridge: Polity Press.

Bauman, Z. (2006) *Liquid Fear*. Cambridge: Polity Press.

Bauman, Z. (2007) *Consuming Life*. Cambridge: Polity Press.

Beck, U. (1992) *Risk Society: Towards a New Modernity*. London: Sage.

Benjamin, W. (2003) 'The work of art in the age of its technological reproducibility [third version]', in W. Benjamin *Selected Writings. Volume 4: 1938–1940*. Cambridge, MA: Harvard University Press, pp. 251–83.

Birch, K. and Tyfield, D. (2012) 'Theorizing the bioeconomy: Biovalue, bio-capital, bioeconomics or ... what?'. *Science, Technology, and Human Values* *38*(3): 299–327.

Blackshaw, T. (2008) 'Bauman on consumerism – living the market-mediated life', in M. H. Jacobsen and P. Poder (eds) *The Sociology of Zygmunt Bauman: Challenges and Critique*. Aldershot: Ashgate, pp. 117–35.

Bourdieu, P. (1977) *Outline of a Theory of Practice*. Cambridge: Cambridge University Press.

Bourdieu, P. (1984) *Distinction*. London: Routledge.

Bourdieu, P. (1997) 'The forms of capital', in A.M. Halsey, H. Lauder and A. Stuart Nells (eds) *Education: Culture, Economy, Society*. Oxford: Oxford University Press, pp. 46–58.

Bourdieu, P. (1988) *Homo Academicus*. Cambridge: Polity Press.

Bourdieu, P. (1995) Physical space, social space and habitus, Lecture delivered to the Department of Sociology, University of Oslo, May 15. Report 10. Oslo: Institutt for sosiologi og samfunnsgeografi.

Bourdieu, P. et al. (1999) *The Weight of the World. Social Suffering in Contemporary Society*. Cambridge: Polity Press.

Bourdieu, P. and Passeron, J.-C. (1977) *Reproduction in Education, Society and Culture*. London: Sage.

Bourdieu, P. and Wacquant, L. (1992) *Invitation to Reflexive Sociology*. Chicago, IL: University of Chicago Press.

Butterfield, B. (2002) 'The Baudrillardian symbolic, 9/11, and the war of good and evil'. *Postmodern Culture* *13*(1). Available at: http://pmc.iath.virginia.edu/issue.902/13.1butterfield.html

Callinicos, A. (1999) *Social Theory: A Historical Introduction*. Cambridge: Polity Press.

Callinicos, A. (2001) *Against the Third Way*. Cambridge: Polity Press.

Campain, R. (2008) 'Bauman on power – from "solid" to "light"?', in M. H. Jacobsen and P. Poder (eds) *The Sociology of Zygmunt Bauman: Challenges and Critique*. Aldershot: Ashgate, pp. 193–208.

Clifford, J. and Marcus, G. E. (eds) (1986) *Writing Culture: The Poetics and Politics of Ethnography*. London: University of California Press.

Clough, P. T. and Schneider, J. (2001) 'Donna J. Haraway', in A. Elliot and B. S. Turner (eds) *Profiles in Contemporary Social Theory*. London: Sage, pp. 338–48.

Connor, S. (1989) *Postmodern Culture: An Introduction to Theories of the Contemporary*. Oxford: Basil Blackwell.

Couldry, N. (2005) 'The individual point of view: Learning from Bourdieu's The Weight of the World'. *Cultural Studies, Critical Methodologies* *5*(3): 354–72.

Davidson, A. I. (2003) 'Introduction', in M. Foucault *Abnormal: Lectures at the Collège de France, 1974–1975*. New York: Picador, pp. xvii–xxvi.

Davidson, A. I. (2006) 'Introduction', in M. Foucault *Psychiatric Power: Lectures at the Collège de France, 1973–1974*. New York: Picador, pp. xiv–xxii.

Davis, M. (2016) *Freedom and Consumerism: A Critique of Zygmunt Bauman's Sociology*. London: Routledge.

de Vries, G. (2016) *Bruno Latour*. Cambridge: Polity Press.

Durkheim, É. (1982) *The Rules of Sociological Method. And Selected Texts on Sociology and Its Method*. London: Macmillan.

Elliot, A. (2001) *Concepts of the Self*. Cambridge: Polity Press.

Esposito, R. (2011) *Immunitas: The Protection and Negation of Life*. Cambridge: Polity Press.

Foucault, M. (1976) *Histoire de la Sexualité 1: La Volonté de Savoir*. Paris: Gallimard.

Foucault, M. (1981) *The History of Sexuality, Volume 1: An Introduction*. London: Penguin.

Foucault, M. (1991) *Discipline and Punish: The Birth of the Prison*. London: Penguin.

Foucault, M. (2003) *Abnormal: Lectures at the Collège de France, 1974–1975*. New York: Picador.

Foucault, M. (2004) *'Society Must Be Defended': Lectures at the Collège de France, 1975–76*. London: Penguin.

Foucault, M. (2006) *Psychiatric Power: Lectures at the Collège de France, 1973–1974*. New York: Picador.

Foucault, M. (2009) *Security, Territory, Population: Lectures at the Collège de France, 1977–78*. Basingstoke: Palgrave Macmillan.

Foucault, M. (2010) *The Birth of Biopolitics: Lectures at the Collège de France, 1978–79*. Basingstoke: Palgrave Macmillan.

Frank, A. W. (2001) 'Can we research suffering?'. *Qualitative Health Research* 11(3): 353–62.

Gane, N. and Haraway, D. (2006) '"When we have never been human, what is to be done?" Interview with Donna Haraway'. *Theory, Culture & Society* 23(7–8): 135–58.

Genosko, G. (1998) *Undisciplined Theory*. London: Sage.

Genosko, G. (2006) 'The spirit of symbolic exchange: Jean Baudrillard's 9/11'. *International Journal of Baudrillard Studies* 3(1). Available at: https://www2.ubishops.ca/baudrillardstudies/vol3_1/genosko.htm

Giddens, A. (1990) *The Consequences of Modernity*. Cambridge: Polity Press.

Giddens, A. (1994a) 'Living in a post-traditional society', in U. Beck, A. Giddens and S. Lash (eds) *Reflexive Modernization: Politics, Tradition and Aesthetics in the Modern Social Order*. Cambridge: Polity Press, pp. 56–109.

Giddens, A. (1994b) *Beyond Left and Right: The Future of Radical Politics*. Cambridge: Polity Press.

Giddens, A. (1998) *The Third Way: The Renewal of Social Democracy*. Cambridge: Polity Press.

Giddens, A. (1999) *Runaway World: How Globalisation is Reshaping Our Lives*. London: Profile Books.

Giddens, A. (2000) *The Third Way and Its Critics*. Cambridge: Polity Press.

Giddens, A. (2011) *The Politics of Climate Change* (2nd edn). Cambridge: Polity Press.

Goux, J.-J. and Wood, P. R. (1998) 'Introduction', in J.-J. Goux and P. R. Wood (eds) *Terror and Consensus: Vicissitudes of French Thought*. Stanford, CA: Stanford University Press, pp. 1–10.

Gudmand-Høyer, M. and Lopdrup Hjorth, T. (2009) 'Review essay: Liberal biopoloitics reborn'. *Foucault Studies 7*: 99–130.

Haraway, D. (1988) 'Situated knowledges: The science question in feminism and the privilege of partial perspective'. *Feminist Studies 14*(3): 575–600.

Haraway, D. (1991) 'A cyborg manifesto: Science, technology and socialist-feminism in the late twentieth century', in D. Haraway (ed.) *Simians, Cyborgs, and Women: The Reinvention of Nature*. New York: Routledge, pp. 149–81.

Haraway, D. (1993) 'The biopolitics of postmodern bodies', in L. Kauffman (ed.) *American Feminist Thought at a Century's End: A Reader*. Oxford: Blackwell, pp. 199–233.

Haraway, D. (2004a) 'Introduction: A kinship of feminist figurations', in D. Haraway (ed.) *The Haraway Reader*. London: Routledge, pp. 1–7.

Haraway, D. (2004b) 'The promises of monsters: A regenerative politics for inappropriate/d others', in D. Haraway (ed.) *The Haraway Reader*. London: Routledge, pp. 63–124.

Hobbes, T. ([1914] 1947) *Leviathan, Or The Matter, Forme and Power of Commonwealth Ecclesiastical and Civil*. London: J.M. Dent.

Horkheimer, M. (1972) 'Traditional and critical theory', in M. Horkheimer *Critical Theory: Selected Essays*. New York: Continuum, pp. 188–243.

Horkheimer, M. and Adorno, T. W. (2002) *Dialectic of Enlightenment: Philosophical Fragments*. Stanford, CA: Stanford University Press.

James, P. and Steger, M. B. (2014) 'A genealogy of "globalization": The career of a concept'. *Globalizations 11*(4): 417–34.

Jaulin, R. (1967) *La Mort Sara: L'Ordre de la Vie ou la Pensée de la Mort au Tchad*. Paris: Plon.

Jenkins, R. (1992) *Pierre Bourdieu*. London: Routledge.

Kant, I. (1991) 'An answer to the question: "What is enlightenment?"', in I. Kant *Political Writings* (2nd enlarged edn). Cambridge: Cambridge University Press, pp. 54–60.

Kaspersen, L. B. (2000) *Anthony Giddens: An Introduction to a Social Theorist*. Oxford: Blackwell Publishers.

King, K. (1987) *The Passing Dreams of Choice... Once Before and After: Audre Lorde and the Apparatus of Literary Production, Book Prospectus*. University of Maryland at College Park.

Kirby, V. (1997) *Telling Flesh: The Substance of the Corporeal*. London: Routledge.

Klein, N. (2015) *This Changes Everything: Capitalism Vs. the Climate*. London: Penguin.

Kleinman, A., Das, V., and Lock, M. (eds) (1997) *Social Suffering*. Berkeley, CA: University of California Press.

Kunzru, H. (1996) 'You are cyborg'. *Wired*. Available at: http://archive.wired.com/wired/archive/5.02/ffharaway_pr.html

Lagrange, J. (2006) 'Course context', in M. Foucault *Psychiatric Power: Lectures at the Collège de France, 1973–1974*. New York: Picador, pp. 349–67.

Lane, J. (2006) *Bourdieu's Politics: Problems and Possibilities*. London: Routledge.

Latour, B. (1988) *The Pasteurization of France*. Cambridge, MA: Harvard University Press.

Latour, B. (1993) *We Have Never Been Modern*. Cambridge, MA: Harvard University Press.

Latour, B. (2004) *Politics of Nature: How to Bring the Sciences into Democracy*. Cambridge, MA: Harvard University Press.

Latour, B. (2005) *Reassembling the Social: An Introduction to Actor-Network-Theory*. Oxford: Oxford University Press.

Latour, B. (2013) *An Inquiry into Modes of Existence: An Anthropology of the Moderns*. Cambridge, MA: Harvard University Press.

Latour, B. (2015) *Face a Gaia*. Paris: La Découverte.

Latour, B. and Woolgar, S. (1986) *Laboratory Life: The Construction of Scientific Facts*. Princeton, NJ: Princeton University Press.

Leach, B. (1998) 'Industrial homework, economic restructuring and the meaning of work'. *Labour/Le Travail* 41: 97–115.

Lemke, T. (2011) *Biopolitics: An Advanced Introduction*. New York: New York University Press.

Lyotard, J.-F. (1979) *La Condition Postmoderne: Rapport sur le Savoir*. Paris: Les Éditions de Minuit.

Lyotard, J.-F. (1984a) 'Answering the question: What is postmodernism?', in J.-F. Lyotard *The Postmodern Condition: A Report on Knowledge*. Manchester: Manchester University Press, pp. 71–82.

Lyotard, J.-F. (1984b) *The Postmodern Condition: A Report on Knowledge*. Manchester: Manchester University Press.

Lyotard, J.-F. (1993) *Moralités Postmodernes*. Paris: Éditions Galilée.

Lyotard, J.-F. (1994) *Das Postmoderne Wissen: Ein Bericht*. Vienna: Passagen.

Lyotard, J.-F. (1997) *Postmodern Fables*. London: University of Minnesota Press.

Lyotard, J.-F. (1998) 'Terror on the run', in J.-J. Goux and P. R. Wood (eds) *Terror and Consensus: Vicissitudes of French Thought*. Stanford, CA: Stanford University Press, pp. 25–36.

Mackenzie, D. (1993) *Inventing Accuracy: A Historical Sociology of Nuclear Missile Guidance*. Cambridge, MA: MIT Press.

Malpas, S. (2003) *Jean-François Lyotard*. London: Routledge.

Marcuse, H. (2002) *One-dimensional Man: Studies in the Ideology of Advanced Industrial Society*. London: Routledge.

Martuccelli, D. (1999) *Sociologie de la Modernité*. Paris: Gallimard.

Marx, K. (1990) *Capital. Volume 1*. London: Penguin.

Mauss, M. (1979) 'The physical effect on the individual of the idea of death suggested by the collectivity (Australia, New Zealand)', in M. Mauss *Sociology and Psychology (Essays)*. London: Routledge and Kegan Paul, pp. 35–56.

Mauss, M. (2002) *The Gift: The Form and Reason for Exchange in Archaic Societies*. London: Routledge.

McRobbie, A. (2002) 'A mixed bag of misfortunes?: Bourdieu's Weight of the World'. *Theory, Culture & Society* 19(3): 129–38.

Merrin, W. (2005) *Baudrillard and the Media: A Critical Introduction*. Cambridge: Polity Press.

Michaels, M. (2016) *Actor Network Theory: Trials, Trails and Translations*. London: Sage.

Morgan, D. and Wilkinson, I. (2001) 'The problem of suffering and the sociological task of theodicy'. *The European Journal of Social Theory*, 4(2): 199–214.

Muecke, S. (2012) '"I am what I am attached to": On Bruno Latour's "Inquiry into the Modes of Existence"'. *Los Angeles Review of Books*. Available at: https://lareviewofbooks.org/article/i-am-what-i-am-attached-to-on-bruno-latours-inquiry-into-the-modes-of-existence/#!

Munnik, R. (1997) 'Donna Haraway: Cyborgs for earthly survival', in H. Achterhuis (ed.) *American Philosophy of Technology*. Indianapolis, IN: University of Indiana Press, pp. 95–118.

Murray, M. (2007) 'Xenotransplanation and the post-human future', in M. Sque and S. Payne (eds) *Organ and Tissue Donation: An Evidence Base for Practice*. Milton Keynes: Open University Press, pp. 152–68.

Norton, M. B. (2013) 'Review of AIME'. *Interstitial Journal: A Journal of Modern Cultural Events*. Available at: https://interstitialjournal.files.wordpress.com/2013/10/norton-latour.pdf.

Oakley, A. (1979) *Sociology of Housework*. Oxford: Basil Blackwell.

Palumbo-Liu, D. (2000) 'Fables and apedagogy: Lyotard's relevance for a pedagogy of the Other', in P. A. Dhillon and P. Standish (eds) *Lyotard: Just Education*. London: Routledge, pp. 194–214.

Parsons, T. (1970) *The Social System*. London: Routledge & Kegan Paul.

Pawlett, W. (2007) *Jean Baudrillard: Against Banality*. London: Routledge & Kegan Paul.

Pawlett, W. (2016) *Violence, Society and Radical Theory: Bataille, Baudrillard and Contemporary Society*. London: Routledge.

Poder, P. (2008) 'Bauman on freedom – consumer freedom as the integration mechanism of liquid society', in M. H. Jacobsen and P. Poder (eds) *The Sociology of Zygmunt Bauman: Challenges and Critique*. Aldershot: Ashgate, pp. 97–115.

Riesman, D. (1953) *The Lonely Crowd*. Garden City, NY: Doubleday Anchor.

Senellart, M. (2009) 'Course context', in M. Foucault *Security, Territory, Population: Lectures at the Collège de France, 1977–78*. Basingstoke: Palgrave Macmillan, pp. 369–401.

Sheridan, A. (1990) *Michel Foucault: The Will to Truth*. London: Routledge.

Skeggs, B. (1997) *Formations of Class and Gender*. London: Sage.

Skeggs, B. (2004) 'Context and background: Pierre Bourdieu's analysis of class, gender and sexuality'. *The Sociological Review* 52(S2): 19–23.

Sullivan, A. (2001) 'Cultural capital and educational attainment'. *Sociology* 35(4): 893–912.

Sullivan, A. (2002) 'Bourdieu and education: How useful is Bourdieu's theory for researchers?'. *The Netherlands Journal for Social Sciences* 38(2): 144–66.

Tierney, T. F. (1997) 'Death, medicine and the right to die: An engagement with Heidegger, Bauman and Baudrillard'. *Body and Society* 3(4): 51–77.

Urry, J. (2009) 'Sociology and climate change'. *Sociological Review* 57(2): 84–100.

Wacquant, L. (1989) 'Towards a reflexive sociology: A workshop with Pierre Bourdieu'. *Sociological Theory* 7(1): 26–63.

Wacquant, L. (2008) 'Pierre Bourdieu', in R. Stones (ed.) *Key Sociological Thinkers*. Basingstoke: Palgrave Macmillan, pp. 261–77.

Wacquant, L. (2015) 'For a sociology of flesh and blood'. *Qualitative Sociology* 38(1): 1–11.

Weasel, L. (2001) 'Dismantling the self/other dichotomy in science: Towards a feminist model of the immune system'. *Hypatia* 16(1): 27–44.

Weber, M. (2001) *The Protestant Ethic and the Spirit of Capitalism*. London: Routledge.

Webster, A. (2007) *Health, Technology and Society: A Sociological Critique*. Basingstoke: Palgrave Macmillan.

Wilcox, L. (2003) 'Baudrillard, September 11, and the haunting abyss of reversal'. *Postmodern Culture* 14(1). Available at: http://pmc.iath.virginia.edu/issue.903/14.1wilcox.html

Wilkinson, I. (2005) *Suffering: A Sociological Introduction*. Cambridge: Polity Press.

Williams, J. (1998) *Lyotard: Towards a Postmodern Philosophy*. Cambridge: Polity Press.

Willis, P. (1983) 'Cultural production and theories of reproduction', in L. Barton and S. Walker (eds) *Race, Class and Education*. London: Croom Helm, pp. 107–38.

Winner, L. (1993) 'Upon opening the black box and finding it empty: Social constructivism and the philosophy of technology'. *Science, Technology, and Human Values* 18: 362–78.

Winograd, T. and Flores, F. (1986) *Understanding Computers and Cognition: A New Foundation for Design*. Norwood, NJ: Ablex.

Wittgenstein, L. (1953) *Philosophical Investigations*. New York: Macmillan.

Index